Investing in a Post-Enron World

Investing in a Post-Enron World

Paul Jorion

McGRAW-HILL
New York Chicago San Francisco Lisbon
London Madrid Mexico City Milan New Delhi
San Juan Seoul Singapore Sydney Toronto

The McGraw·Hill Companies

1234567890 DOCDOC 09876543

ISBN 0-07-140938-6

Printed and bound by R.R. Donnelley.

This publication is designed to provide accurate and authoritative information in regard to the subject matter covered. It is sold with the understanding that neither the author nor the publisher is engaged in rendering legal, accounting, or other professional service. If legal advice or other expert assistance is required, the services of a competent professional person should be sought.

—From a Declaration of Principles jointly adopted by a Committee of the American Bar Association and a Committee of Publishers

McGraw-Hill books are available at special quantity discounts to use as premiums and sales promotions, or for use in corporate training programs. For more information, please write to the Director of Special Sales, Professional Publishing, McGraw-Hill, Two Penn Plaza, New York, NY 10121-2298. Or contact your local bookstore.

Library of Congress Cataloging-in-Publication Data

Jorion, Paul.
  Investing in a post Enron world / by Paul Jorion.
    p. cm.
  ISBN 0-07-140938-6 (pbk. : alk. paper)
  1. Investments—United States. 2. Stocks—United States. 3. Corporations—Accounting—Corrupt practices—United States. 4. Accounting firms—Corrupt practices—United States. 5. Enron Corp. I. Title.
  HG4910 .J67 2003
  332.63'2042—dc21
                        2002152468

Contents

Acknowledgments   vii

Introduction   ix

1   Enron 101   1

2   Holding the Accounting Firm Accountable   13

3   Capitalism 101   29

4   Sharing Capital Growth—or Not   37

5   The Price and Value of a Share of Stock   49

6   How Shares Are Priced   65

7   How Enron Got Earnings-Obsessed   81

8   Stock Options:
The War Between Management and Shareholders   97

9   Wretched Excess   123

10   Aggressive Accounting   137

11   Massaging Financial Reports   151

12   Reading (or Ignoring) Analysts' Recommendations   165

13   The Perils of Cliffs   181

14   Employees as Shareholders   197

15   The Last Word   211

Notes   223

Index   233

Acknowledgments

My thanks go to Jeffrey Krames, the editor of the series, who achieved two major things. First, he showed me that it was not enough that I liked my own book; second, he convinced my wife Homa that she would be the perfect reader who would help me to make sense of what I was putting on paper.

Homa Jorion, née Firouzbakhch, did a remarkable job structuring the book and constructing the chapters so that the ideas come across clearly. Also, she persuaded me time after time that, although there were many more insightful people and sources that I wanted to cite, the reader deserved the benefit of my analysis and insight.

In various ways, this was also the message I got from Jeff Cruikshank. Many thanks to you, Jeff.

Kelli Christiansen at McGraw-Hill made me understand two major points about writing: that a book should be appealing even when only thumbed through and that it should look like a good read when only glanced at.

I learned to look below the surface in economic matters when Chris Gregory encouraged me to read a fellow Cambridge man: Piero Sraffa's *Production of Commodities by Means of Commodities*.

Philippe Jeanne and I struggled together in the pioneering days of swaps and "swaptions"; my understanding of financial instruments is owed to him in large part.

Alain Caillé decided on repeated occasions that my views on price formation were thought provoking enough to be debated at Paris-Sorbonne. And Pierre Marchand believed that they would thrill the students of the Paris-Sorbonne MBA program. I can only hope that they did.

Introduction

The recent months and years have been a tough time for investors—tough in part because after a disheartening decline, the stock market has been slipping mostly sideways, refusing to take a cue from all the pundits who keep spotting the long-awaited recovery. It also has been tough because a lot of people—myself included—were appalled at the recent series of revelations about slippery dealings in the corporate world. *Enron* has become a catch-all term for the sleazy dealings of a basketful of companies that did not seem to know right from wrong, could not seem to make an honest buck, and did not hesitate to report their numbers in creative (read *dishonest*) ways.

I remember vividly from my early childhood the sight of buildings that had been ravaged by the aerial bombardments of World War II. In some cases, a bomb exploding close at hand had caused the front wall of a house to drop down, like a too-heavy stage curtain, revealing the relatively intact contents of the house. The tables would still have their tablecloths on them. The paintings would still be on the walls. The bathtub—although now inaccessible to would-be bathers due to the collapsed stairwell below it—would be gleaming white in the daylight.

The collapse of Enron created a somewhat similar impression. The once-proud company imploded with astonishing speed, leaving behind a hulk that on the face of it seemed fairly well preserved. You could almost see the porcelain of the bathtubs, metaphorically speaking, waiting to be pressed back into service.

Meanwhile, of course, 20,000 Enron employees—not counting the senior executives—had seen their retirement savings reduced to rubble. And many of the rest of us, taken in by the hype and dazzle, were also co-owners of the wreckage.

But the story does not end there, thank goodness.

The inhabitants of a bombed-out city find a way to pick up the pieces and move forward. They rebuild, taking into account some of the lessons learned during the recent disaster. The city comes back to life. Eventually, when enough time has gone by and enough new investments have been made, only the trained eye can spot traces of the former devastation.

The investment community—you and I—are beginning a similar process of rebuilding. For now, we are still gun-shy and skittish. We should be. (If we can't trust the numbers that these corporations put out, why should we put our much-reduced savings into them?) Eventually, though, we will go back into the markets. And when we do, we will have the great advantage of having learned a lot about the way things actually work: how they can go wrong and how they can be set right.

This is what this book is about. We are entering into the "post" world, as in postwar (the word Enron is in the title of this book, but it could just as easily have been post-WorldCom or post-Adelphia or post-Vivendi). The key question is, What lessons are we going to take with us?

I have taken a somewhat unusual tack in the structure of this book. I have used Enron as a sort of case study, off of which I hang analysis and observations. However, rather than laying out the entire mosaic of the Enron debacle—which is the stuff of a multivolume set and which no one in the world grasps in its entirety—I have decided to alternate between glimpses of the main actors in the recent dramas (Enron, Arthur Andersen, and so on) and explanations of the mechanisms behind the drama.

Thus, for example, I will describe Enron's business model and how it changed over time. I will then talk about regulated and unregulated markets. Then I will talk a bit more about how Enron decided to plunge into an unregulated market of its own making. And then I will try to draw some lessons for investors out of this story line.

The point, in other words, is not to make you an expert on Enron. That can be left to the juries and the historians. You and I have to figure out where to go next with our money.

The challenge in this approach, of course, is striking the right balance. I hope that most of my readers find the balance between "too elementary" and "too complex" to be just about right for them. I have tried to keep in enough complexity to underscore just how difficult it was for the investor in the "Enron world" to protect his or her interests.

Note my deliberate use of the past tense when I refer to the "Enron world." I strongly believe that we have entered into the post-Enron world, although to a great extent that world remains to be defined. And I also believe that this new world is going to function more efficiently and equitably than what came before. One reason for this optimism is that corporations have embarked on self-policing to an unprecedented degree. Another reason is that the politicians and regulators have jumped on the bandwagon, albeit belatedly, and there are now strong signals that genuine reforms are underway.

Most important, however, I believe that you and I—and the millions of other individual investors like us—are going to demand that the post-Enron world be different. Yes, we investors can be a little too greedy or a little too lazy at times. Fundamentally, though, we understand the importance of playing in a fair game, in which the rules are clear, apply to everyone, and do not change unexpectedly. And I believe that we are going to demand—and get—this kind of a game in the post-Enron world.

And meanwhile, of course, we will walk carefully through the wreckage, putting our feet down one at a time in safe places and looking for outstanding opportunities to rebuild.

1

Enron 101

One reason that some look beyond Enron is that a
fundamental question remains unanswered: Was
the company the imperfect child of a healthy
financial system or the perfect product of an
unhealthy one?

—STEVE LIESMAN, *Wall Street Journal*[1]

If the point in this book is to think through the implications of being an
investor in the post-Enron (or post-WorldCom, post-Adelphia, or post-etc.)
world, it makes good sense to take a close look at what actually happened
to Enron and why. However, the goal of this chapter is not to make you an
expert on the enormously complex scheme that was Enron. (Perhaps *no one*
other than a few insiders can grasp the entire picture or needs to.) Instead,
the point of this chapter is to give you a feel for how a business model that
had some interesting, innovative, and maybe even sustainable components
evolved into a beast that deserved to die.

When a cascade of debt-related woes knocked Enron off its feet, the
company's innards were exposed to the light—for all the world to see. It
was only at this point that it became clear that the Houston energy-trading
giant had been playing the "bubble game." When things turned sour—when
the company's debt load became overwhelming—there was only one strat-

egy left to play: Turn the machine into what I call a *stock-price pump,* and hope that the company could stay at least one step ahead of the posse.

Enron did not invent the speculative bubble. Nor was it the first company to turn itself into a stock-price pump, manipulating its numbers to artificially inflate its appeal to "The Street." It *was* unlucky to get caught in the spotlight, held up to intense scrutiny, and numbered among the vanquished. Perhaps Enron and its legacy will be forgotten quickly. Or perhaps "Enron" will enter the annals of corporate greed and excess—like "Teapot Dome," for instance, or "ITT" in the Nixon era—and be remembered as the company that made the investor understand bubbles and stock-price pumps and forced corporate America to leave the casino and go back to creating value.

So let's look at some telling details.

The Debacle

The high-speed implosion of swashbuckling Enron—in the late 1990s, Wall Street's poster company—over a mere 46 days left the investment world shell-shocked. But the implosion was just the beginning.

The company filed for bankruptcy protection on December 2, 2001. Only a few weeks earlier, it had ranked as the seventh-largest public company in the United States; now it was on the reef and taking on water. Then began the *real* torrent of disquieting news. Internal Enron review committees began releasing their findings. Investigative reporters poured fuel on the fire as they turned up a wealth of seamy facts. Senate subcommittees summoned the main actors of the drama to appear before them, and some of those actors told shocking stories. Most of us—from senators to scholars to investors with hard-earned money on the table—could not believe what we were seeing.

What became clear quickly was that Enron's executives, or at least some among them, were as aghast as we were. Evidently, they had *shared* in the mass delusion that Enron was the "Mother of All Corporations." After all, it was fast-moving, savvy, trendy, and *in the deal stream.* At its peak, it had a market capitalization of *$80 billion.* However, as the analysts (belatedly) started to bear down on the failing company's numbers, we learned finally that Enron had never really been very good at making money. The "Mother of All Corporations" was an underperformer at best.

It also became clear that the proximate cause of Enron's death—the "discovery" that a partnership created mainly for accounting purposes had been improperly capitalized—was not a particularly significant problem and not necessarily a mortal blow. Most likely, with a little help from Wall Street, the company could have gone on more or less indefinitely, playing its shell games with its purposefully complicated partnerships. However, when scrutinized under the glare of an intense national spotlight, Enron simply could not stand up. The undercapitalized partnership was part of a bigger pattern—including, as we will see, collusion by a prominent accounting firm—and almost nobody liked the picture. We saw a tapestry of edge skirting woven by people who were undeniably smart and unforgivably greedy.

Pretty quickly, in the days that followed December 2, 2001, the main focus of the investigation shifted. The question became, *To what extent is Enron an isolated case—the one rotten apple in the barrel?* Almost everyone with a stake in the economy hoped that the bad smell arising from the Houston energy-trading giant would turn out to be an aberration. Soon, though, equally offensive odors began emerging from other hotshot companies. Tyco International, Global Crossing, Qwest, Adelphia, and World-Com—to name but a few—came under scrutiny and held up no better than (or only slightly better than) Enron.

Enron, though, remained a special object of scorn. And wherever probing eyes looked within the company, a similar picture emerged: naked greed and raw selfishness, testing every definition of *honesty* and *legality.* The whole company seemed to have been put together by its executives for the purpose of cheating people—clients, shareholders, and even its own employees. Over the years, Enron's employees had their contributions to their 401(k) plan matched (50 cents to the dollar) with Enron stock, and for a while, this looked like a great deal. People counted their paper earnings and believed that they were getting rich or at least setting the stage for a comfortable retirement. Then the hammer came down on Enron, and all that wealth simply vanished. And worse, in the eyes of the public, Enron's rank-and-file workers were stuck with their worthless stock, while its leaders were able to gut the hulk, pulling assets out of the disaster.

To be fair, Enron and its executives got no special treatment during this stage of final unraveling. The company simply took full advantage of two fail-safe mechanisms available to any company in its death throes. The first—a provision of the Chapter 11 bankruptcy law designed to encourage companies to reorganize rather than lock their doors—permitted the payment of retention bonuses to key employees so that the firm could keep functioning. Understandable? Yes, under certain circumstances. However, did it pass the sniff test in Enron's case? Hardly!

The second fail-safe mechanism that Enron invoked was not codified in the law but in place in a majority of U.S. corporations. In the event of a corporate bankruptcy, executive retirement plans tend to be *far better protected* than those of lower-ranking employees. In fact, they may be fully sheltered from the winds of misfortune. Again, this is not illegal. However, what the public saw on the evening news, night after night, was tearful Enron employees—now effectively robbed of their retirement savings—juxtaposed with stories about executive bonuses and disaster-proof executive pension plans. We saw a company punishing people who had played by the rules and rewarding people who were incompetents, scoundrels, or both.

The Innovators at Enron

OK, I have finished my screed against the evils of Enron—at least for the time being. Now let me make the case that Enron was not foredoomed to be a train wreck. Let me make the case that, at least to some extent, Enron actually *was* what its leaders thought it was: an innovative company that had arrived at some interesting solutions to contemporary business problems. My goal, of course, is not to let Enron and its leaders off the hook—where they well deserve to be—but rather to help you, the gun-shy but persistent investor, to better understand the process of value creation in the contemporary economy.

Many journalists (especially lazy ones) have used the phrase "house of cards" to describe Enron. But Enron was far from that. At one point, the company was thriving, awarding $30 million in commissions in one year, for example. (To do this, Enron either had to be doing something right or else had be engaged in an active swindle, which it was not.) At least in the early days, Enron's stock price rose as a reflection of the value the company was creating. Yes, the corporate culture was swaggering and aggressive. But it was doing well at its chosen game, which was energy trading. Then, as we shall see, the company got snared in the tail end of the dot-com bubble and started into its death spiral.

The result, of course, is that we are tempted to brand *all* companies that bear a resemblance to the early Enron as "deadbeats" and "ne'er-do-wells."

Recently, for example, a *Wall Street Journal* writer recommended that we investors restrict ourselves to acquiring stock in "boring and simple" companies.[2] However, this is akin to throwing away the baby with the bathwater. Better that we learn to spot and invest in "Good Enrons" and stay as far as possible from "Bad Enrons."

In my opinion, far too few investors read enough history. Yes, investors have to be present- and future-oriented, but in many cases history can help us discern the kinds of patterns that we need to plot our course. One book I often recommend is *Dangerous Dreamers: The Financial Innovators from Charles Merrill to Michael Milken*.[3] The author is the late Robert Sobel, a thoughtful and prolific writer on the history of finance. Sobel was quite purposeful in including the name *Milken* in his book title. Milken, as you may recall, was the so-called junk bond wizard who was, in his day, the pariah that Enron is today. (He had a large part of his fortune confiscated by the government and served time in jail for his excesses.) Say what you will about Milken's faults and failings, Sobel advises us, but do not overlook the fact that he was a brilliant innovator in the realm of corporate finance.

So, too, was Enron. Enron was more innovative in the exotic field of energy trading than any other company, bar none. Enron dove into the complex world of "derivative" financial instruments and figured out a way to use those instruments in their full complexity to manage risk in very sophisticated ways. I am aware that kind words about Enron—*any* kind words—may surprise some and offend others. The truth is, though, that Enron made itself into an expert player in the management of risk. It had its fingers badly burnt in its early days, way back in 1987, mainly because it failed to manage risk. Its leaders resolved that this fate would never again befall the company, and they succeeded in that resolution—as long as they stayed on their home turf, that is.

My point is that there may be a book one day about the history of financial innovation that invokes the name Enron in a positive light. It is even possible that some revisionist historian will redeem the reputation of Enron Chief Executive Officer (CEO) Jeffrey K. Skilling. (All right; this is a little harder to imagine, but it is *possible*.) As investors, we have to figure out (1) what went right and (2) what went wrong. We have to distinguish the baby from the bathwater.

Let's begin this process by looking more closely at Enron's fall from grace.

Bandwidth and Stock Prices: A Cautionary Tale

In the mid-1990s, the Internet burst into the economic landscape. All of a sudden, all bets were off. The game had changed dramatically.

A little-noticed but remarkable side effect of this revolutionary development came in the energy sector. Within about 5 years of the emergence of the Internet and the Web, electricity consumption linked to this new phenomenon had surged to 8 percent of total consumption. Naturally enough, this caught the eye of the prosperous energy trader down in Houston. How could Enron play in this exciting new game?

In order for a firm to have a reasonable chance of success in the realm of the Internet, it needed to be able to control its risks. Well, this was something that Enron was in a very good position to do. In fact, very few companies in the 1990s were as well positioned as Enron to play in this game (or so it seemed). "What Enron has been about for a long time," said Jeff Skilling, then Enron's chief operating officer, "has been making and restructuring markets. If you look at the present phenomenon, the Internet, it also comes into existing markets and dramatically overhauls them. That's something we started doing in the mid-1980s. The Internet just gives us the juice to extend more products across more markets more quickly."

In particular, Enron got interested in the exotic-sounding world of *broadband,* which is a catch-all term for high-speed access to the Internet through the use of fiberoptic cable.[4] Broadband is little more than a data pipeline of great *bandwidth,* or carrying capacity. (Or more precisely, bandwidth "determines the speed at which data can flow through computer and communications systems without interference."[5])

Even at the time—even amid all the Internet hype and hoopla—people knew that the nascent broadband/bandwidth industry was a dicey proposition. "The market will not be for the faint of heart or the ill-prepared," one observer commented. "Success will require careful consideration of the appropriate market entry strategy. Organizations must ask the tough questions, such as 'what's my appetite for risk?'"[6]

Well, in Enron's case, the answer was "*big* appetite." In the spring of 1999, Enron created a company called Enron Communications, Inc., that soon changed its name to Enron Broadband Services (EBS). It began selling a standardized bandwidth product, effectively turning the elusive concept of bandwidth into a commodity.

For a while, and especially from a particular perspective, it worked. That perspective, of course, was the price of a share of Enron stock. People *loved* the idea of Enron and the Internet converging. Within 9 months—that is, the period between year-end 1999 and September 2000—Enron's stock price soared. In fact, it more than doubled—from $44 to $90.

This brings up a central theme of this book: For a group of ambitious and self-impressed executives—especially those with heavy stock options—stock-price fever is something like heroin addiction. It goes from being a nice-to-have to the be-all and end-all. And over time, you need more and more of the stuff to get those good feelings. (In fact, when you *do not* get the stuff, you start feeling bad.) Management got accustomed to a high and rising stock price—and so, by the way, did Wall Street.

When stock-price fever sets in, lots of other temptations begin rearing their heads. One of them is trading in company stock. As you will see in Chapter 7, Enron turned trading in company stock into a modest cottage industry—or more accurately, an *immodest* cottage industry.

It is worth noting that in the dizzying stock market context of that time, Enron's stock performance was not unique or even especially remarkable. Enron's stock price consistently tracked the rising trend of the Nasdaq Index, which specializes in technology stocks (the "stock exchange for the twenty-first century," as some long-vanished ads used to put it). If you draw a diagram with two curves—one being the ascent of Enron's stock price over the period 1997 to mid-2001 and the other the Nasdaq Index for the same period—you find that, for the most part, Enron simply rises along with the hyperinflated Nasdaq. It is only in 2000 that Enron's stock price gains more momentum and keeps rising for another 6 months—attaining a 300 percent growth rate—while the Nasdaq stops short at a relatively paltry 250 percent.

OK, so now Enron has created an extraordinary track record and has set expectations that are simply impossible to sustain in the long run. (Companies cannot grow 300 percent every 4 years; there is not enough universe to go around.) Meanwhile, of course, for reasons that are beyond the scope of this book, the broadband market began to collapse around Enron. And, oh by the way, Enron's international investments were not holding up very well either.

Enron's Securities and Exchange Commission (SEC) quarterly filing for the third quarter of 2001 described the twin calamities in cool "corporate-speak": "Non-Core businesses are businesses that do not provide value to Enron's core businesses. These primarily are part of Enron's global assets and broadband services segments. Enron has approximately $8 billion invested in these businesses, and the return from these investments is below acceptable rates. Accordingly, Enron is developing a plan to exit these businesses in an orderly fashion."

When you encounter corporate-speak about "noncore businesses," you can be sure that a management team is trying to wash its hands of a venture that is going nowhere fast.

Does "Asset-Light" Equal "Corporate-Lite"?

It is time to introduce another bit of jargon, this one fairly specific to the Enron debacle. Enron prided itself on being an "asset-light" company. This should have come as no surprise to those who tracked corporate genealogies. Jeff Skilling was a partner with the consulting firm of McKinsey & Company, and McKinsey & Company had long been touting the advantages of being knowledge-heavy and asset-light. The first volume of *The McKinsey Quarterly* for 1998, for example, celebrated knowledge as the corporate asset of the future: no costs related to manufacturing or distribution, increasing returns as initial development costs are spread across rising volumes, and so on. This is fairly predictable stuff, clearly derived from and tied to those heady Internet/Web days.

Not surprisingly, McKinsey & Company had some specific observations about Enron, which had subscribed heavily to McKinsey's asset-light thinking:

> Enron: Creating a new industry from embedded knowledge. . . .
>
> Some companies succeed in defining new industries by exploiting knowledge opportunities that are overlooked in existing products and processes. . . .
>
> Until the early 1990s, Enron was a gas pipeline transmission company like many others. But its managers realized that embedded in what appeared to be a commodity gas business was valuable information about product flow, supply, and demand. They established Enron Capital and Trade Resources to exploit this information through an innovative range of risk management contracts. The enterprise helped Enron grow its sales by 7 percent per year and its shareholder returns by 27 percent per year between 1988 and 1995.[7]

In an interview in 2000, Skilling talked confidently about his company's (and former company's) asset-light philosophy:

> People like assets; they can go in the field and kick them. It gives people a certain warm feeling. What's becoming clear is that there's nothing magic about hard assets. They don't generate cash. What does, is a better solution for your customer. And increasingly that's intellectual—not physical-assets-driven. The market is sending us a very clear signal. We are in a new economy, and the market is willing to pay for market position, not necessarily assets.[8]

This is true enough for what turned out to be a relatively short-lived and exceptional (in the sense of *unusual*) era in business history. Two weeks after Enron filed for bankruptcy, *New York Times* commentator Paul Krugman wrote a devastating piece entitled, "Death by Guru." Krugman derided the notion that the future belonged to "fabless" (that is, nonfabricating) asset-light companies with *attitude.* He voiced particular scorn for the analysts who fell for—or actively promoted—this twaddle:

> Admittedly, there is a chicken-or-Enron question: Was Enron so admired because it embodied faddish management ideas so perfectly, or did those ideas become so faddish because of Enron's apparent success? Probably both. The point is that the stock market rewarded Enron for following such a fashionable business strategy, and few analysts were willing to fly in the face of fashion by questioning Enron's numbers. Enron executives had every incentive to turn the company into a caricature of itself—a 'giant hedge fund sitting on top of a pipeline,' as one critic said. And the power that came with fashionability shielded the company from awkward questions about its accounts.[9]

Say what else you will about assets, but they do have one really nice redeeming feature: They act as a welcome buffer when hard times set in. When your banks and institutional investors want reassurance about your staying power, it is helpful to be able to point to your factories, your distribution systems, and so on. At such moments, you do not want to appear to be "corporate-lite."

I do not dismiss asset-light thinking out of hand, and neither should you. As investors, we have to be open to new ways of thinking. Some of the great innovations in business history have been met with scorn and derision—often because some minor negative consequence obscures the beauty of the innovation. The invention of paper currency, for example, fits this pattern.

Is there anything inherently bad about an asset-light company? No. The real problem with Enron is that there is, as of yet, no good ways to assess the value of an asset-light company. It is relatively easy (if tedious) to assess the value of a steel mill and to report that value to your shareholders and

lenders. There is as yet no meaningful ways to assign value to an innovative approach. And investors need to seek out *value*, either present or future.

So this is our case history in a nutshell: Enron got *really good* at using
derivatives to ply its trade of energy trading. (More on derivatives later.)
Then, tempted by the siren song of the dot-com universe, it stepped sideways into the complicated world of broadband. This did not work out very
well, to put it gently. (More on this ill-fated move later, too.) Then the company began using its inventiveness with derivatives to hide the growing
mountain of debt derived from the unsuccessful foray into broadband. Then
came December 2001—and misery.

However, can we really fault Enron for stepping sideways and trying to
inject itself into the hot, "happening" sector of the economy? Didn't Enron's
investors expect exactly this kind of bold stroke? And can we fault the company's leaders for making what turned out to be a bad bet? My response is,
"Yes and no." We can fault their analysis—and perhaps their arrogance—
but we probably cannot fault their determination to grow and diversify.

Growth and diversification are tough challenges, however. "Improvements in information technology have created new opportunities for innovative companies," cautioned Federal Reserve Chairman Alan Greenspan
in March 2002, "but an environment of rapid technological change is also
one in which the resulting profit opportunities are difficult to assess and
project. In particular, such rapid change has heightened the potential for
competitors to encroach on established market positions. This process of
capital reallocation has not only increased the long-term earnings growth
potential of the economy as a whole, but has widened as well the degree of
uncertainty for individual firms."[10]

In other words, adventurousness can be good for a company. Diversification can be a good thing. Or it can be *bad* for an individual company (but
still good for the larger economy, which is Greenspan's beat). The fast-moving pace of today's economy, though, and the difficulty of predicting what's
coming next raise the stakes and increase the risks for the adventurous.
Enron bet big stakes in a high-risk game—and lost.

Then there was that *other* piece of the story. . . .

Andersen and the Chronology of Doom

Perhaps you are surprised that I have been able to get this far into the Enron
saga without once mentioning an accounting firm called Arthur Andersen.
Let me bring Andersen on stage by means of a brief chronology.

As already noted, Enron in the late 1990s and early 2000s was spreading its wings. Its audacious venture in broadband propelled its stock price to unprecedented heights, rising from $40 in January 2000 to $70 only 3 months later.

This proved unsustainable, but on October 15, 2001, the price of a share of Enron stock was still a respectable $33.17. The next day, the Houston-based energy-trading company issued a press release stating that it had to report "non-recurring charges totaling $1.01 billion after-tax." Two weeks later, Enron's stock was quoted at $13.90.

Then, on November 8, came a second batch of very bad news. The company issued a restatement of its reported income for the years 1997 to 2000, to the tune of $586 million. This rewriting of history was a drastic step indeed and one that was certain to shake investor confidence. Why did it have to happen? Briefly put, it became inevitable when the company's auditor, Andersen, decided that the financial results of some of those complicated Enron partnerships should have been consolidated with those of the parent company after all.

On November 28, Standard & Poor's and Moody's Investors Service, the principal rating agencies, downgraded Enron's debt to junk-bond status, and this precipitated the company's collapse.[11] "A classic run on the bank," complained Enron's former CEO Jeff Skilling, in his February 2002 testimony before a House subcommittee. "A liquidity crisis spurred by a lack of confidence in the company." By month's end, the company stock was trading at a pathetic 26 cents a share. The Chapter 11 filing that took place 2 days later was only the *coup de grace*.

The question begs asking: *How much longer could the Houston energy-trading company have managed to stay in business had there been no need for the October and November 2001 restatements?* No one can say for certain, but my own opinion is that Enron could have limped along indefinitely. Yes, its debt burden was staggering, and its technology portfolio had lost a great deal of its value. The leverage that Enron had foolishly sought in its own stock was amplifying its difficulties, and the corporation's culture of self-congratulation—premature and financially extravagant—was now playing against its survival.

However, one can make the case that in time things would have turned around for Enron. The economy, then mired in a deepening recession, would rebound eventually. The plunge into broadband ultimately might have been proven to be an excellent bet, although with hindsight it was clearly premature. In short, I believe that Enron could have made it—if not for the calamitous restatements of October and November 2001.

Therefore, the question is, *Who created the need for these restatements?* In my mind at least, the answer to this question is crystal clear—Arthur Andersen. And that ill-starred company is the subject of Chapter 2.

LESSONS FOR INVESTORS

Caveat emptor. If the nation's seventh-largest public company— the darling of analysts, business school professors, and Wall Street alike—can engage in deception and trickery, you need to watch out for your own interests.

Do your homework. It is no longer enough for investors to believe what analysts tell them—and certainly what corporations tell them.

Be prepared to be baffled. Sometimes, even the brightest and most experienced people, working full time, cannot figure out what's going on with the likes of Enron. You cannot ever know everything, or even enough. If you cannot get comfortable with this, stay out of the pool.

Rising tides may not float all boats equally. High-flying companies can make serious mistakes and implode, even in booming economic times. Do not assume that your favorite company's escalator will always go up.

Beware of fads. For several years, all the gurus agreed that "asset light" was the place to be. Now the Wall Street Journal advocates investing in "boring" companies. The best policy is to avoid the fads altogether.

Diversify. As an investor, and certainly as an employee with an employer-heavy 401(k), you must make sure that your portfolio reflects the very real risks of doing business. Cutting-edge businesses carry enormous risks. Why did Enron's stock plummet from $70 a share to 26 cents a share? In part because of chicanery—but also because Enron was involved in highly risky sectors. I will return to the issue of portfolio diversification in later chapters.

2

Holding the Accounting Firm Accountable

In light of the Enron affair and the seemingly endless barrage of news about other firms restating profits, artificially embellishing revenues, and creating obscure 'special purpose vehicles' conveniently off their balance sheet, no one can reasonably doubt that there is a crisis in the accounting and auditing profession.

—PAUL A. VOLCKER, former Federal Reserve Board chairman, chairman of the International Accounting Standards Committee[1]

The accounting firm of Arthur Andersen was indicted on March 18, 2002, for its role in the Enron affair. Shortly thereafter, Andersen personnel took to the streets wearing "I am Arthur Andersen" T-shirts, protesting their company's treatment at the hands of the federal government. They felt that the government was wrong to blame—and perhaps even bring down—an entire company because of the alleged misdeeds of a few. Two days after the indictment, advertisements appeared in major newspapers making the same point: *"Don't condemn us all just because there may have been a black sheep or two in the fold. Which, by the way, we don't think there were."*

"The Justice Department has weighed in with a tragically wrong indictment of our whole firm," proclaimed one of these ads, in part. "The indictment is a political broadside rather than a focus on the facts. Our attorneys are absolutely convinced that no one in this firm committed a crime, and we are confident our firm will be absolved at trial."

Clearly, those who wrote and placed these ads hoped to fan antigovernment sentiment and perhaps turn the tide of public opinion in Andersen's favor. ("There are errors in the Justice Department's case," the ad went on, "which is perhaps why the department refused to even allow Andersen officials to appear before the Grand Jury. Where's the justice in this?") However, the decision to invoke the wisdom of "our attorneys" hints at how out-of-touch with reality Andersen was by this point. Simply put, the accounting firm's leaders had *no idea* how the public was perceiving the Enron affair. The truth was that Americans were furious, and a lot of that fury was directed at Andersen.

Investors in particular were angry. They resented tales of fast-and-loose accounting practices, and for good reason. If you cannot trust the numbers in the back of the annual report—that is, the numbers that are audited, footnoted, and blessed by the corporation's high-priced accounting firm—how are you supposed to make informed investment decisions? A *Los Angeles Times* opinion poll at the time made the point clearly, focusing on people who do the bulk of their investing through 401(k) vehicles: "Americans who own 401(k) plans, though broadly pro-business in attitude, were much more likely than non-investors to support new governmental regulations aimed at accountants and the managers of pension plans."[2]

No, the accounting firm does not work for the individual investor. However, to the extent that the firm works *against* the interests of individual investors, it may be courting disaster.

Perhaps more ominously, the corporate community, too, was losing faith. A *Wall Street Journal* poll released in this same time period revealed that "companies using outside auditors give the accounting profession an overall performance score of 61, or 'D.' By comparison, business-to-business services generally average 80, or a 'B' grade, while top-performing firms with the strongest client relationships score in the 90 to 100 range, or an 'A.'"[3]

Oblivious, Andersen kept serving up the twaddle. In a double-page spread placed in national newspapers on March 22, 2002, the disgraced firm attempted to tug at the nation's heart strings, this time swapping out "our attorneys" and swapping in "family members and retirees" in their place:

Arthur Andersen

Injustice for all

One indictment

28,000 Andersen U.S. men and women

5200 retirees

85,000 family members

All put at risk

It's simply unjust. . . .

But what were the impartial observers—those in a position to know—saying? Was this a case of a vengeful government running amok and looking for a scapegoat? Hardly. Paul A. Volcker, the highly respected former Federal Reserve chairman and chairman of Andersen's independent oversight board, weighed in to the contrary. "The board is fully conscious," he declared in somber tones, "of the serious concerns that resulted in the indictment of Andersen by the Justice Department."[4]

Andersen was in the untenable position of trying to have it both ways. "Andersen's partners and employees all claim that they have nothing to do with Enron," wrote one Internet-based observer. "This rings hollow, since they fell all over themselves to claim even a small association with Enron a couple of years ago, when the energy trader was flying high."[5]

The conclusion: When confronted with a firm-threatening crisis, deny everything—including your former friends—and try to blame it all on an out-of-control federal bureaucracy.

Blameless Victim or Repeat Offender?

Once again, I want to focus on some specifics of the Enron fiasco—in this case, specifics having to do with Arthur Anderson—because I want to equip the individual investor to function more effectively in the post-Enron world. No doubt doctoral dissertations will be written about exactly how and where Andersen went wrong, and I will leave most of the ugly details to those writers. However, we need to look at enough of these details to ask and answer two key questions:

> Was Andersen's role in the Enron affair an aberration or part of a bigger picture?
>
> If it was part of a bigger picture, what does this mean for the community of individual investors (you and me)? What numbers can we trust?

Unfortunately, there is simply no doubt about the answer to the first question. Andersen was *not* a blameless victim but was in fact a repeat offender. *New York Times* correspondent Kurt Eichenwald assembled a devastating portrait of Andersen's track record in the months and years preceding the unfolding of the Enron drama and documented the government's increasing anger with an arrogant Andersen. A Securities and Exchange Commission (SEC) task force had uncovered recent accounting frauds "at a number of Andersen clients," wrote Eichenwald, "including Colonial Realty in Connecticut, the Sunbeam Corporation, and even a nonprofit organization, the Baptist Foundation of Arizona. In those cases, investors and others who believed records certified by Andersen lost tens, if not hundreds, of millions of dollars. In each case, regulators and law enforcement officials had developed evidence that Andersen was, in part, responsible for the financial disasters."[6]

In its dealings with another client, Waste Management, Inc. (WMI), Andersen's auditors for several consecutive years had approved financial statements that they knew to be flawed and had advised the company's directors about that state of affairs. The SEC task force began scrutinizing WMI in 1998, Eichenwald reported, "after the company announced that 4 years of its pretax profit reports had been inflated by $1.4 billion."

Many cases of alleged accounting fraud hinge on the concept of *materiality*. Auditors look over a company's numbers and its explanations of those numbers and make a supposedly independent assessment of whether a particular event, condition, or outcome is *material*, or relevant, to the company's financial health. The standard of materiality is both high and imprecise: If a "reasonable person" would have made decisions about a company—for example, the decision about whether or not to invest in that company—as a result of having known about this particular event, condition, or outcome, then it is deemed to be material.

Materiality was central to the WMI imbroglio. "In its audit in 1995," wrote Arthur A., a Web gadfly who also has assembled a damning case against Andersen, "Andersen uncovered $160 million that the company failed to expense in 1993–1994. At the time, Waste Management also received $160 million in gains from the sale of a subsidiary, 'netted' the gain against the past unaccounted expenses, and avoiding disclosing anything to investors on the basis that the net impact of the two was not material. According to the Securities and Exchange Commission, '[Andersen] reasoned that the netting and the non-disclosure of the misstatements and the unrelated gain were not material to the Company's 1995 financial statements taken as a whole. In fact, these items were material. Andersen's 1995 unqualified audit report was materially false and misleading.'"[7]

In other words, Andersen colluded with WMI's management to paint an overly rosy portrait of reality, and that is not permitted. When it settled with the SEC in June 2001, Andersen paid a $7 million fine and accepted an injunction forbidding the firm from engaging in similar sorts of wrongdoing in the future.

Andersen now knew that it was on the SEC's radar screen. "We cannot afford losses due to failed audits, flawed consulting projects, or unhappy clients," as an internal memo—addressed to partners and dated September 5, 2001—put it. "Our reputation won't tolerate it, and our balance sheet won't support it—certainly not if costs continue to escalate."[8]

We can't afford it; our balance sheet won't support it—are these the lessons that Andersen should have drawn from this initial brush with the feds? Obviously not. Andersen simply did not get the main point: *Mend your ways!* The company had discharged its professional responsibilities very badly, gotten caught, and gotten punished. Instead of looking in the mirror, however, the firm decided that a vindictive government was at fault.

This was the backdrop for those people taking to the streets in those T-shirts and for all those double-page ads in the papers. The truth was that the March 14, 2002, indictment of the accounting partnership should have come as no surprise to those within the partnership.

The claim made by Andersen's "spin-meisters"—that not all should be punished for the sins of a few—has a strange ring to it. It makes sense only if the shredding of documents was the isolated initiative of a small number of individuals—or preferably, a single rotten apple. This is the interpretation that Andersen stuck to consistently. It was David Duncan—a member of the Andersen team working at Enron who had ordered the shredding of documents on October 21, 2001. *He* was the "bad guy," Andersen broadly implied, and 3 months later—on January 15, 2002—the company fired him.

I have worked in lots of contexts, but never a professional partnership, which was Andersen's structure. I suppose that it is conceivable that within that structure there is no sense of shared responsibility and no sense that the "person at the top" has to own up to the shortcomings of his or her subordinates. This is conceivable, but not likely, because corporate clients would not put up with an organization that did not take responsibility for its own actions. And don't forget that Andersen's initial response was to proclaim that *"our lawyers say no one has broken any laws."* Once the partnership had identified a credibly culpable individual, it threw him overboard and then denied that he was in any way representative of the firm.

Skilling to Everybody: *It Was Andersen's Fault*

I can name at least one person in addition to myself who believes that Andersen contributed mightily to Enron's downfall. That person is Enron's former chief executive officer (CEO), Jeffrey Skilling, of "asset-light" fame.

Andersen is the guilty party. This was the line of defense that Skilling erected for himself and to which he clung tenaciously when he was called as a witness before both House and Senate committees looking into the Enron mess. I am not saying that I buy his protestations of personal innocence (see below), but it seemed clear, watching those performances on TV, that his deep belief in Andersen's guilt gave him the enormous measure of self-assurance that he displayed in front of skeptical congressional panels. Indeed, it probably got him talking in front of those committees in the first place, unlike his colleagues in Enron's upper-echelon management, most of whom "took the Fifth."

"I'm not an accountant," Skilling repeated relentlessly. Even when it became clear that he was irritating his interrogators, he stuck with his defense. Here is a typical excerpt from an exchange he engaged in with California Democratic Senator Barbara Boxer:

BOXER: Were you aware of that?

SKILLING: I am not an accountant.

BOXER: I didn't ask you that. Is her statement true?

SKILLING: I think I'd have to be an accountant to know if it's true. I don't know.

BOXER: Wait a minute. You have to be an accountant to know that a company could never use its own stock to generate a gain or

> avoid a loss on an income statement? What was your educa-
> tion, Mr. Skilling? I know I read it was pretty good. What . . .
>
> SKILLING: I have a master's in business administration.
>
> When asked more precise questions about the shaky capi-
> talization of Enron's partnerships, Skilling kept it up tena-
> ciously. It seemed that it *must* be okay, he reiterated, because
> the Andersen accountants had not seen anything wrong with
> it. Here is part of the back-and-forth he had with Illinois
> Republican Senator Peter Fitzgerald:
>
> FITZGERALD: So you didn't see issuing stock as being at all risky to capi-
> talize . . . [a particular partnership] with even an unlimited
> amount of Enron stock?
>
> SKILLING: See it as risky—quite frankly, as long as the accountants had
> told me that they thought this was an appropriate structure, I
> felt comfortable with it.

Well, here is another case where a leader is not exactly jumping to take
responsibility for a problem. And for a Harvard-educated MBA to assert
that he more or less handed the financial reins on his company over to the
outside accountants strains credibility. But he definitely got bad advice. As
the report prepared by Enron's board of directors concluded, "There is abun-
dant evidence that Andersen in fact offered Enron advice at every step, from
inception through restructuring and ultimately to terminating the . . . [sus-
pect partnership]. Enron followed that advice. The Andersen work papers
we were permitted to review do not reflect consideration of a number of the
important accounting issues that we believe exist."[9]

It pains me to agree with the likes of Skilling and his board. Nevertheless, I do. To some extent at least, it *was* Andersen's fault.

The Spirit and the Letter

One interesting aspect of the Enron and post-Enron investigations is the
emergence of low standards disguised as high standards. I am thinking, for
example, of the pundit who applauded SEC Chairman Harvey L. Pitt when
he "admonished accountants and lawyers to follow the spirit, not simply the
letter, of the law."[9]

Why was Pitt reduced to advocating the self-evident? Because so many companies, Enron included, had grown accustomed to playing it cute—playing the "Gee, it didn't look like there was a line where I could mention this" act.

The accounting style that focuses on the *letter* of the law, rather than its spirit, might be described as the "checkbox style" of accounting. Checkbox accounting grows directly out of checkbox management. "Every time a smart chief financial officer (CFO) or investment banker wants to do something," says University of Chicago accounting expert Roman Weil, "they look through the rule book and say, 'this isn't here,' so they design a transaction that is not covered, and then ask the accountants, 'where does it say I can't do it?'"[10] In checkbox accounting, financial reports are prepared against a list of no-nos—practices that are clearly illegal and which therefore have to be avoided. If you can put together the entire report without getting checks in any of your boxes, you are considered successful, even if the resulting information is less than accurate.

Enron's whistleblower, Sherron Watkins, made a similar point in her February 2002 testimony before the House Energy and Commerce Committee. "I think somehow in this country our financial accounting system has morphed into the tax code," she observed. "And, you know, in tax accounting, if you follow the codes, whatever result you get, you are justified in using that treatment. In financial accounting, a number of my accounting friends have said [that] if you follow the rules, even if you get squirrelly results, you know, you have a leg to stand on."[11]

Some commentators argue that these "unholy" trends parallel the increasing complexity of tax law. In his appearance before the Senate, Jeffrey Skilling publicly longed for a shift to what he called the "European structure," in which—he asserted—"it's more what makes sense than what the specific rules are that govern transactions." However, the fact that these same ills are often ascribed by Europeans to *their* tax codes suggests that the explanation lies elsewhere.

In fact, a number of forces have converged to promote checkbox accounting. One is checkbox management, as described earlier. Corporate America's relentless drive for greater earnings is a theme that I will return to throughout this book. When one company spots a loophole, it takes full advantage of it, and other companies quickly follow. The edge goes away at that point; what remains is the letter-of-the-law mentality.

A second factor—Enron's whining notwithstanding—is a relatively lax regulatory environment, particularly at the SEC. President Clinton's SEC chairman, Arthur Levitt, Jr., was widely regarded as a fierce advocate of investors. On taking office in August 2001, George W. Bush's chairman, Harvey Pitt, announced that he wanted a "kinder and gentler" SEC, meaning that he wanted a less adversarial relationship between his commission and the companies it regulates. Those words have since come back to haunt him, of course, but that *was* his avowed starting point.

Too Cozy for Comfort

There is yet another contributor to the emergence of checkbox accounting, and that is the alarming coziness between corporation and auditor—in the case at hand, between Enron and Andersen. At the risk of stating the obvious, the whole notion behind an independent audit of financial statement is *independence*. The corporation acts, and the auditor passes judgment on the financial implications of the action.

This, emphatically, was *not* the relationship between Enron and Andersen. It is worth noting that as the details of that relationship came to light, Andersen felt compelled to lay claim to the role of a noncombatant. "Andersen auditors provide accounting advice," company spokesman Patrick Dorton told *The Wall Street Journal*. "They don't structure or promote transactions."[12] However, this does not go far enough when it comes to the kind of checkoff accounting that sanctioned Enron's undercapitalized partnerships. Enron proposed, and Andersen disposed. With one notable exception (described below), I have never seen a shred of evidence that the two companies disagreed on the appropriateness of any aspect of these deals. They were accomplices—with shared responsibility for what ensued.

What makes an *accomplice*? In the narrow sense, it means working together toward a mutual goal. In a deeper sense, however, it means subscribing to a shared value system, building a common culture, *thinking alike*. Those working the Enron account at Andersen subscribed wholeheartedly to the Enron culture—so much so that others at Andersen's main Houston office considered the Enron team members as outsiders in their own firm. They were *Enron* types.

It is true that a rift developed between Andersen's Enron team and Carl Bass, who headed up Andersen's own internal Professional Standards Group in Houston. What happened next was illuminating: Enron wanted Bass out of the picture—and Andersen complied. Bass was dismissed. The message came through loud and clear that the union between Andersen and Enron was of overriding importance, and whoever failed to understand this and act accordingly would be eliminated from the picture.

Why does all this matter? Because at the end of the day, Enron and Andersen would be held up to an *ethical* standard rather than a technical one. This is a point that Enron and Andersen (and to some extent, the congressional inquisitors who came along in the wake of the mess) seemed to miss consistently.

Consider the following excerpt from the "Powers Report" produced by Enron's board: "When Enron and Andersen reviewed the transaction closely in 2001, they concluded that Chewco did not satisfy the SPE accounting rules and—because JEDI's non-consolidation depended on Chewco's status—neither did JEDI. In November 2001, Enron announced that it would consolidate Chewco and JEDI retroactive to 1997." What the public hears, when it hears this sort of stuff, is not the specifics of a complex transaction. It hears *collusion*, *accomplices*, *the fox in the henhouse*, and so on.

The public, in other words, was interested in the moral, rather than the mechanical, aspects of the Enron/Andersen affair. And in part through their collusion, both companies came up short.

Beyond "Marking to Market"

Once upon a time, not so long ago, some ingenious financial types began suggesting that the world of business should leave behind the concept of *book value*—that is, a stated value of a given corporate asset that is based on depreciation and other generally accepted accounting practices. For perfectly legitimate business reasons, the tax code allows companies to write down the value of certain assets—real estate, equipment, and so on—according to predetermined schedules. The book value of a given asset, therefore, can be well below its market value.

And so these ingenious financial types began making the case that assets should be *marked to market*. This, they argued, would be the only accurate way to report the actual worth of an asset. Marking to market would paint a picture of *true* economic value—far more realistic than focusing on a purchase price that might have been paid many years ago, less depreciation, and so on and so on. This is also the principle behind *write-downs* of assets: When the marked-to-market value of an asset drops below its book value, the difference must be accounted for as a write-down.

Marking to market was intended in part to serve as a safeguard against speculative behavior, especially on the junk-bond market. And in fact, the Financial Institutions Reform Recovery and Enforcement Act, passed in August 1989, required thrifts to mark their junk bonds to market, thus letting people know how big a junk-bond exposure (or actual loss) each thrift had incurred.[13]

This sounds sensible, right? However, marking to market turned out to have its own problems, especially when there is no good sense of "market." If you own a stock that has not traded in many years, for example, you may have next to no idea what that stock is worth. Yes, this is an unusual situation, but what about the case where the market for a given stock is relatively thin, limiting its liquidity, so that the most recent trade in that stock resulted in a distorted price? Or what if there is as yet no proven market for your company's innovative new product? Or what if you have a clear bead on today's market, but that market can change dramatically the day after tomorrow?

Thus, even if you are determined to act in good faith vis-à-vis your investors, current and potential, you may still face major challenges as you assign values to assets. Depending on your particular sector, those challenges may be acknowledged in the "rules of the road." For example, energy companies—which, of course, do business in a particularly volatile sector— play according to accounting rules that give them "wide leeway to make assumptions about the direction of the market."[14]

All of this goes to say that valuing corporate assets—and auditing those valuations—is complicated, full of value judgments, and—at the end of the day—somewhat arbitrary. The results you get will depend to some extent on the assumptions that you make. Again, this argues for a good old-fashioned arm's-length relationship between the auditor and the audited.

From Enron to Andersen—To the Swoon

It started as the Enron affair, and then it became the Andersen affair. Then it became the Global Crossing affair and the WorldCom affair and the Qwest affair and the WorldCom affair revisited, and so on, and so on ad nauseum. In each case, the details were different, but the patterns were very similar.

And the patterns were *scary*. The enormous swoon of the stock market in the first half of 2002 was in part the result of overprice stocks meeting a faltering economy. (A Dow-Jones study of the first-quarter results of 1146 firms found that, on a collective basis, they were in the red for the first time in 10 years.) It was also an aftershock of terrorist attacks and anxiety about future terrorist attacks. Most observers, however, myself included, believe that the most important cause of the stock market plunge was investors' growing lack of confidence in the numbers that were being reported by corporations.

When buying and selling shares of stock, investors have to base their decision making in part on the information in the corporation's financial reports. There is really nowhere else to go. If those financial reports cannot be trusted, then we either have to buy and sell without the information we need—or we have to get out of the game. This is what a lot of investors did in the first half of 2002—they got out.

The Enron debacle made it clear that there were several reasons why financial reports could not be trusted any longer. Some of those reasons were superficial; others were deep-rooted. Among the superficial reasons was the inclusion in the most visible parts of financial reports of items with no real impact on the company's earnings, such as the marking to market of derivatives used in hedging. (This painted an overly rosy picture.) Among the deep-rooted reasons was the nonexpensing of executive stock option plans, which can have an impact on earnings in a nonnegligible way—as much as 10 percent, according to Standard & Poor's.

Efforts are now underway to address some of these abuses and get the numbers closer to right in the future. As investors, we have to monitor these reform efforts, but the good news is that corporate America now understands that if it wants us to get back in the game—and it does!—then it will have to give us a much more accurate version of the truth.

You and I Played a Part, Too

There's one last factor that I want to introduce at this point. I said earlier that the complexity of the tax code does not lead directly to the excesses of the Enrons and Andersens of this world. There *is* a piece of that code, however, that can be blamed for many of those excesses.

Simply put, in our system, dividends are taxed more heavily than capital gains. The not-so-surprising result is that investors prefer to earn their returns in the form of capital gains rather than dividends. This, in turn, means that corporations do their best to pump up their stock prices. In theory, of course, a rising stock price can (and *should*) reflect a company that is increasing in value. Far too often, though, a company's leaders are tempted to play games with their earnings in order to get stock-price increases that they have not actually "earned."

Companies like Enron make an unhealthy transition when they play this game. They start out by playing some sort of genuine role in the economy—producing valuable goods or services, creating value—and slowly turn into caricatures of themselves. They begin playing the "bubble game." This transition is accelerated when external circumstances go bad or the business model proves to be less robust than was anticipated. Rather than retrenching—or, God forbid, giving up!—they become what I call *earnings-obsessed.*

I should distinguish here between earnings-*focused* and earnings-obsessed. During the dot-com craze, the more conservative voices in the investment community—the Warren Buffett types—persisted in asking an embarrassing question: *Exactly how and when are these high-flying companies going to make money?* As it turned out, the answer in many cases was "never." The survivors in the dot-com universe (the Amazons and eBays) accepted their responsibility to make a buck. They became earnings-focused, and this was a good thing—for themselves and for their investors.

Earnings-obsessed is different—in fact, it is almost the opposite. *Earnings-obsessed* means *manipulating the reporting* of value rather than *creating* value. In many cases, it works—but only for a while. Enron's executives had the heady experience of having their stock price double in 6 weeks. "The Street" loved them. Somewhere along the line, they started believing their own propaganda. They believed that they had discovered a money machine—capitalizing subsidiaries or pseudosubsidiaries on call options on the price of their stock—and that henceforth the sky was the limit.

So yes, Enron (aided and abetted by Andersen) soiled its own nest through its earnings obsession. However, let's go back to the beginning of this section. Can't you make a strong case that we, the investors of the world, have to share some of the blame? If we investors make it clear that we are no longer interested in dividends, why wouldn't corporations tilt toward pumping up the stock price? Keep in mind that executive stock options—another subject to which I will return later—push in the same direction. The shareholders would rather see their portfolio value soar than be paid healthy dividends, management reasons, and if we go in that direction, we personally get richer.

It's a system with no checks and balances—at least until the bubble pops. And like it or not, we investors are accomplices to that system.

LESSONS FOR INVESTORS

The "appropriate" role of the accounting firm is undergoing a rapid evolution—toward the past. The auditor is supposed to provide independent assessments of a company's finances. The auditor is *not* supposed to help pick strategies or structure deals. The recent trend of accounting firms unloading their consulting arms reflects the collective realization that having an accounting firm propose a course of action (consulting) and then passing judgment on the outcome of that course of action (accounting) is riddled with potential conflicts of interest.

The development of a merged and exotic culture between a high-flying company and its accounting firm is almost always a bad thing. This is hard for the individual investor to pick up on, of course, but there are sometimes clues pointing to excessive coziness.

It is increasingly difficult to assign values to assets. Some of the time-honored valuation techniques, such as marking to market, simply do not work well in many contemporary circumstances. The accelerating pace of change, the increasing technology component of many products and services, the difficulty of assessing the future value of an innovation—all make the task of valuation far more difficult.

Beware the disconnect between value and valuation. Maybe the price-earnings ratio is, indeed, old-fashioned and out of touch for today's markets—or maybe it is not.

Regulation and legislation, although well intentioned, can lead to damaging distortions. For example, taxing dividends more heavily than capital gains provides a huge incentive for "bubble thinking."

Investors share some of the blame. To the extent that we ignore dividends—a boring but accurate measure of a company's value-creation abilities—in favor of stock-price appreciation, we may be forcing corporate America into bubble thinking.

Capitalism 101

At the beginning of this book I implied that we would sometimes go slowly in order to go fast. This is one of those cases. In this chapter I want to get some fundamentals in place as a foundation for later discussions. If the territory I cover is already familiar to you, feel free to move on.

The territory of this chapter is capitalism—specifically, capitalism as a system of investing money in enterprises. As you will see, a seemingly simple process can become complex quickly.

Buying, Selling, Leasing

Capitalism presumes the existence of private property. If I see something I need, I am supposed to strike a deal with its legitimate owner. Conversely, if I own something that someone else needs, that person has to come up with a proposition that will appeal to me.

Depending on the nature of the bargain that is struck, the transaction may or may not change the ownership of the object of the negotiation. If the deal entails a transfer of ownership, the transaction is called a *sale*. If there is no transfer of ownership, it is a *loan*. So far, so good, right?

In our modern economies, things generally are exchanged for money. This is not necessarily a given; other economies are barter-based. In fact, the question of whether or not a *capacity swap*—a complex derivative instrument used by several of the companies that have hit the regulatory rocks recently, including Global Crossing and Qwest—is actually a barter transaction became a focus of the Securities and Exchange Commission (SEC) investigations early in 2002.[1]

The amount of money agreed on between the trading parties for transferring ownership or use is the *price,* and anything that has a price associated with it is a *good* or a *commodity.* If the transfer of ownership takes place before the price is paid, the transaction is a *credit* purchase. If the opposite is true—that is, if the price is paid before ownership or use changes hands—the transaction is a *forward* purchase. And finally, of course, the place where a commodity is traded (for the amount of money that its price expresses) is called a *market* and, in some circumstances, an *exchange.*

Loans 101

Continuing along with our fundamentals, we need to talk briefly about the characteristics of loans. Borrowing a commodity has an appeal mainly because it is cheaper to gain the *use* of that commodity if you are not also acquiring ownership. Having borrowed something, you can act as if you own it for a set period of time. You are committed to returning the good in working condition at the end of that period (that is, when the loan comes to *maturity*). Sometimes you borrow something for so long that you are bound to damage the good to some extent. This effectively transforms the loan into a sale, which is the case with many *leases.*

Sometimes the ownership of a loan is transferred to a third party. This automatically creates what is called a *secondary market* for the commodity in question. The current circumstances of the loan constrain its transfer price: the time remaining to maturity, the attractiveness of competing loans of similar length, and so on. The financial concept of *present value*—that is, calculating the current value of a future cash flow—is used to determine a sale price for an outstanding loan; it is also useful for marking a commodity to market, as discussed in Chapter 2.

Let's call the thing that is being lent *capital.* There is a price attached to the loan of capital, called the *face value* of the loan, that is the price that one would to pay for the full transfer of its ownership. The *face value* of a $1 million loan, obviously, is $1 million.

Capitalism at Work

Some uses of capital have the capacity only to diminish in value. If you put your money into a car, it loses value (lots of value!) in that first tenth of a mile that you drive away from the showroom. This reduction in value is *depreciation*. Some other types of capital hold a capacity for growing or *appreciating*. (Your car may in fact appreciate if it becomes a collectible antique, but you will have to wait a very long time to find out if this kind of fortune will smile on you.) Although capital may grow on its own, more often than not, capital will grow through the industry of individuals. Let's call a person who possesses a particular gift for making capital appreciate an *entrepreneur*.

Any type of productive activity on the part of entrepreneurs requires a putting-together of resources—the "advances," in the word of eighteenth-century French economist François Quesnay. The concept of an advance holds within it the notion that putting up a stake will sooner or later produce some sort of return, which is hopefully bigger than (or at least equal to) the advance. Today we capitalists take this for granted as the way of the world—the way things work—but when you think about it, the notion of making a profit is part of a belief system, grounded in nothing more than our profit-loving hearts.

Some capitalists find this annoying and seek to ground their secular religion in the natural order. The Physiocrats, for example—a group of French economists from several centuries back—ascribed profits to the benevolent action of the sun. They argued that although an individual producer might be able to make the sun deliver a return solely through his or her own industry, most producers in the real world needed advances. They needed an investment of capital by a third party. And this is how we capitalists become part of the natural order of things.

Any type of productive activity requires a certain time to unfold. During that period of unfolding, all kinds of things can happen that can render the outcome of the activity uncertain. In other words, there is a *risk* attached to advancing capital: The advances often get refunded, but sometimes they do not. The longer the time period that is needed before a return can be generated, the greater is the risk.

When capital is examined over a period of time, and when its initial value is compared with its value at the end of that time period, there are only three possible outcomes: The value is higher at the end of the period (*profit* or *income*), the value is lower (*loss*), or it is the same.

A profit or a loss generally is expressed as an amount of cash associated with a given time period: "There was a profit of $30,000 over the year." The time element is critical, of course, because there is an enormous difference between a $30,000 profit made over a year starting with capital worth $3 million and a $30,000 profit made over a month growing out of a $15,000 investment.

There is a conventional way of making profits (and losses) comparable: assessing them over a standard period of time—typically a year—with the profit (or loss) being calculated as a proportion of the invested capital, which translates into a rate of return. Thus, in the first example, the *profit rate* is 1 percent ($30,000 divided by $3 million) per year. In the second example, the *profit rate* is 200 percent ($30,000 divided by $15,000) per month. Moreover, if one ignores the fact that a monthly profit can be reinvested the following month, thus making the pot bigger, the profit rate is 2400 percent (200 percent times 12) per year.

Capital Growth Through Diversification

It is time to complicate things a little bit and thereby make things a little more exciting. Let's look at an example of how capital grows when one factors in the power of something called *diversification*. I will use a hypothetical example involving two entrepreneurs named Julie and Percy.

Last year, Julie managed in her business to make her capital grow from an initial investment of $1 million to $1.2 million. The yearly profit rate of her business, therefore, was 20 percent [(1.2 − 1)/1]. Percy, meanwhile, managed to make an initial capital of $2 million grow into $2.2 million, so he made a yearly profit rate of 10 percent [(2.2 − 2)/2]. The actual profit they each made last year was $200,000, but those identical amounts represented different rates of return on their businesses.

Let's suppose that Julie, Inc., is *undercapitalized*. In other words, Julie does not have enough "advances" behind her business. If she did, she is convinced—and for the sake of our argument, we will assume that she is right—she could double the size of her business in the coming year and still maintain her 20 percent profit rate. Not surprisingly, she is on the lookout for an additional $1 million. Of course, she is prepared to hand over part of her expected additional profit to the person or organization that advances this additional money. (More definitions: The actual cash she will borrow will be the *principal* of the loan; the price of the capital, as we have seen, will be its *nominal amount* or *face value*; and the amount she will return as payment to the lender will be the *interest* on the loan.)

Let's describe a situation in which Percy turns out to be the ideal candidate for striking a deal with Julie. The 10 percent profit rate he made last year through Percy, Inc., is not impressively lucrative in the current economic environment. Maybe his company is *overcapitalized*. Maybe he can get a better return by taking $1 million out of his business and investing it instead in Julie, Inc. Instead of simply continuing to make widgets, or whatever, maybe Percy, Inc., should go into the lending business.

Thus Percy does his due diligence, finds out that this is indeed the case, and submits to Julie the following proposal: He will lend her $1 million for a year. At the end of the period, she will return to him his $1 million (the principal) and an additional $150,000 in interest. In other words, Percy offers Julie the opportunity to borrow $1 million in capital at an annual interest rate of 15 percent.

Let's say that Julie agrees, and everything proceeds according to plan. Because it is invested in Julie, Inc.—with its 20 percent profit rate—Percy's $1 million expands by the end of the year to $1.2 million. Julie repays the loan—$1 million principal and $150,000 interest—and keeps for herself $50,000, which is the difference between the $200,000 profit Julie, Inc., has managed to make from an injection of $1 million in capital and the $150,000 returned to Percy as interest. In the meantime, Julie, Inc., made the same profit return as it did the preceding year on its initial capital, that is, $200,000, so the total profit of Julie, Inc., for the year is $250,000 ($50,000 + $200,000), amounting to a 25 percent profit rate.

Meanwhile, Percy is able to add the $150,000 that he has made in interest on the loan to Julie, Inc., to the $100,000 that Percy, Inc., made on the traditional part of its business on the remaining $1 million at the same profit rate of 10 percent as last year. By diversifying the activity of Percy, Inc., into lending, in other words, Percy has managed to make $250,000 in profit this year, which corresponds, with an initial capital of $2 million, to a 12.5 percent profit rate.

It is almost magical, right? Last year, Julie, Inc., and Percy, Inc., together made a total profit of $400,000; this year, the two companies made a combined profit of $500,000. The profit rate for Julie, Inc., grew from 20 to 25 percent and that of Percy, Inc., grew from 10 to 12.5 percent (the combination of a *profit rate* of 10 percent on $1 million and an *interest rate* of 15 percent on the second $1 million that was loaned out). Julie managed to make more money by putting additional capital behind her successful business concept. Percy managed to make more money through a different allocation of his capital—in other words, through *diversification*, complementing the profit he made through Percy, Inc., with the *rent* he collected through lending capital.

A final observation on this homely but telling example: At the outset, before the arrival of Percy on the scene, Julie had $1 million in capital. That capital, as noted, grew in 1 year to $1.2 million. The $200,000 difference was the profit she made as an entrepreneur; there was no need for her to share it.

Out of the $200,000 she made through borrowing $1 million from Percy for a year, she returned $150,000 to him as an interest payment and kept $50,000 for herself. That $50,000 is her profit on the capital she borrowed, it is the reward she gets for being a successful entrepreneur. Percy's $150,000 is his reward for being a successful investor, or capitalist.

When the entrepreneur himself or herself is the sole source of capital, the whole surplus resulting from capital growth is a profit that goes solely to him or her. However, when an investor advances capital to an entrepreneur, the surplus must be shared between them. One part goes to the entrepreneur as *profit*; the other part goes to the investor as *rent*. This is a zero-sum game: If a larger share of the capital growth is assigned to the entrepreneur, then the capitalist necessary gets less. I am laboring this point because the notion of a fixed pot of money will become relevant in later chapters when we consider both capital gains and stock options.

Why Julie and Percy Are Interesting

The story of Julie and Percy illustrates several points. First, of course, we see that investment is a great thing if you can find the right business concept to back. Second, investment is even better if it involves reallocating capital out of a less productive use (Percy, Inc.) and into a more productive use (Julie, Inc.). Less obvious but even more important, the story of Julie and Percy begins to contradict some common misgivings about *interest cash flows*.

A traditional view about loans is that the interest paid on a loan is simply the compensation the lender receives for the *inconvenience* he or she experiences from having loaned out his or her capital. In other words, the interest cash flow is perceived as a compensation for his or her temporary dispossession of the amount lent, which could have been put to alternative uses.

However, what we saw in the example was that the interest cash flow results from the combining of the varying capacities of several entrepreneurs to expand the capital they have in their possession. This shifting of funds toward their highest possible profit rate is the fundamental principle of investment. The mechanism that lies behind it is known in the financial literature as the *price-discovery process.* In simple terms, it is the mechanism whereby economic units with extra money lying around meet and find an optimal point of equilibrium with units that could put that extra money to good use.[2]

And finally, it is clear that investors are mainly out to maximize their own income. By so doing, though, their investment creates value and benefits the economic system—*our* system, capitalism—as a whole.

LESSONS FOR THE INVESTOR

Because this chapter was mainly a definitional exercise, there aren't as many lessons for investors as I would normally aim for. But here are a few to consider:

Capitalism is an act of faith. We capitalists like to think that we are part of God's plan, but in fact, we are the (lucky) subscribers to an economic faith. This is one reason why losses of faith—such as those caused by the shenanigans at Enron and Andersen—can do so much damage to the stock market. At least temporarily, we lose our faith.

Diversification of capital and reallocation of assets can be powerful. Using capital differently can increase the size of the pot for everyone involved.

It is still a zero-sum game. Despite the magic of diversification and reallocation, the pie still has to be divided. A larger share of capital growth for the entrepreneur means a smaller one for the investor. Stock options—as you will see—mean a larger share for the entrepreneur.

Self-interest can be good for us all. Our individual acts of self-interest as investors are what collectively make a vibrant economy possible. When people lose faith, hunker down, and stop placing individual bets—which constitute votes of confidence in capitalism—you get the great depression.

C H A P T E R

Sharing Capital Growth—or Not

The method by which we accumulate capital in this country is to have an investor in Bismarck, North Dakota—or anywhere in the country, for that matter—buy a share of stock based on the belief that the financial statements represented by that corporation and approved by the accountants is a fair representation and an honest representation of what is happening inside that corporation. If that trust is broken—and I believe it was in the Enron Corporation situation—when that trust is broken it undermines the method by which you accumulate capital for our system of capitalism.

—SENATOR BYRON DORGAN (R., North Dakota)[1]

Most investment books devote one or two lines, or at most a whole paragraph, to a discussion of exactly what a *share of stock* is. Bonds, meanwhile, are rarely even mentioned.

My guess is that the authors of these books assume that their readers already know—or perhaps do not *need* to know—what a stock is and that they are not interested in bonds in any case. These assumptions do not necessarily track with my experience. In my experience, many investors do not have a clear idea of what their options are or of what they are buying when they buy a share of stock or a bond.

I will use the same ground rules here that I invoked in Chapter 3. If you are confident that you already know enough about the subject at hand, skip to the next chapter. However, at least take a look. You needed to understand these fundamentals well before Enron, and in the wake of Enron and other recent upheavals, it is even more important that you understand them now.

The Two Ways You Get Compensated

As an investor, you are loaning capital to an enterprise. There are two ways to get compensated for that loan: prorated on the loan amount (*rent*) or prorated on capital growth (*share*).

Chapter 3 introduced an example of a business deal between Julie, Inc., and Percy, Inc., in which Percy lent Julie $1 million for 1 year at a 15 percent interest rate. At the end of the year, Percy received $150,000 in interest. (More likely, he would have gotten two semiannual payments of $75,000 each, but I chose not to complicate things too much.) Because Julie managed to replicate in the second year the 20 percent profit rate she had hit the year before, she took home $50,000 as her reward for successfully investing and managing the $1 million she had borrowed for a year from Percy.

One way of looking at this transaction is that Percy was paid *rent* on the advance in capital he made. Percy made what is called a *fixed-income investment,* in which a predetermined return was his return for his decision to loan money to Julie. This is the same logic that underlies all debt instruments, such as Treasury bonds; corporate and municipal bonds, notes, and bills; and a whole host of similar investment opportunities. Because they involve relatively little risk for the investor—the exception being such things as junk bonds—they generate relatively modest returns. Percy did a lot better with his fixed-income investment than most of us could expect to do with ours!

Suppose, however, that Percy had wanted to take a different approach to doing business with Julie. Suppose, for example, that he decided that Julie was really onto something, with her business model and that he wanted to find a way to share in the upside potential of her thriving business. How would he do that?

This is an arena in which humankind has shown itself to be remarkably inventive. It has come up with two entirely different answers to the question of how Percy might be rewarded for loaning money to Julie. In the first method of compensation, which is the one we have explored already, the return is fixed and prorated on the amount of the loan. In the second method, compensation is prorated on the capital growth that occurs during the lifetime of the loan. The first method is called receiving *rent;* the interest rate sets the basis for the prorating. The second method—as you may have guessed—is called holding a *share.* Its basis for prorating is often formulated as "so many parts out of so many"—for example, "one part out of six." In the case of the stock market, the return on a share is called a *dividend.*

Getting Compensated on a "Share" Basis

Although we tend to think of shares in enterprises as modern inventions, they are in fact a pretty old mechanism for raising capital for investment. In fact, they can be linked to some of humankind's earliest and most fundamental economic activities.

To make the point, let's imagine a situation in which Julie owns arable land, and Percy has none. Let's further imagine that should Percy get access to some good farmland, he would know how to grow crops on it. Julie, meanwhile, is not much of a farmer.

Here are two possible arrangements. First, Percy can agree to pay Julie $600 every month for use of the land, which is more or less the terms under which Percy loaned Julie money in Chapter 3. Or—in the second arrangement—come harvest time, Percy can agree to hand over to Julie an agreed-on share of the crops that he generates on the land. If the crop is wheat, for example, Percy may agree to hand over 1 out of every 3 bushels that he succeeds in growing.

This second system is called *sharecropping*; Percy is the *sharecropper*, and Julie is the *shareholder*. The land is an *advance* made by its owner to the sharecropper. Julie, lending use of the land to Percy, remains its owner; there is no transfer of property. In the real life of a sharecropper, however, Julie's advances most likely also would consist of various items of equipment, housing for the sharecropper and his family, and so on. To the extent that Percy's access to capital was extremely limited—as it was for almost everybody back when sharecropping was invented—the Julies of the world had to advance not only the land but also everything else needed to make the land productive.

The Chance of Gain; the Risk of Loss

Over time, capital either grows or gets depleted. Capital growth translates into a profit; capital depletion means a loss. Phrased slightly differently, the occurrence of profit materializes the *chance* of gain, whereas the occurrence of loss materializes the *risk* of loss.

The preceding example focused on farmed land as a form of capital. This was so in part because sharecropping is one of the oldest kinds of contract in agriculture and also because it is still the most common system worldwide for sharing profit in many agricultural industries, small-scale fisheries, traditional salt production from salt marshes, and so on. Why this continuing popularity? Because, generally speaking, sharecropping makes for a fair deal in productive activities in which there is a high volatility (or chance of dramatic variation) in yearly returns.

There are lots of other realms in which this is true. Think of Columbus setting sail at the end of the fifteenth century. He proposed to sail west to go east, in three relatively tiny ships, to do business on the other side of the world. He was confident that he would succeed, but he lacked the resources to mount the expedition. Fortunately, he was able to persuade Ferdinand and Isabella that this business venture made sense—despite the unpredictable length of the voyage and all the perils associated with it. Never mind shipwrecks, piracy, disease, or perhaps sailing off the edge of the world, Columbus argued; we can make a *profit* on this one. He was surely a salesman as much as he was a navigator.

Therefore, productive activities combine two distinctive features: the uncertain nature of the return and the required provision of advances. Historically, two ways—*rent* and *share*—have been used to deal with the occasional necessity for the producer to borrow advances. The essential distinction between rent and share lies in their different ways of dealing with the chance of gain on capital growth: Rent ignores it, whereas share divides it between lender and borrower.

In neither case is the lender exposed to loss. With rent, his or her return is entirely independent of capital growth or depletion. In a share system, the lowest possible income for his or her share is zero. A parallel can be drawn here with a call option that gets "in the money" if the value of the underlying financial product increases and is "out of money," meaning that it is worthless, if the value of the underlying position decreases.

Rents: Who Profits, and How?

Let's return briefly to the Julie and Percy example presented in Chapter 3 and move it forward a few more steps.

Although Julie managed to run her business last year at a 20 percent profit rate, she has no guarantees that she will do as well this year. In the scenario laid out in Chapter 3, she has agreed to borrow $1 million from Percy at a 15 percent rate on the assumption that the capital will grow by 20 percent. However, this is nothing more than an informed bet on her part, right? Maybe the economy will go south or a new and ferocious competitor will burst on the scene.

Or maybe she will do even *better* than 20 percent.

So let's look at two more scenarios. In the first, Julie only manages to make a 10 percent return on Percy's $1 million; in the second, she makes a whopping 30 percent.

Julie has committed herself to an interest rate of 15 percent on the amount borrowed. If the revenue from the investment is less than 15 percent—say, 10 percent—she will be forced by the terms of her contractual commitment to Percy to find another source for the "missing" $50,000. That source most likely would be the profit she has made on her own capital.

In other words, assuming that she still managed to make $200,000 on her initial capital, she can tap her continuing/underlying profit for the missing $50,000. At the end of the day, her profit on $2 million of invested capital would be $150,000, or 7.5 percent [($200,000 − $50,000)/$2 million]. In other words, her decision to look for further investment in her business turned out to have been a bad one; Julie, Inc., was not undercapitalized and was unable to put additional capital to productive use. However, Percy is feeling no particular pain. He invested $1 million at a 15 percent rate and got back the interest cash flow he was counting on. Clearly, the agreement put all the risk on Julie's shoulders, and she paid the price for her misplaced optimism.

In our second scenario, Julie is much happier. She reaps profit at a rate of 30 percent on the $1 million she borrowed—much better than the 20 percent she was hoping for. Her profit is $300,000. Her plan was to pay $150,000 in interest and keep the $50,000 remainder for herself. Instead, there is a surplus of $150,000. Her profit at the end of the day is $350,000, amounting to a profit rate of 17.5 percent [($200,000 + $150,000)/$2 million]. What happens? Percy gets the same $150,000 that he was guaranteed contractually through his 15 percent interest rate. In this scenario, Julie benefits significantly from the structure of the deal, which assigns all the additional gain to her.

In short, in a *rent*-based deal, the variation in income is borne entirely by the borrower. Variation materializes alternatively as either *risk of a loss* or *chance of a gain*.

Shares: Who Profits, and How?

The other possible approach to investment, the share system, draws on the sharecropping model described earlier. In this approach, the lender retains the opportunity to share in the chance of gain.

To see this approach in action, let's suppose that the contractual arrangement between Percy and Julie has not been stated as a 15 percent interest rate but rather as a *share in profit of three out of four* for the lender. If Julie manages to achieve in the second year, on a capital that is double in amount, the same return she achieved in the first year, she obtains a profit of $200,000 on the $1 million she borrowed from Percy. If Percy gets his three-out-of-four share, this means that he is getting $150,000 of this $200,000, and Julie is getting the other $50,000—in other words, the same outcome achieved by the 15 percent interest rate described in Chapter 3.

What happens, however, if the return on capital is something other than 15 percent? Obviously, the answer depends on whether the variation is on the high side or the low side. If the return on capital is 40 percent, for example, Percy's return on capital doubles to 30 percent. If the return on capital is as low as 10 percent, his share drops to 7.5 percent, or half of what the he would have received through a straight rent agreement.

Winning Strategies for Lenders and Borrowers

Thus the sharing of gain proceeds very differently in a rent system than in a share system. Let's examine in more detail the two share-based scenarios just described—the one in which Julie makes a profit of only 10 percent on Percy's money and the other in which she makes 30 percent on his money.

Let's look first at the situation that is unfavorable for Julie, in which the rate of capital growth is only 10 percent. Percy gets three out of four of the $100,000, or $75,000, and Julie gets one out of four, or $25,000.

In the second case, far more favorable to Julie, the rate of capital growth is 30 percent on the $1 million that Percy invested in the company. In this case, Percy gets three out of four of $300,000, or $225,000, and Julie keeps $75,000 for herself.

The comparison between rent and share systems—drawing on our Percy and Julie example—can be seen clearly in Table 4-1. Three rates of capital growth are shown: 10, 20, and 30 percent.

TABLE 4-1	
Rent (15% Annual Interest Rate)	**Share** (Three Parts Out of Four)
10% CAPITAL GROWTH	
Lender: $150,000; borrower: −$50,000	Lender: $75,000; borrower: $25,000
20% CAPITAL GROWTH	
Lender: $150,000; borrower: $50,000	Lender: $150,000; borrower: $50,000
30% CAPITAL GROWTH	
Lender: $150,000; borrower: $150,000	Lender: $225,000; borrower: $75,000

In the case of rent—the left-hand column—the agreed-on interest rate determines the yield, and that yield is a proportion of the loan's face value. The variation in capital growth is entirely supported by the borrower. In the first case, when the rate of capital growth is lower than the rate of the rent, the borrower incurs a loss.

In the case of a share system—the right-hand column—variation in returns occurs for both investor and borrower. When the rate of capital growth is low, the lender gets less than with rent, but he or she spares the borrower the pain of incurring a loss. Conversely, whatever profit is made is shared by both. When capital growth or appreciation is high, the investor gets more than he or she would have gotten under the rent contract because he or she shares in the capital growth. The borrower gets less than under rent, but this foregone upside is the equivalent of an insurance premium paid by the borrower in return for not taking a hit when the capital growth is low.

What conclusions should the Percys and Julies of the world draw based on this table? Here are a few of the obvious ones:

Rent allows the lender to fix his or her revenue at the time the contract is drawn up.

As far as the borrower is concerned, the share system reduces fluctuation in returns (volatility).

When there is low capital growth, it is in the interest of the lender to charge rent and in the interest of the borrower to promote a share system. The only case where there is an actual loss—what we understand by *risk*—for the borrower is one where he or she pays rent.

Conversely, when there is high capital growth, it is in the interest of the lender to obtain a share and in the interest of the borrower to pay rent.

The Straight Story on Bonds

So far I have been using the word *rent* to describe the funding approach that presumes a fixed rate of return. In the real world, the tools in this toolkit—all debt instruments such as bonds, notes, bills, certificates of deposit (CD), municipal or corporate bonds, corporate junk bonds, and shares—can be aggregated under the general term *bond*.

Bonds are called *Treasuries* when they are backed by the government's guarantee. A long-term Treasury is one that involves government debt obligations for 10 years or more, a medium-term Treasury is called a *note* and matures in between 2 and 9 years, and a short-term Treasury is a *bill* and matures in between 3 months and 1 year. They are all similar debt instruments involving loans in cash that an investor grants to the U.S. government in exchange for a guaranteed rate of return. In the case of a Treasury, the borrower is the U.S. government, and there is a 100 percent guarantee that the borrower will not default. (Be aware that this is *not* true in every country and may not be true forever in *any* country.) Beyond this rather fundamental fact, there is no difference between a Treasury bond and a corporate bond; henceforth, I will simply refer to a *bond* when writing about these kinds of instruments.

With a long-term bond, interest cash flows are paid on a regular basis, typically semiannually. The value of future coupons is calculated easily: It is the bond's yield multiplied by the principal. A 7 percent bond with a principal of $10,000, for example, pays $700 annually. Because coupons are paid semiannually, there is a payment of $350 due every 6 months.

Short-term Treasuries, like bills, are sold at a *discount.* In other words, they are sold below their face value and are reimbursed at their full face value at maturity. The interest earned constitutes the difference between the face value of the bill and the purchase price. Thus, for example, a $10,000 one-year Treasury bill with a coupon of 7 percent would sell for $9345.80. Why? Because 7 percent of $9345.80 is $654.20, so principal ($9345.80) plus interest ($654.20) makes $10,000, which is the face value of the bill. Seen from the other end of the telescope, a $10,000 Treasury bill is sold at a discount for $9345.80; that capital makes 7 percent over a year (that is, $654.20), and at the end of the year, principal ($9345.80) plus interest ($654.20) is being paid back to the borrower.

Thinking Straight about Shares

A *share* of stock is for its buyer a share just like a stake in any other share system: the compensation of a loan, prorated on capital growth. The loan is granted by an investor in a corporation. There is no transfer of ownership of the capital; there is a transfer of usage of the cash. The shareholder remains the owner of the advances he or she is making to the corporation.

However, things can get complicated if and when the company goes bankrupt. In such a case, *all loans from shareholders to the corporation come to an end.* Yes, the company pools its assets—including all investors' contributions—in anticipation of distributing them on a proportional basis among its shareholders. Here's the bad news from an investor's standpoint: *Shareholders' rights to assets cannot be exercised until after the corporation's creditors have been compensated.* This makes sense if one acknowledges that the company's debt is nothing but the loans it has obtained from other sources—loans on which it pays *rent* in most cases. In other words, you have to pay off your debts before you can fairly assess your riches.

Back to the nonbankruptcy scenario: The share's return is typically distributed as an annual dividend. Dividends constitute a set proportion of the net earnings (capital growth) that the company has managed to make with the help of the contribution in capital that the share represents. It is logical, therefore, that the shareholder receives a dividend only if the company has made a profit over the preceding year. In other words, you get a dividend only when your contribution in capital has managed to grow.

The price paid by an investor for a so-called common share of stock is the price paid for a share in a corporation's capital growth. The price of the share is the price of the *advance* made to the company to provide it with the cash needed to perform its business.

There is another kind of stock that we need to take a quick sideways look at before this chapter comes to an end. This is the so-called preferred stock. A preferred share is actually not a share at all in the sense that I have been using the term in this chapter. It is actually a form of debt incurred by the corporation that is prorated on the capital's face value rather than on the company's capital growth. The dividend paid on a preferred share, in other words, amounts to the payment of rent.

Watch what happens the next time a major corporation goes under. Almost inevitably someone will complain about the "preferred shareholders" getting their needs met before anyone looks after the needs of the "common shareholder." No matter that the corporation has entered these obligations with its eyes open. No matter that, for the most part, preferred shareholders (unlike common shareholders) hold nonvoting stock and therefore have no say in the overall direction of the corporation. People almost certainly will wonder out loud who these preferred types—read "fat cats"—are.

And this is one justification for including this chapter on the realities of rents and shares and bonds and stocks. Before you can deal with the complexities of the universe populated by the Enrons, WorldComs, and so on, you have to understand the fundamentals on which that universe is based.

LESSONS FOR THE INVESTOR

Understand your options as an investor. There are two ways of being compensated for a loan to a corporation: charging *rent* prorated on the loan amount or claiming a *share* of capital growth. When charging *rent,* investors are only exposed to default of the borrower, which means that their risks are relatively low. At the same time, they do not stand to benefit from potential capital growth. When holding a *share,* the investor (the *capitalist*) shares capital growth with the borrower (the *entrepreneur*).

Understand how your advantage shifts in changing corporate and economic circumstances. With low capital growth, it is in the interest of the investor to buy *corporate bonds* and in the interest of the entrepreneur to issue *shares of stock.* With high capital growth, it is in the interest of the investor to buy *shares of stock* and in the interest of the entrepreneur to issue *corporate bonds.*

Issuing shares of stock may be advantageous to the entrepreneur. The entrepreneur will never incur a loss when issuing *shares of stock* but may incur a loss when issuing *corporate bonds* because—once again—the rate of capital growth of his or her business may be lower than the *corporate bond*'s coupon. And issuing shares of stock instead of corporate bonds reduces fluctuation in returns (or *volatility*).

Bonds, although never popular during bull markets, hold some clear advantages to the investor. True, bonds cut the investor out of the capital-growth calculation, but they allow the investor to fix his or her future revenue at the time the contract is purchased. (Those seeking a dependable source of income or those who anticipate a significant cash payment—such as a tuition payment—in the near future therefore prefer bonds.) And if and when a corporation gets into trouble, the bondholder is first in line. A shareholder's right to a corporation's assets is a right to its actual wealth, meaning after debt has been accounted for.

Not all stock shares are true "shares." Preferred stock is actually a type of debt and typically is a nonvoting stock (but make sure to read the fine print!).

5

The Price and Value
of a Share of Stock

*Dividends historically represent the dominant part
of the average return on stocks. The reliable return
attributable to dividends, not the less predictable
portion arising from capital gains, is the main
reason why stocks have on average been such good
investments historically.*

—ROBERT J. SHILLER, *Irrational Exuberance*[1]

What makes for *value* in a share of stock, and how does that relate to the
price of that share? Surprisingly, the answers to these questions are not
always obvious. In fact, they have been the basis of heated debate in recent
decades. As we work our way toward investment strategies in the post-Enron
world, let's reflect briefly on the value-price relationship.

The two predominant views about the value of a share of stock are the
dividend-stream theory and the *castle-in-the-air theory*.[2] The dividend-
stream theory has a number of alternative names, such as the *fundamentals*

explanation of stock price, the *firm-foundation assessment of price* (Burton Malkiel),[3] the *expectations theory* (Alfred Rappaport),[4] and so on. With small variations, these are the same.

The dividend-stream theory and the castle-in-the-air theory are usually presented as competing notions. Very briefly, the dividend-stream theory holds that the fair price of a stock is the present value of all future cash flows—in other words, all expected dividend payments and a final proportional share in the asset value of the company, should it choose or be compelled to liquidate. (I will return to the dividend-stream theory later.) The castle-in-the-air theory, credited to John Maynard Keynes, holds that there is no such thing as a *fair* or *rational* price for a share of stock and that price translates into—bluntly put—*whatever the next sucker is prepared to pay*. Logically, there is no immediate valuation of a share of stock in the castle-in-the-air theory; and in fact, it is not really a theory at all. It is more an expression of despair about the seeming impossibility of objective valuation.

Neither of those two views is wrong, and to see them as competing views miscasts the role they play within an overall framework. As I will argue in this chapter, the dividend-stream theory should govern a stock's initial price—that is, the price it commands on its initial public offering (IPO). The castle-in-the-air theory accounts convincingly for the price of a share of stock on the secondary market for stocks, also called the *aftermarket,* when a buyer purchases shares on the open market from a seller. (As a general rule, individual investors acquire their stock on the secondary market.) Unfortunately, the reason why the castle-in-the-air theory accounts fairly well for the price of many stocks is that they are caught in a speculative bubble—and a stock in a speculative bubble is truly a castle in the air.

Primary and Secondary Markets: IPOs and Aftermarkets

I have already talked about buying stock as the contemporary equivalent of engaging in a share system like sharecropping. There *are* some interesting differences, however. In most of the traditional environments in which share-cropping was a common mode of sharing resources, the shareholder rarely, if ever, asked the question of how to value the share. This was because the owner of capital was in a dominant social position within the economic system. In fact, he or she likely was in a monopolistic position, being an aristocrat at a time when only the upper class owned land. The sharecropper had to settle for whatever terms the aristocrat put forward, whether they were just or not.

There were some practical limits on the price demanded by the aristocrat, of course. At the end of the day, the sharecropper and his or her family had to be able to make a good enough living to survive. In truly terrible growing years, the enlightened shareholder generally saw it as being in his or her long-term interest to lend additional resources to the sharecropper, thereby enabling him or her to survive until the following year's harvest.

I have already introduced the idea of primary and secondary markets. In a primary market, one party is the producer—someone who delivers a product or a service, tangible or intangible—whereas the second party is the buyer of that product. (In this case; the buyer is called a *primary buyer.*) In the case of the stock market, the role of a producer is played by the corporation issuing its own stock, either acting on its own in a *private placement* (or a direct public offering), in which the company offers its shares directly to institutional and accredited investors, or through an intermediary (the underwriter) in an IPO. In almost all cases, the management of the corporation is heavily involved in the structure and timing of the IPO.

In a traditional share system, such as sharecropping, the farmer would be the seller, and the landlord would be the primary buyer. You can imagine an "IPO" in such an environment; it would sound something like the following: "OK," the farmer/sharecropper would announce, "I can farm 40 acres in a year, and I'm prepared to work on the basis of a 'two parts out of three' shareholder arrangement. Anyone interested?" Together, the initial shareholder and the sharecropper would define a *primary market.*

A secondary market develops when a third party wishes to buy the share from the initial shareholder and offers to purchase from the shareholder his or her position within the existing deal. That is, someone comes around and says, "You've got the rights to a 'two parts out of three' arrangement with this farmer on his or her crop. I would like to buy you out. I had something like $500 in mind." Should a deal ensue, a *secondary market,* or *aftermarket,* is automatically created.

In the early stages of a secondary market, logically, one of the parties is likely to be a *primary buyer,* and the other party—the person or institution that purchases from the primary buyer—is a *secondary buyer*. After a while, as the primary buyers leave the game, all buyers on a secondary market are secondary buyers.

The Primary Market for Shares: The IPO

When it comes to the stock exchanges, there is precious little room for small investors in the primary market, which consists of the IPOs of companies. Most or all of the shares put forward in IPOs are snapped up by powerful primary buyers—in many cases, institutional investors such as pension plans and college endowments. It is interesting to surf the Web and see the "little people"—the individual investors—coming to grips with this unpleasant fact. A visitor to the *www.IPO.com* Web site asks, plaintively, "How can I purchase shares at the offering price?" And the answer is that "in today's market, it is extremely rare for the small investor to purchase shares of an IPO at the offering price. The big-time players boasting a significant wealthy status have the best chances of getting shares."

A second IPO Web site (*http://www.hoovers.com/ipo/*) reaches similarly discouraging conclusion. "If you want to invest in an IPO but don't have a relationship with one of the managing banks," suggests one correspondent, "you can also try to start an account, making it a condition that you receive some shares in the new issue you're interested in, but you may not have much luck with this tactic. IPO shares are saved to reward a firm's biggest, most active, and longest-standing customers."

Does this sound to you like a rigged game? If so, you may be right. Two investigations relative to dubious IPO practices were made public in April 2002. The first, initiated by the National Association of Securities Dealers (NASD), focused on whether some investment banks had assigned privileged investors large allotments of IPO stocks on condition that they would kick back part of their IPO profits as inflated commissions on later trades with the same banks. The second, initiated by the Securities and Exchange Commission (SEC), explored whether some investment banks imposed an interesting precondition on investors who wanted IPO shares: Those investors would be required to place orders for the same stocks at higher prices on the first day of trading. Such a practice, known as *laddering,* aims unambiguously at artificially inflating the stock price. There is simply no other credible explanation for laddering.[5]

Using the Dividend-Stream Theory

The dividend-stream theory, as noted earlier, holds that a stock price should be the present value of all future cash flows associated with the stock (and perhaps with a bump at the end added on, representing a proportional share of corporate assets). In the words of financial pioneer Benjamin Graham and coauthors:

> Distributed earnings have had a greater weight in determining market prices than have retained and reinvested earnings. The "outside," or non-controlling, stockholders of any company can reap benefits from their investment in only two ways: through dividends and through an increase in the market value of their shares. Since the market value in most cases has depended primarily upon the dividend rate, the latter can be held responsible for nearly all the gains ultimately realized by investors.[6]

For the sake of completeness, let me also include an afterthought by Graham's recent coauthors: "We may suggest an extension of the 'dividend stream theory' to read: a common stock is worth the discounted value of future expectable dividends over any assumed period of time, plus the discounted value of its expected market price at the end of the period."[7]

Clearly, this little afterthought—the one about the "expected market price at the end of the period"—leaves some room for taking into account in the dividend-stream theory the appreciation of the stock price or capital gains. However, as I will demonstrate in Chapter 6, there is no way to compute the increased value of a share of stock that results from capital gains. The castle-in-the-air theory accounts for what happens at that point, and it does not offer any direct valuation method. (It only hints at what to look at, which is, essentially, actual price changes.) There is no effective way to assess that "expected market price at the end of the period."

Think back to our earlier discussion of rents. Calculating the present value of the cash flows of a fixed-income debt instrument (the *rents*) is a relatively easy exercise. At the risk of getting too technical too quickly, one works out a zero-coupon curve from the current-yield curve, and on that basis, all future cash flows are discounted to their present value. Those present values are then added up to determine a fair value of the fixed-income instrument as a whole.

Attempting to perform the same exercise with a dividend stream is much, much tougher. Almost by definition, dividends are variable cash flows (because companies have bad years and good years). Also, unlike the rents paid to a bondholder, the dividends paid to a shareholder are not necessarily limited in time. In theory at least, the series is potentially infinite.

This is why Graham's associates arbitrarily set a time horizon and end the series with an "expected market price at the end of the period." As we have seen, the asset value that can be included as the end point of a time series of dividends is that of the net asset value of the company divided by the number of outstanding shares. Investors may want to make their own assessments more sophisticated—for example, by generating scenarios in which future dividends granted are higher or lower than their current level. They also should remember to build into their divisor the number of shares in the company's executive stock option plan—an issue that has come to the fore in recent months and which deserves all the scrutiny it has been getting.

The present value of all returns to come—dividends and share in assets—would constitute a valid upper limit for the price one might choose to pay to take part in the share system that a particular corporation's stock constitutes. I say *upper limit* because the present value of all future cash flows is the *maximum* an investor should be willing to pay. Why? Easy: Because the sum of future cash flows amounts indeed to a *breakeven* outcome, which should never be regarded as a bold enough objective when one is acquiring stock to build wealth.

Thus what we have here is another case of good news masquerading as bad news. Let's agree that the investor should compare the current price of a stock with a best-guess dividend-stream theory valuation and simply abstain from buying if the current price is equal to or higher than the breakeven level. What's the good news? Various studies in recent years have shown, however, that the prices paid through IPOs *tend to be higher than the breakeven price*, as determined by the dividend-stream theory. So yes, you are being frozen out of the primary market that IPOs represent—but the fact remains that this is not a market you want to be in if your goal is to own stocks that trade at a fair price level.[8]

Valuing the Stock of Companies That Do Not Pay Dividends

So what happens if a company does not pay dividends? How can the value of *that* stock be assessed?

Obviously, dividend-stream theory will not work. Yes, the current value of the company's assets is presumed to be something higher than zero, but as we have already seen, any point in time that you pick to make such an assessment is likely to be a very arbitrary one. Ten years out? Twenty? Thirty? *Why?*

Jeremy Siegel, in his influential *Stocks For the Long Run*, claims that valuation of stock price for a company that does not pay dividends should be performed just the same way it is for a company that grants them: Stock value, he argues, should be the discounted value of the *forthcoming* dividend cash flows because, he assumes, there will necessarily be a time when there *will* be dividends. "It makes absolutely no difference what dividend policy management chooses," Siegel writes. "The reason for this is that dividends not paid today are reinvested by the firm and paid as even larger dividends in the future."[9]

I admire Siegel's optimism, but not necessarily his logic. Why would a company that does not pay dividends ever revise its policy? One (optimistic) view holds that promising young companies are so burdened with debt early in their existence that they cannot afford to be encumbered with dividends. They are no less attractive, this argument goes, just because they are younger and poorer.

To this I reply, *Why wait and see if they live up to all that potential?* Weren't all those dot-com wonders saying more or less the same thing about their inability to make a buck and pay a dividend? Did we like the way *those* bets turned out?

Yes, a wait-and-see strategy would have made you miss out on the early and most explosive growth of, say, Microsoft. Microsoft stock has turned out to be a very good bet, particularly for those who got in real early. The difficulty, of course, lies in distinguishing the real Microsoft from all those little would-be "Microsofts" that came to nothing. And in my experience, people *always* talk about their own personal "Microsofts," and they *never* talk about the 10, 20, or 30 other risky bets they made that turned out to be losers. (An interesting question, in many cases, is: *Are they ahead of the game from an overall standpoint?*)

Don't read me wrong. I certainly do not mean to say that there is no safe way to play stocks like Microsoft (more about this later in this chapter). I *am* saying that there is no method that allows for a meaningful evaluation of such stocks in a way similar to discounting the value of their dividend cash flows—which, as we have seen, is only the best tool in a relatively bad bunch.

You have heard this before (in Chapter 4), but my personal view is that companies that do not pay dividends should be encouraged—*strongly*—to start doing so or at least to present a plan for how and when they will. Investors should demand dividends. Companies that do not pay dividends cannot be evaluated; their value may be anywhere, and their price is likely to be everywhere. They are flouting the spirit (if not the letter) of the share system. As they do, moreover, they keep pulling investors into speculative bubbles that almost always obliterate hard-earned savings.

Long Run or Short Run?

"Dividends not paid today are reinvested by the firm and paid as even larger dividends in the future," Jeremy Siegel tells us. There are two logical flaws here. The first is the assumption that any player in a game can keep playing that game forever or at least as long as needed. This is almost never true for investors, whose investment strategies necessarily change over time.

The second flaw is the implicit assumption that corporations are immortal. Not true! The longer a corporation has been around, the more likely it is that the odds will catch up with it, and it will die from some happenstance. Corporations are something like trees in this regard: Most trees do not have a biological clock (that we know of) and therefore do not tend to die of old age. And yet, they do die—from disease, after being struck by lightning, from collapsing under their own weight, and so on. Five hundred companies made up the Standard & Poor's (S&P) 500 in 1957 when that index was introduced; only 74 of those companies remained on that list in 1997.[10]

Even the advocates of looking to the long run recognize the fallacy inherent in this strategy. In his *Stocks for the Long Run*, Siegel lists the companies that were part of the Dow Jones Industrial Average in 1896, 1916, and 1928. Most notable is the rapid *turnover* on this list. What happened to Feeding—a once-proud member of the 1896 index? (What *was* Feeding?) What about Studebaker (from the 1916 list) and Victor Talking Machine (from the 1928 list)? My point is that if you wait long enough, you may find that your high-flying company has crashed and burned before it ever paid a dividend.

The Problem with Buying Recycled Shares

The individual investor on the stock market buys and sells in the environment of a secondary market. When you or I buy stock, shares are already out there on the open market, and whatever shares we buy have been recycled from previous buyers turned sellers. Their price is also set at a particular level, which we are in no position to negotiate: It is take it or leave it.

So what? Well, that nonnegotiable price may bear little or no relationship to the price that would be suggested by a dividend-stream-theory valuation. For all practical purposes, therefore, the dividend-stream theory is not particularly relevant for stock price valuation in the secondary market for shares in public corporations.

And this is probably just as well because—as Alan Greenspan has pointed out—individual investors do not have the capacity to perform the necessary analyses in any case: "Apart from a relatively few large institutional investors, not many existing or potential shareholders have the research capability to analyze corporate reports and thus to judge the investment value of a corporation."[11]

The big players, the institutional investors, employ scores of analysts who are replaying the IPO every day, who are recalculating a price based on the dividend-stream theory and then playing the market accordingly. The decisions they make involve huge quantities of stock and actually may shift the market up or down. Wherever these moves leave stock prices is where you, the individual investor, will find them. You simply cannot play in this game.

The authors who have performed the most thorough analysis of dividend-stream theory, in my view, are Alfred Rappaport and Michael Mauboussin, the authors of *Expectations Investing*.[12] I recommend that you read this impressive book, which focuses on future changes in earnings as a key factor in shifting stock values. Again, as an individual investor, you are not going to break new ground or move markets; you are likely to succeed by understanding and mimicking the techniques of some of the bigger institutional investors.

The bottom line is that investors can use dividend-stream-theory valuation as a reference point—an indication of what price a share of stock might command in a perfect marketplace—but they should not count on it as a broadly applicable base for decision making. I do believe, along with many other analysts and observers, that a stock will sooner or later "find its level" somewhere near the price suggested by dividend-stream theory. However, there are so many distortions in the stock market—including investor psychology—that this process may take years or even decades. And most of us, as noted, are not going to be in this game indefinitely.

The Role of Capital Gains

In 1997, the tax rate on long-term capital gains was capped at 20 percent. This compares with the maximum rate of 39.6 percent that applies to dividends. In addition, capital gains can be deferred until the stocks are sold, giving the investor more flexibility in terms of tax planning. In these two ways, wealth derived through dividends is at a disadvantage to capital gains.

During the 1986 tax-reform debates, a proposal to reduce or remove these relative disadvantages got pretty far along before it was killed. Recent circumstances—Enron and others—have revived this debate and have reinforced the long-standing belief of many (including me) that it is time to revive the proposal that died in 1986. We need to stop tipping the scales in favor of capital gains.

In a March 2002 speech, Federal Reserve Board Chairman Alan Greenspan drew a portrait of the recent evolution of dividends and earnings. He explained in very clear terms why dividends are—in the current context—irrelevant to stock valuation. He also indicated clearly an alternative candidate for valuation and why assessment from that basis is nearly impossible. In Greenspan's words:

> Dividend payout ratios, which in decades past averaged about 55 percent, have in recent years fallen on average to about 35 percent. But because share prices have risen so much more than earnings in recent years, dividend yields—the ratio of dividends per share to a company's share price—have fallen appreciably more than the payout ratio. A half-century ago, for example, dividend yields on stocks typically averaged 6 percent. Today such yields are barely above 1 percent.
>
> The sharp fall in dividend payout ratios and yields has dramatically shifted the focus of stock price evaluation toward earnings. Unlike cash dividends, whose value is unambiguous, there is no unambiguously "correct" value of earnings. Although most pretax profits reflect cash receipts less out-of-pocket cash costs, a significant part results from changes in balance-sheet valuations.
>
> The values of almost all assets are based on the asset's ability to produce future income. But an appropriate judgment of that asset value depends critically on a forecast of forthcoming events, which by their nature are uncertain. A bank, for example, books interest paid on a loan as current revenue. However, if the borrower subsequently defaults, that presumed interest payment would, in retrospect, be seen as a partial return of principal. We seek to cope with this uncertainty by constructing loan reserves, but the adequacy of those reserves is also subject to a forecast.

Depreciation charges against income, based on book values, are very crude approximations of deterioration in the economic value of physical plant. The actual deterioration will not be known until the asset is retired or sold. And projections of future investment returns on defined-benefit pension plans markedly affect corporate pension contributions and, hence, pre-tax profits. Thus, how one chooses to evaluate the future income potential of the balance sheet has a significant impact on current reported earnings."[13]

In other words, it is a logical path to an unattainable destination: Capital gains are taxed more lightly than dividends. Therefore, the basis for stock valuation shifts away from dividends in favor of an estimate as to whether a rising stock price will create capital gains. However, there is simply no good way to value stock based on capital gains, either realized or potential. There are far too many variables involved. At best, it is a tall stack of wild guesses.

One More Time: Seek Out Dividends!

Because I criticized Jeremy Siegel's work earlier in this chapter, it is only fair to applaud him when he hits the nail on the head. So here goes: "A strategy based on the highest yielding stocks in the Dow Jones Industrial Average," reports Siegel, "outperformed the market."[14] Siegel's analysis was confirmed in a study by James O'Shaughnessy, in which he demonstrated that in the period between 1951 and 1994, among stocks with a capitalization of $1 billion or more, the 50 highest dividend-yielding stocks had a 1.7 percent higher annual return.[15]

By now it should be clear why earlier chapters went all the way back to the days of sharecroppers and aristocrats and explored the differences between a rent system and a share system. Today, investors are after capital gains, even though from a historical standpoint it is *dividends* that have made stocks a good investment.

And this is precisely the core of what some journalists have labeled "Enronitis." For the fickle, capital-gains-obsessed investor to remain captivated by a company such as Enron, the share price has to keep going up. It needs to go up for a good reason, a bad reason, or no reason at all. When there is no *good* reason, the company's management has little choice but to make the stock price rise for no reason at all—or for a bad reason.

This is the context within which the Enron affair started developing as early as 1999, when there was no good reason left for Enron's stock price to rise. Enron's managers pulled out their stock price pump and put their investors in the position of being speculators, pure and simple. There is no other message to be inferred. Unfortunately, thousands of people went along with the scheme.

In other words, as an investor in the post-Enron world, you need to be skeptical about the motivation of management teams. I am not saying that you have to assume the worst about them—but do not extend them your blind faith either.

Back at the height of the dot-com frenzy, I was interviewed for a senior position with an Internet company. Curiously, the interviewer did most of the talking, focusing on all the exciting times the company was going through. It would all come to a head, he said, in less than a year, when the company floated its IPO.

Toward the end of the interview, I was asked the standard question: "Is there anything you'd like to ask about the company?"

"Yes," I said. "What is going to happen *after* the IPO?"

"Oh, well ," the interviewer replied, "there will be some difficult times. For one thing, there will be a serious continuity issue, since all the executives plan to retire."

Needless to say, this powerful evidence about the motivations of this particular management team persuaded me to take another job. I am not sure whether that particular IPO ever took place. I wonder how many people would have invested in that company if they had the same window into the corporation's guiding principles that I had.

The Legacy of Carlo Ponzi

Charles ("Carlo") Ponzi founded a financial company in Boston in 1919 that set out to "arbitrage" the price of an international postal reply coupon between the United States and Spain. Simply put, Ponzi discovered that he could buy for 1 cent in Spain an international postal reply coupon that would buy six 1-cent stamps in the United States. Talk about a "money machine"!

An *arbitrageur* is a trader who finds different quotes for the same product and buys where the ask is low and resells where the bid is higher. Traditionally, as in Carlo Ponzi's day, the trading activity of arbitrage involved buying a product on one regional market and selling it on another regional market where the quoted price is higher. With the globalization of markets and the instantaneous dissemination of quoted prices through new telecommunications media, traditional arbitrage has virtually ceased to exist.

The current activity of the arbitrageur consists of the more sophisticated equating of complex financial instruments with structures of simpler instruments in order to attempt the arbitraging of one or more of the components of the structure. However, this is inherently self-limiting. Because of the constant activity of arbitrageurs, arbitrage opportunities tend to vanish. In other words, if a complex financial instrument can be equated with a structure of simpler instruments, the price of the complex instrument will converge with that of the structure of the simpler ones. This is called the *law of one price* and, sometimes, the *rule of no arbitrage*. Once this convergence is achieved, the pricing methods used for the simpler instruments can be combined to calculate the *fair price* of the complex instrument.

So whatever happened to arbitrageur Carlo Ponzi? Well, he promised investors that he would use his international postal reply coupon scheme to double their stake in 90 days. And, in fact, he did—at least for a while. The problem was that he did not generate his big returns through the international postal reply coupon trade, as advertised. Instead, he used the new capital that kept pouring in to reward earlier investors. In such a situation, sooner or later sales growth falls off, and this becomes unsustainable.

Interestingly, Carlo Ponzi became very rich, was caught and convicted, spent some time in jail, and died in poverty in 1949 in the charity ward of a Rio de Janeiro hospital.

Ponzi's legacy was his name, which now stands for any scheme that rewards yesterday's investors with the buy-in fees of investors. This is also known as *pyramiding*. In French, it is called *la cavalerie*, referring to a cavalry charge—a maneuver that usually ends in a brutal and bloody manner.

In late November 2001, a mere 10 days before Enron filed for Chapter 11 protection, Web correspondent Peter Eavis raised an interesting question. "Could Enron be setting up new trusts," Eavis asked, "to pay off damaged old trusts?"[16] The question hinted at a Ponzi scheme. As it turned out, the answer to the question was "yes." This was *exactly* what Enron was doing.

Enron used pyramiding in another context as well. This time it was Robert F. McCullough—formerly an Arthur Andersen partner and subsequently of McCullough Research—who spotted it. Here is how a *New York Times* article by Gretchen Morgenson summarized it:

> Enron may have found a way to paper over its problems, Mr. McCullough said, with an accounting technique known as "mark to market." That would

have allowed it to realize immediately the earnings it forecast on energy deals, even though the costs and revenue on those deals might stretch over long periods. A result would be high earnings but little actual cash coming in. The inherent risk in such an arrangement is that the price of energy could fall. If that happened, the contract struck previously would become less valuable than the company had forecast, creating a loss on the deal. Salvation from having to show the loss could present itself, however, in an even bigger power contract at current prices. The new contract, Mr. McCullough explained, would provide enough mark-to-market earnings to offset the loss on the contract struck when prices were higher. "With sufficient growth in volume, earnings can be positive in each year," he said, "while cash flows continue to deteriorate." But such an approach fails when sales growth falls, he said, "like any other pyramid scheme." [17]

There is a commonly held delusion that the entrepreneur and the investor together can be rewarded by more than a company's capital growth. (Absent this view, no one would have ever bought a share in a dot-com.) "The rewards came from the market in the form of capital gains," as one observer put it, "this being the least expensive way for any management to earn shareholders' gratitude."[18]

In other words, management keeps investors happy by generating capital gains, which may be entirely unrelated to capital growth. However, if capital gains exceed capital growth, where does this additional wealth come from? From the market, of course—meaning from you and me.

And this is where the castle-in-the-air theory comes in—AKA "whatever the next sucker is prepared to pay." The additional wealth comes from the next buyer who is prepared to pay more for the same share of stock. One reason why he or she is prepared to pay more is because he or she assumes that there is another buyer coming soon who is prepared to pay even more. This is the stuff that speculative bubbles are made of. Robert J. Shiller calls it a "Naturally Occurring Ponzi Process."[19] Like Carlo Ponzi's scheme, however, this only works until it stops working. Then it crashes and burns.

Two Fish Stories

Let me conclude this chapter with two fish stories, both of which come to bear—more or less—on the lessons of this chapter and set us up for the next several chapters. Back in the 1970s, I spent a year as a professional fisherman. I was fascinated, and sometimes even stunned, by the amazing intuitive knowledge that many fishermen have about their environment. I was predisposed to hear all their utterances as deep and profound.

One day I was on a tiny fishing boat, hauling up prawn pots, when my skipper/friend said to me, "Paul, I predict that this will be a great year for shrimp!"

"But Jean-Michel," I replied with great interest, "how do you *know* this will be a great year for shrimp?"

"Well," he replied, "It's only February, and we've already got a real good catch!"

My second story occurs in the late 1980s. There was a fish auction in a port in Brittany, on the west coast of France. I have lost the clipping from the trade paper that reported on the auction, but it went something like this: "Surprisingly high price obtained yesterday for scallops at Le Croisic Port. The explanation rests with a group of journalists visiting the auction hall, who were mistaken by those present for potential buyers."

The lessons? What goes up does not keep going up—it goes down. Ponzi schemes are self-limiting. In the wake of one market crash, J. P. Morgan was asked to explain what had happened. "There were more sellers than buyers," he coolly replied. Just as at the fish auction, all those extra bodies created a level of excitement that in turn drove prices up to unnatural levels.

So don't get stampeded. And place a standing order with your broker to sell as soon as the stock price hits a particular level on its way down. More on this in Chapter 6.

LESSONS FOR THE INVESTOR:

Understand the tools that are available to you for relating value to price—and understand their limitations. The dividend-stream-theory valuation of a share of stock suggests a *breakeven* value of a stock; it is therefore the maximum an investor should pay for the stock. However, this technique for valuation is most relevant for IPOs, which you—as an individual investor—are highly unlikely to get involved in.

Do not bemoan your inability to "get in on the IPO action." By any reasonable measure, IPOs are overpriced. Wait a few months and see what happens. (In most cases, the price will go down.)

Do not encourage—that is, invest in— companies that do not pay dividends. Based on studies conducted over several decades, dividends are the only reliable indicator of a stock's value. Insist that your companies play by the rules and make a buck. "The reliable return attributable to dividends," writes Robert J. Shiller, "is the main reason why stocks have . . . been such good investments historically."

Do not get stampeded. Just because the fish catch is up this month, it may not be next month. The best strategy at an auction—including an online auction—is to set a price and stick with it. Do not bid more than you think something is worth just because there is a castle-in-the-air type bidding against you.

Know exactly when you are going to sell. To get the nerve factor out of the picture, leave a standing sell order with your broker. Then go find a good book to read.

How Shares
Are Priced

From the investor's perspective, this is a pretty simple picture: Prices go up, and prices come down. The average investor knows very little about what actually happens in the process of price formation. Shareholders know and care only about *why* prices move rather than how.

This might be an acceptable state of affairs if there *were* a "why"—for example, the price is going up because the company has announced a plan to pay higher dividends, or conversely, the price is going down because the company is moving to a lower dividend rate. However, with dividends an endangered species, as we have seen, there is no such "why." In most cases today, a stock price only goes up because a majority of investors *believes* it is going up.

So there is no "why" other than the "how." This chapter will focus on the how and show you how this understanding leads to practical advice for investors. In particular, this chapter will show you how a *filter strategy* (also known as *swing trading*) can help you deal with the excesses of earnings-obsessed corporations—the Enrons of the world—while succeeding in the investment game.

The Tug of War

Picture a game of tug of war, with a rope being pulled on by a team on each of its ends. Today's stock price is a point in the middle of the rope. Ignoring such things as the relative weights and strength of the players, how the price moves today and tomorrow depends on how many players there are on each team. So, too, with stocks: A stock price level reflects the current power balance between sellers and buyers.

Some versions of tug of war involve the drawing of a centerline on the ground between the two teams, past which each team tries to drag the other. Again, there is a rough equivalent with stocks: Price is a *boundary* phenomenon—it takes place where sellers and buyers meet.

I like the tug-of-war analogy more than constructs such as "supply" and "demand," which only "meet" in an abstract sort of way. Buyers and sellers, by contrast, are real people. They meet and create price through their interactions and through their speculations about the other party's intentions. It happens in a specific place: the *open outcry,* that strange and largely misunderstood trading-floor setting where grown men shout at each other, arms are waved, and prices are born.

On a superficial level, price formation is a little bit like an electrical discharge—a spark, a bolt of lightning, or whatever. A tension exists between the price asked by potential sellers and the price offered by potential buyers, something like the tension between a positively charged body and a negatively charged one. The closer the *ask* and the *bid*—the stronger the positive and negative charges—the greater is the tension, and the more likely it is that a *settle price* (a price acceptable to both parties) will materialize.

In making subsequent decisions, buyers and sellers respond as that price goes up or down, buying low and selling high. For every price reached, pre-existing buy and sell orders add automatic volume to the trading. A high volume of sell orders pushes prices downward, and a high volume of buy orders pushes prices upward.

On a superficial level, this is about all there is to it.

Is There a Pattern?

We are interested in price formation once—the first time a stock is offered for sale—and subsequently, we are interested in the *variation* in that price.

If you think about it, in a stable world, price variation would make no sense. After all, the fluctuating price applies continuously to the same underlying commodity. For a whole host of reasons, though, this is not the way our world works. The price of gold used to be fixed at $35 per ounce. This is what gold was deemed to be "worth." Then the gold standard was abandoned, and the price of gold was unfixed and allowed to vary according to market conditions. And it is this variation that creates both opportunity and risk for investors.

Price variation has been studied in economics and in finance using methods borrowed from physics. (Economists often look to the "hard" sciences for conceptual help.) The formation of a price has been equated, for example, to the trajectory of a body moving through space—for example, a bullet or an interplanetary probe. However, there were problems with this analogy. Because price variation is known to be somewhat erratic, economists were forced to describe that trajectory as being subject to significant vibrations (technically called *noise*). From a conceptual point of view, this was a case of making the best of a bad situation.

Another framework described price as the result of a random motion—like the diffusion of gas in a volume of space, the diffusion of heat through a solid body, or the percolation of a liquid through a porous substance. The widely accepted Black-Scholes valuation method for options, for example, is based on the physics of gas molecules diffusing into a volume of space.

In fact, it was the striking similarity between two sets of diagrams—one from physics representing a particular type of randomness (brownian fractal noise, if you are interested) and the other showing actual price variations from the real world—that led to what is called the *random-walk view of price formation.* Simply put, the random-walk view holds that price variation is an effectively unstructured phenomenon.

This raises another troubling question, however. If price variation behaves in a way that is indistinguishable from randomness, how can it be assumed that the pricing process is "efficient"? How can economists assert that the pricing process reflects the best information available to buyers and sellers? No matter whether this information leads to "rational" decision making or to emotional, herdlike decision making, we should still be able to detect *some* kind of structured behavior instead of randomness, right?

Well, no. As it turns out, there is no reason why structure should be visible in price formation, even though buyers and sellers may be acting in a structured way. The reason is twofold. First, the sheer number of interactions obscures the structure that underlies them. (Think of the chaotic structure of a beehive.) Second, their consequences are constrained by thresholds (*nonlinearity,* in the words of the economists). It is like riding a bicycle: You cannot do much until you get to a certain speed. Below that speed, there is activity without much result.

Types of Markets: Organized and Over-the-Counter

Financial operations take place either in *organized markets*—the smooth operation of which is ensured by *clearinghouses*—or on a private basis between two or more parties in what is called *over-the-counter* (OTC) *operations.*

The clearinghouses of organized markets match potential buyers with potential sellers; they also make sure (for their own protection and to protect soundness of the market) that every participant is solvent at the end of the trading day. Each participant's position is "marked to market" at market closure to determine whether that player's equity is positive or negative. If a trader's account is depleted, that player is required to produce additional cash. In this way, all players are protected against an individual's potential default. Participants in organized markets, therefore, need not worry about the solvency of their counterparts.

OTC financial operations, by contrast, are private deals between two parties. Among other things, this means that there is a risk that one party to a deal may fail to fulfill its financial commitments. This risk has been mitigated somewhat by the evolution of new mechanisms. For example, as corporate borrowers have become rated by professional rating agencies—a subject to which I will return in Chapter 13—it has become possible for them to protect themselves in their mutual dealings through so-called credit swaps, which are based on their respective credit ratings and act as an insurance against default risk.

Traders

Let's take a look at the trading floor. In the *pit*—the area reserved for the auction of financial instruments—stand a number of traders acting in one of a number of different capacities. Some, the so-called specialists, are there on their own account. (In other words, this is how they make their living.)

Others are there representing the account of a bank or a brokerage house. In this latter case, the trading is either *proprietary*—that is, aimed at making a profit for the institution itself using its own resources—or conducted on behalf of the house's clients. Traders quote *bids,* which are price levels at which they are prepared to buy a definite number of shares, and *asks,* which are price levels at which they are prepared to sell a definite number of shares.

Most traders are allowed to quote only either bids or asks. The exception—and it is an important one—comes in the case of so-called market makers. Market makers are contractually obligated (through an agreement with the clearinghouse holding responsibility for that market) to have at all times both a plausible bid and a plausible ask for the market's product. This more or less guarantees that the market will be active and that products that get to the market will sell. (For markets to work, sellers of stocks need to believe that someone will want to buy when they want to sell, and vice versa.) Being a successful market maker is a delicate exercise, and clearinghouses offer various incentives (such as commission rebates) to those specialists and brokerage houses that are prepared to play the role of market maker.

If trading on their own account, traders follow their own personal strategies for buying cheap and selling dear. If they are trading on behalf of their clearinghouse, they generally follow the instructions recorded on their *deck*. This is nothing more complicated than a deck of cards showing each proposed trade, including clients' special orders that must be executed at a specific price or in a specific market situation.[1] The entire set of a financial firm's orders—in a sense, its collection of decks—is called its *trading book.* The trading book is kept secret from competitors because it constitutes valuable information about triggers that—depending on volume—are likely to push prices up or down.

Package buying or selling refers to large orders from institutional investors that are usually sliced to ease market absorption with minimal *slippage.* Slippage is the move in price that an order creates against itself due to its volume—in other words, the more you sell, the lower the price drops. Conversely, the more you buy, the higher the price rises. Neither case is good, unless, of course, you complete your transactions—that is, get all your buying and selling done—before the slippage starts to show up.

Already you can start to see how complicated and ethically slippery this can get. Brokerage houses and banks know about their clients' large-volume orders, right? Armed with this information, they might just decide to drop their own (*proprietary*) trades right in alongside any significant package buying that they are conducting on behalf of their clients. Some brokerage houses have been caught performing these types of manipulations and have gotten their knuckles rapped as a result.

The value of a given trading book is difficult to assess with any certainty because it depends entirely on where the market will be heading in the future—and as we just saw, a trader's own trading book influences the market. In January 2002, one month after Enron filed for bankruptcy, UBS Warburg acquired Enron's trading deck and trading book. There was no upfront payment from UBS to Enron. Instead, the agreement took the form of a share agreement: Enron would receive in the future 33 to 45 percent of the profit over the next 10 years. Asked to assess the value of Enron's share in the deal, Enron's advisor—the Blackstone Group—valued it to be worth anywhere between $40 million and $2.87 billion.[2] This enormous range in possible valuations shows just how difficult it is to make such estimates.

What Actually Happens

As noted, a *transaction* is the meeting of a buyer and a seller at a particular price level for a particular number of shares. A specific settle price is created every time a transaction takes place at that particular price level. The volume of the transaction that takes place is necessarily the lower of two numbers: the number of shares specified by the potential buyer (quoting the *bid*) and the number of shares offered by the potential seller (quoting the *ask*). The existence of more than one settle price at any one point in time is anomalous and short-lived; an exchange tries to guarantee the existence of a single settle price at any one time.

When a transaction takes place, *pit recorders* enter into the computerized quote system of the exchange the price, volume, and houses involved in the transaction. The price data are then displayed on electronic screens within the exchange and relayed by news agencies (such as Bloomberg or Bridge-Telerate) to the quote screens installed in financial firms. The quote screens display the ask and the bid price levels that are closest to each other, the last price and the previous one, the highest price and the lowest price in the current session, and often the open price of the current session and the close price of the prior session.

Traders' Responses to New Prices

Of course, a trader's deck is dynamic. It keeps changing because transactions are being triggered automatically whenever the market hits the particular price level that they are associated with. Traders adapt to the new price levels reached in the trading process—either on their own initiative or following standing instructions from their bank or brokerage house. Meanwhile, clients of the banks and brokerage houses react to the new price levels displayed on their quote screens by placing new orders. Spurious patterns of price evolution may take shape when trading is hectic and multiple prices are traded within very short time intervals. Sometimes it may appear that a sequence of nearly simultaneous transactions is fraught with significance— a run toward this stock, perhaps, or a run away from that one—but this is rarely the case. The order in which the pit recorders enter these nearly simultaneous transactions is truly haphazard, so patterns that seem to emerge minute to minute are most often not patterns at all—more like clouds briefly converging to create a recognizable shape.

Clients who have specific goals (buying or selling) in mind or specific investment horizons on which they are focused enter *special orders*. These orders may have been preexisting for some time—they may have been entered months ago—or they may be responses to price changes that have occurred only in the last few minutes. The issue of special orders was raised prominently by Martha Stewart's sale of ImClone stock on a day when insiders had become aware of a soon-to-come drop in the stock price. The issue was whether or not there was an extant order from Martha Stewart to sell the stock if its price dropped to or below $60? If there was, the sale was legitimate; if there wasn't, the likelihood is that the sale order came as a consequence of knowledge that the Food and Drug Administration was about to turn down the application for ImClone's primary cancer drug.

Bid, Ask, Settle Price, and Volume

What constitutes a *price*? Actually, there are three types of prices: asks, bids, and settle prices. Logically, all asks should be higher than all bids; otherwise, they would overlap. When they do overlap, asks and bids match at those price levels, and transactions take place, generating new settle prices.

This applies to the entire price region in which bids and asks coincide, and the exchange quickly returns to a status quo in which all remaining asks are higher than all remaining bids. The fast dynamics of the open outcry—in which dozens of traders interact efficiently—guarantee that an overlap of asks and bids never lasts for more than a couple of seconds.

Both asks and bids are potential *(or virtual)* prices only. Not until they coincide in a settle price is there a transaction, at which point there is an exchange of cash for the transfer of ownership of the shares. Therefore, what is important is the spread between the ask and the bid that are closest to each other. The asks and bids not within this spread have no direct influence; they remain virtual. This is why a single share traded within the range of the current spread is very significant, whereas thousands of shares on offer or on demand some distance away from the spread are of no current significance. Again, price formation is a *boundary* phenomenon created between buy orders and sell orders where they stand closest to each other. Everything away from that boundary is unimportant, at least for the time being.

Once a flurry of transactions has exhausted the potential of a new settle price, another process begins. Market players try to figure out what has just happened and—based on this analysis—what they should do next. On their screens, they see (among other things) the most recent *settle* price and the two previous ones. The questions they ask themselves are, "What does this latest development suggest is coming next? What should *I* do next?"

In other words, this is a feedback loop: A decision is implemented that changes the playing field to some extent, and this leads to analysis and a new round of decision making and action. Each new settle price signals the end of an individual "game" played by two traders who have entered an ask and a bid since a settle price was last generated. At the same time, each settle price sets the level from which new (or the same) traders can start new individual "games."

Alternatively, the market for an individual stock may go dormant. The fact that a market may become dormant for an indefinite period each time a settle price has been set underscores that fact that prices have no inherent momentum and no internal dynamics. It is the prospect of future profits or losses that relaunches the play (or fails to relaunch the play) on the exchange. This also demonstrates the major difference between the motion of a body in space—like the bullet or the interplanetary probe mentioned before—and the motion of a stock. The trajectory of a stock is defined by a series of consecutive "games," separate but linked, each involving only two traders. These individual "games" cannot be considered entirely independently of each other because each grows out of the previous game, and yet each game is closed unto itself. Unfortunately for economists, there aren't any great parallels in the natural world.

With this background under our belts, we can see more clearly why some traditional interpretations of stock price formation do not work. Supply and demand, for example, presupposes a static view of price formation that does not reflect the volume and rapidity of the feedback that takes place in the context of an open outcry. Supply and demand are implied in the existing standing orders, of course, but such orders *do not determine price directly*. As we have seen, prices are determined on a boundary, where a particular ask level and a particular bid—those closest to each other—are facing each other across a spread.

Supply and demand collapse two elements of a different nature: first, the volumes associated with the closest ask and bid that will materialize into a settle price when a trader makes them meet and, second, the "pull" created in one direction or the other when standing orders on both sides of the market get activated when new settle prices reach them. Again, this is a contingent, dynamic universe—not at all like the static world of the supply-and-demand model.

Also undermining a supply-and-demand explanation is the fact that the quantities of shares associated with particular asks and bids may very well be small. Hence, under certain circumstances, *it is relatively easy to move the market one way or the other* and thereby to define the location where the next price "game" will occur. Monroe Trout, of Trout Trading Company, explains (in an interview in an interesting book called *The New Market Wizards)* how he moves the market while trading very small volumes. You can safely ignore the technical details, but try to follow Trout's tactics:

> For example, if I'm long one thousand S&P contracts and it's 11:30 Chicago time, I'm probably going to want to put in some sort of scale-down buy orders, like buying ten lots every tick down, to hold the market in my direction. It doesn't cost me that many contracts at that time of day to support the market, because there are not a lot of contracts trading."[3]

What's going on here? Trout is holding the market with small lots of 10 contracts at lunchtime, which is a time of day when trading tails off significantly. No, such small pushes are unlikely to have a lasting influence, especially if subsequent heavy trading swamps them. Still, in a thin trading context, they may very well end up bending the market in the hoped-for direction. Remember: What makes this possible is that *every change in price is regarded as significant by the actors in the drama*, no matter what the volume that is associated with that particular settle price.

We also can see more clearly why the notion of *equilibrium* comes up short in the real world. Equilibrium theory assumes that there is a natural disposition for a stock price to return to its *mean* or average value—therefore, *mean reversion*. However, the stock market is not mean-reverting because stocks do not *have* an average price. Think about the logic here: If stock prices were mean-reverting, investors whose interest is in capital gains would have noticed this unhappy reality a long time ago and would never buy stock for the long run.

Of course, the case is very different with interest rates, which tend to move within a range of, say, 1 and 15 percent. If you are looking at either of those extremes, it is a safe bet that interest rates eventually will revert to their mean. Stocks, however, simply do not work this way.

Uncertainty and the Market

There is a commonly expressed view that holds that "uncertainty fuels the market." This is a misreading of reality. Uncertainty actually paralyzes the markets. When investors are uncertain, they keep a low profile. It is only when investors are reasonably certain that they make decisions.

How do investors get to certainty? They tend to draw on evidence in one (or both) of two categories: intrinsic and extrinsic. *Intrinsic* means focused on or derived from the history of price variation for this particular stock. This is the evidence that so-called technical analysts rely on, working with charts of all types and flavors. Of course, people have been searching for the Rosetta stone of the stock market since the invention of the market, and—not surprisingly—a near infinity of techniques has been developed to use past price variation to infer future price evolution. Most employ some type of statistical processing: trends, moving averages, Elliot waves, oscillators, wavelets, fractal interpolation, and so on.

Extrinsic evidence comprises not only company information but also data from the overall economy's fundamentals: gross national product (GNP), level of unemployment, consumer confidence, housing starts, monetary mass, and so on.

Too much certainty can be a bad thing as well. If all the players *agree* in their certainty, there may be only buyers or only sellers, and trading stops. However, the occasions most likely to make a change are those in which two types of certainties clash—the certainty of those who are sure that prices will go up and the certainty of those who are positive that prices are bound now to come down.[4] *Volume* goes up as the number of people in both "camps of certainty" increases.

We buy in the hope that the price goes up and sell in the fear it will come down. Fortunately, buying and selling are self-fulfilling prophecies: Through buying, we help the price go up, and through selling, we help the price come down. There is one condition, however: For us to have any impact, *we have to be siding with the majority view.*

The reason is that there is a threshold at which the majority adjudges and "takes all." The pushing in one direction or the other is short-lived; it materializes through the formation of one single settle price. With large buying and selling volumes, such as with package buying and selling, a trend line of successive prices may be created (*slippage*) due to the fact that each price exhausts a number of standing orders.

Prices will move up as long as there are renewable surpluses of buy orders over sell orders; conversely, prices will move down as long as there are renewable surpluses of sell orders over buy orders. The difficulty lies in guessing what will result from the complex combination of standing orders and new decision making deriving from the recent evolution of the price. And once again, unfortunately, *there is no other logic to stock price when it is determined by capital gains.*

The good news is that figuring out if there is a surplus of buyers over sellers or the reverse is not as difficult as you might imagine. The institutional investors mentioned earlier make up the bulk of buyers and sellers of shares of stock; their influence in the market far outweighs that of any individual investor. If you can figure out what the "big boys" are doing, you are a big step ahead of the game. Tracking the behavior of institutional investors is a service provided by some research firms on a subscription basis. Here are the addresses of a couple of Web sites where this kind of service can be purchased:

http://www.ia-dpm.com/
http://www.investools.com/

The Filter or Swing Trading Strategy

In fact, I do not think that you should drive yourself crazy trying to figure out whether there are current surpluses of buy and sell orders. This kind of analysis can—and therefore *should*—be automated with the use of a computer. If you go this route, you should devote a certain amount of time on a schedule of your own choosing—every month, week, day, hour, or minute (God forbid!)—to figuring out what the market is trying to tell you.

Broadly speaking, the market is trying to tell you one of two things: Either the market is selling and the price has gone down, or the market is buying and the price has gone up.

And even more broadly speaking, your response should be to travel with the herd: *Buy or hold if the market is buying, and sell if the market is selling.*

The buying and selling method just sketched out is called a *filter.* It takes market behavior at face value and sends buy and sell signals accordingly. How, exactly, does it work? You define what constitutes an upward trend—say, a 5 percent upward movement in a particular period of time—and you buy into that upward trend. When a stock peaks and begins moving in the opposite direction (down!), you watch closely to see if it hits your predetermined downward-trend number (which could again be 5 percent). If and when it gets there, you sell. Then the game starts all over again: You determine the bottom of the valley and start buying again when the next upward trend establishes itself.

On the "long" part of this strategy, there are two signals: the *upward-trend buy*—which decides when you move in—and the *trailing sell order* or *stop-loss*—which is the drop you will permit in price before cutting your losses.

On the "short" part of this strategy, things are reversed. The downward-trend sell may be the same signal as the trailing stop-loss of the long part of this strategy. When applied "short," a trailing stop-loss applies when the stock price goes up. The two percentages for upward-trend buy and trailing stop-loss need not be identical.

The "long" part of this strategy succeeds because more often than not by the time the automatic trailing stop-loss has been triggered, the price will still be higher than the price you paid when you bought on an upward-trend buy.

The reason why the filter strategy works should be intuitively clear: There is an intentional asymmetry built into the way that profit and loss are dealt with. As we have seen, there is no cap on profit, but there is a set floor on allowable losses: the trailing stop-loss.

Let me hasten to add, however, that although the basic tenets of the filter system—*let your profit grow; cut your losses*—are logically compelling, this is no guarantee that people will embrace them. Why? First, because people are not logical. We humans are slow to embrace our successes and quick to defend our mistakes. "Don't get out too soon," we tell ourselves on the ride up. "Don't worry, the price will be back," we reassure ourselves on the long slide down.

These psychological observations are not original to me, by the way. In his 1930 publication, *The Art of Speculation*, Philip L. Carret remarked on ". . . the timidity of the average trader in the face of a profit, [and] his [or her] stubbornness when faced with a loss. The explanation is probably to be found in the tardiness with which the mind adjusts itself to changing ideas of value."[5]

And second, there is an enormous amount of propaganda to the contrary. Many of the players in the game—corporations and financial advisors among them—have a stake in the "buy, hold, and buy more" strategy. Mutual fund salespeople tell us to "dollar cost average," which means putting the same amount into a bad market that you put into a good one. This is presented as the *prudent, long-term* approach to investing. I say that it is silly on the face of it.

The highly respected economist Burton Malkiel describes the filter method in *A Random Walk Down Wall Street*. He first remarks that the method is "very popular with brokers" but then immediately derides it: "When the higher transaction charges incurred under the filter rules are taken into consideration, these techniques cannot consistently beat a policy of simply buying the individual stock (or the stock average in question) and holding it over the period during which the test is performed."[6]

I grant that constant trading to track tiny fluctuations of the market up and down will wind up costing the investor a certain amount in commissions—although the cost of the average commission is far less today than it was even a decade ago. And yes, the effectiveness and efficiency of the method depends on multiple factors above and beyond transaction fees: what level of upward trend you move on, what level down from the peak you place your trailing stop-loss, and so on.

Malkiel's preferred alternative of "buy and hold" is demonstrably worse, however, because it can only work in a bullish market (that is, when things are headed upward). When things are headed in the opposite direction, you *definitely* should be willing to pay a few extra commissions to unload plummeting stocks.

And yes, to determine which decision levels stand to optimize capital gains, professionals perform elaborate computer simulations, trying out various combinations of values for "upward-trend buy" and "trailing stop-loss" over the past history of the stock. Getting access to this expertise can be very expensive. I maintain, however, that to work reasonably well, the fil-

ter method requires only the application of some good old-fashioned common sense. Since your buy and sell signals are triggered automatically by
stock price levels, you will not need the (expensive) advice of any broker
or financial advisor. Use a deep-discount brokerage—and the lower the
transaction fee, the better.

So why does Malkiel try to dissuade investors from using the filter?
"The individual investor would do well to avoid using any filter rule," he
writes, "and, I might add, any broker who recommends it." Myself included,
I suppose.

The only explanation that I can offer is that Malkiel believes that it
would damage the market if too many people used this trading method
simultaneously. If a large number of investors used the filter in concert, it
certainly would amplify market movements and add volatility. Drops in
price would encourage *more* selling—and additional drops in price. Conversely, overheated buying would trigger more overheated buying.

For that type of amplification to be noticeable, however, large numbers
of buy and sell orders would have to be identical. Practically speaking, this
will never happen. Investors necessarily will have different thresholds for
trend buying and trailing stop-losses based in part on what commission fees
they are charged on trades. In addition, their time horizons will differ—from
the individual investor's month to the intraday trader's minute.

And by the way, why is it your responsibility, or mine, to make up for
market shortcomings that are created indirectly by earnings-obsessed companies? Why should *we* take the hit? Why shouldn't we look after our own
interests as carefully as the corporations, brokerage houses, and exchanges
look after theirs?

All I know—and I know it from personal experience—is that the filter
strategy serves disciplined investors extremely well. In the early 1990s, I
designed an automated system based on the filter strategy for a French commodity and trading advisors firm, and its overall rate of return was surprisingly high.

The filter strategy works. And—speaking directly to the underlying
theme of this book—it is an effective way to deal with earnings-obsessed
companies that may not have their investors' best interests at heart.

In Chapter 7, which focuses on the specifics of the Enron death spiral,
I will draw on some of the information presented in this chapter and show
what happens when an aggressive (and increasingly desperate) company
sets itself up as a market maker in an OTC exchange.

LESSONS FOR THE INVESTOR

Buy and hold as long as there is a renewable surplus of buy orders over sell orders. But *sell* when there is evidence of a renewable surplus of sell orders over buy orders. In other words, *go with the crowd.* Do not be afraid to sell when the time comes.

Other investors' motives are not pertinent. Do not worry about them; you can't figure them out in any case. Only their disposition to buy or to sell is relevant to you.

Institutional investors are the source of most buy and sell orders. To find out about surpluses of buy or sell orders, track the behavior of institutional investors using appropriate subscription services.

Explore the appropriateness of a filter strategy for your investments. If it feels right, use it.

In any case, buy or hold if other investors are buying (because the stock price is going up); sell if other investors are selling (because the stock price is dropping).

Only buy the services you need. Buy and sell strategies that are dictated by stock price level should be pursued using deep-discount brokerages. Keep your commission costs down to keep your profits up.

7

How Enron Got
Earnings-Obsessed

*I have always tried to do the right thing, but where
there was once great pride, now it's gone.*

—From the suicide note of JOHN CLIFFORD BAXTER,
Enron's former vice chairman

We humans are optimistic creatures. We believe in outcomes that we *want*
to believe in despite all kinds of compelling evidence to the contrary. For
example, we believe today (or at least many of us do) that inflation is a thing
of the past—that we have vanquished it and put it to rest forever. This is
absolutely, positively not the case. And yet, we go on being optimistic.

At the turn of the century, similarly, we believed that recessions were a
thing of the past. In a chorus led by Federal Reserve Chairman Alan
Greenspan, we celebrated the constant rise in productivity due to the com-
puterization of business and agreed that this meant the "death of recession."
After all, by 2000, the economy was in the eighteenth year of a bull market. This time, certainly, the bear was not hibernating but was properly dead.

Down at Enron's headquarters in Houston, there were powerful people
who shared in this optimism. Some time in 1999, these people—and perhaps

a number of more cynical colleagues who saw no reason *not* to go along with the optimists—began devising business policies that would *only* work in a bull market. From 1999 on, Enron's business could only operate in an environment where the price of its stock was constantly moving upward.

Was this so wrong if the bear was dead?

How culpable was Enron?

Was it optimism or cynicism that got Enron into the mess that ultimately destroyed it?

The Benefit of the Doubt?

As of this writing, only one Enron higher-up has admitted to involvement in any fraudulent activities. More may follow. However, I think that when the final story of Enron is written, it will be less about outright fraud and more about culture. It will be a story about recklessness and arrogance on a massive scale.

The interesting thing is that in this imperfect world of ours, recklessness and arrogance do not necessarily hurt corporate profits. Under some circumstances, they can help jump-start a company and move it forward.

As noted earlier, there *was* a time when Enron was going in the right direction. Then, beginning some time around 1999, the company got caught in a web of adverse circumstances. The harder Enron's leaders tried to wriggle out of the trap they had created, the more deeply they got enmeshed. From then on they started cutting corners and pyramiding in a forward flight, and the company went downhill—to the end that we have all been reading about.

Part of the Enron story hinges on a corporate reliance on something called *synthetic leases,* a model that Enron used when creating its shaky partnerships. Synthetic leases are specifically designed to deceive. (They serve no other useful purpose.) I personally would prefer that business be done without intentional trickery. All the same, if much of the business community is resorting to the use of synthetic leases, and the regulators bless this tactic, is it fair to point the finger of blame at Enron?

Therefore, let's give Enron the benefit of the doubt, at least in its pre-1999 incarnation. Let's say that there was once a "Good Enron." Let's presume that if the company had not had the misfortune of getting caught in the final flares of the dot-com bubble, Good Enron might have adopted a different line of defense and avoided making many of the mistakes that ultimately brought the company down.

At the same time, however, let's also try to figure out why there had to be a "Bad Enron." Let's figure out why the company became earnings-obsessed. Let's figure out why Enron had to "run twice as fast to stay where it was," as energy-industry analyst Robert F. McCullough described it to a *New York Times* journalist.[1] Our goal, again, is to identify danger signs and keep future Bad Enrons out of our portfolios.

I will point to six critical factors in the decline and fall of Enron.

Factor 1: An Entrepreneurial Culture Run Amok

Enron was a company that prided itself on its freewheeling entrepreneurial culture. However, there is a clear difference—or there should be—between entrepreneurship and buccaneering. Here are a few data points that, in retrospect, are simply amazing:

> Enron's chief financial officer (CFO), Andrew S. Fastow, got himself named head of several of the shaky partnerships mentioned in previous chapters (including, for example, LJM Cayman and LJM2 Co-Investment) and yet remained on as the company's CFO. Apparently no one saw any potential conflicts of interest in this dual role.

> Fastow also was in command of the Raptors partnership—ultimately a half-billion-dollar loser—and, through one of his subordinates, of the equally disastrous Chewco.

> Fastow awarded himself $30 million in commissions from LJM2 after Raptor 1 had only been in existence for a couple of weeks. No one among Enron's senior executive ranks objected.

Again, I'll use the word *amazing* to summarize these facts—alone and especially in combination. It is amazing that no one inside the company objected to this stuff. And it is amazing that no external analysts were willing or able to "pierce the corporate veil" and call a spade a spade.

My point here is not to beat up on Andrew Fastow. Yes, the Powers Report singled out Fastow as the main culprit of the unmitigated disaster. (The recent plea bargaining by one of his chief lieutenants points in the same direction.) however, it is interesting to note that former Chief Executive

Officer (CEO) Jeffrey Skilling—despite the opportunity afforded by his many hours of testimony before Senate subcommittees—placed no blame at the doorstep of his former CFO. One explanation had it that Skilling first wanted to review the numbers himself before condemning his freewheeling CFO.[2] I think, however, that this explanation misses the point. Skilling did not condemn Fastow's overreaching because Fastow simply was embodying Enron's vaunted entrepreneurial culture.

According to a *New York Times* report, "a culture of 'earnings management' permeated Enron. They said it went far beyond the efforts of Andrew S. Fastow. . . . 'Every unit was doing this,' said one former energy services official. 'We were entrepreneurial, and one thing people thought we could do better than anyone else is structured finance.' Former employees in Enron's broadband and retail energy services operations said the company's financial management strategies were first developed at Enron Capital and Trade, a unit that prospered in the 1990s under the leadership of Jeffrey K. Skilling, who helped set up a 'gas bank' to finance struggling gas producers."[3]

In other words, Fastow and others like him simply were following the entrepreneurial template laid down by CEO Skilling. No wonder, then, that Skilling was reluctant to disown his protégé's excesses.

Factor 2: The Failure of Project Summer

According to a lawsuit filed by some Enron's investors in April 2002, the debacle at Enron began in 1997 when the company "experienced a severe financial shock because of a $400 million loss in a British natural gas transaction and a $100 million charge relating to deals involving a fuel additive. By autumn of that year, Enron stock lost one-third of its value."[4]

I sympathize with the investors' pain, but I think that this is too early a date to point to as the "beginning of the end for Enron." At that time, the company had not even started its online trading of energy. Its disastrous broadband venture was still only a scheme on paper.

In my view, *New York Times* correspondent David Barboza identified the true "beginning of the end" in a March 2002 article entitled, "Enron Sought to Raise Cash Two Years Ago." In 2000, according to Barboza, there was a failed attempt—known to insiders as "Project Summer"—to raise cash for Enron, which at the time had started incurring considerable losses in its forays abroad. "Less than two years ago," Barboza wrote, "the company failed to complete a deal to sell the bulk of its international energy holdings for about $7 billion to a group composed primarily of wealthy Middle Eastern investors."[5]

In order to shield Enron from the risks associated with those overseas investments, a plan was hatched to carve out Enron's foreign operations from the rest of the company and create a new global entity. According to Barboza, "Enron had been negotiating to sell a majority of its foreign holdings to a group of investors that was led by Amin Badr el- Din, a special adviser to Sheik Zayed bin Sultan al-Nahayan, the longtime president of the United Arab Emirates, according to former Enron executives. The investors came from the United Arab Emirates, Saudi Arabia and Europe."[6] The deal would have involved most of Enron's large international holdings in the Caribbean, South America, Turkey, Gaza, Qatar, India, and Japan.

The project came to nothing in the summer of 2000 when Sheik Zayed was forced to travel to the United States for a kidney transplant and treatment of a fractured hip. Barboza claims that what happened in the aftermath was that "company executives gave the task of improving the company's finances to Andrew S. Fastow, the chief financial officer. . . . In late 2000, Mr. Fastow began selling foreign assets to a variety of off-balance-sheet partnerships as a temporary measure to improve the company's cash holdings at the end of the year, former executives say. 'It's now clear Fastow's tricky partnerships were bailing out the company,' one former high-level executive said. 'These big transactions take six to nine months to do, minimum. Fastow would close this in two to three weeks; his people didn't have to do due diligence.'"[7]

Although there is no hard evidence supporting Barboza's account, it has the indisputable merit of making sense of a number of otherwise outlandish features, such as the implausible creation by CFO Andrew Fastow of partnerships such as Chewco and Raptors, the relief by the board of directors of any conflict of interest for him doing so, and the healthy compensation he would soon receive for the service rendered—with no recorded objections raised.

Factor 3: Broadband and Model Risk

In the hearing before the Senate's Subcommittee for Consumer Affairs, when asked by Missouri Democratic Senator Jean Carnahan to explain why

Enron's stock price had plummeted, former CEO Skilling cited several causes, including the foreign investments just mentioned. The *first* cause he pointed to, however, was broadband: "The first one," he told the senators, "was that the collapse in optical-fiber stock started in February and March of the year 2001. We were viewed as a player in that optical-fiber business, and that immediately hit our stock."

Enron set out to create a bandwidth market on its own. It would launch a product and—to draw on the terms introduced in the last chapter—trade that product over the counter, as well as be that product's market maker. In other words, it would be prepared to sell bandwidth to whomever wanted to buy it and purchase it from whomever wanted to sell it. On both sales and purchases, Enron would make a small profit. And because the transactions would be over the counter—in other words, not regulated by a stock exchange—and because of the structure of the energy industry, where players are either buyers or sellers, the spread between Enron's buying and selling would remain a private matter.

Enron did not lack ambition. As in the energy field, Enron aimed to *be* "the market" in broadband. And based on its track record, it had cause for optimism. At one point, as noted earlier, Enron managed to trade *25 percent* of the U.S. domestic electricity consumption—an astounding accomplishment for a once-obscure pipeline company in Houston.

It is worth noting that in its conquest of the electricity market, Enron had some good friends who wielded a lot of influence. For example, for Enron's strategy to succeed, the company had to remain the main player in the market. A switch to an organized market, open to independent traders, would have been death to this strategy. In 1992, Wendy L. Gramm—chairwoman of the Commodity Futures Trading Commission—played an instrumental role in ensuring that the trading of energy derivatives (such as the forward contracts that were Enron's bread and butter) would remain unregulated. A year later she joined Enron's board of directors and also became a member of the board's audit committee.

On the broadband side of the shop, Enron was trading with its counterparts over the counter, defining the terms of the trades, and trying to meet expectations that it would do as well as a bona fide exchange. A large piece of this, of course, was coming up with standardized products to trade. Give the devil his due: In this realm, Enron pioneered, coming up with the first standardized bandwidth product.

This deserves some explanation. In order for a commodity to qualify for standardization, two conditions must be met: The good needs to be *con-*

sumable and *fungible*. The second criterion means that there needs to be a true and reliable unit of measure that makes trades strictly comparable. Thus, for instance, if bandwidth between New York and Los Angeles is chosen as the fundamental unit for bandwidth consumption, then it becomes possible to state that bandwidth between New York and London represents so many of those New York–to–Los Angeles units. And this is precisely what Enron managed to achieve.

On an organized market set on an exchange such as the New York Stock Exchange, the role of the market makers is clear. When they are asked where they will place their bid and ask, they cast their eyes on the electronic tote board where quotes are displayed—ask, bid, last settle, and so on—and make their decision based on what they see other traders doing.

However, when, like Enron, you try to do it all on your own, over the counter, there is no reliable place to cast your eyes. In order for the market you have set up to have any chance of surviving, you need to know with some assurance where to locate your bid and your ask. In other words, you need to make good guesses about the level where buy orders and sell orders are likely to meet in somewhat similar quantities. The risk involved here if you are wrong is called *model risk,* which simply means the risk that grows out of an inaccurate representation of the fundamentals of the market—a bad model that leads to locating the bid and ask quoted to your over-the-counter counterparties at the wrong level.

Kenneth Lay, Enron's last CEO, understood this well. He emphasized in an interview that Enron did not really need to care about how high or how low the prices were as long as it knew *where* they were: "Whether the price is high or low is not that important to us; it's mainly a matter of matching up transactions."[8] Again, at what level would a near-equivalent number of buy and sell orders meet?

In previous chapters I have compared debt instruments (for example, bonds) with equities mainly to cast light on how equities work. In order to calculate accurately the present value of a bond, you need to be able to discount accurately the different interest cash flows associated with that bond. In order to do this, you need to derive a *zero-coupon yield curve* from the market yield curve; simple multiplication and division then permit you to calculate all needed forward rates, such as 3 months in 6 years.

This is a relatively easy task. But how do you calculate a forward 3 months in 6 years for electricity?

Some risks can be managed using new financial instruments. For example, default risk of counterparties can be hedged with *credit swaps,* which act as insurance against insolvency. Risk linked to spikes in energy demand can be managed with *weather swaps,* which act as insurance against unexpectedly good or unexpectedly bad weather upsetting time-in-the-year consumption patterns. Pollution risks can be managed through *emissions swaps,* which act as insurance against pollution exceeding regulatory thresholds. And these were the paths that Enron took.

In contrast, in order to protect itself against the uncertainties of its modeling of energy yield curves, Enron and other players in the energy-trading business decided to manage the inherent risk in the most traditional manner: through insurance and reinsurance.

In April 2002, Michael Brick reported in the *New York Times* that "because Enron was dealing in commodities where there was no established public market to set prices, a trader had to decide on a price curve—the expected direction of prices in the future—on which to value each deal in the present."

However, there is a trap and a temptation in this, as Brick reported: "'The further out you go on a forward curve, the values are less known,' one trader said. 'The further out you go, there's some potential that there's a less objective value.' Some traders took advantage of this subjectivity to set unreasonably high curves, and later to change those curves to establish even higher values, which they could report as profits immediately, a former manager on the trading desk said. 'The curve moved constantly,' this manager added, 'especially toward the end of the quarter, to generate reported income.'"[9]

Calculating a *forward* for energy products—and certainly for novelties such as bandwidth—proved to be very, very difficult. This became painfully clear during the energy crisis in California in 2000–2001. If the forward turns out at some point to have been way off the mark, then the irate customer is likely to demand contract renegotiations. And this is exactly what happened in April 2002 when California renegotiated the energy forwards it had purchased at the high point of the crisis in 2000. Why? Because by April 2002, the electricity forwards that had been bought in 2000 were priced at *three times* the spot price for electricity.

Did Enron fall victim to model risk? The answer is "yes." And worse than that, Enron's bad guesses may have been influenced by their growing need to show profits. As utility industry analyst Robert F. McCullough phrased it, "Their [Enron's] financial problems might have been intervening in their day-to-day trading activities."

Factor 4: California, Energy, and Nomads

According to Jeffrey Skilling, the third reason why Enron stock started plummeting was the California energy crisis and its potential impact on the recently deregulated energy market. "Because of the California power problems," Skilling told his Senate inquisitors, "there was a fear that the wholesale markets might put in price caps and re-regulate the natural-gas industry, and I think that was viewed as negative for Enron in the long term."

The California energy crisis had unfolded in the summer of 2000, when—in a confusing context of apparent shortages—electricity prices spiked dramatically. Unexplained plant shutdowns helped drive up the prices that the California Independent System Operator (Cal-ISO), the agency acting as a dispatcher, paid for emergency power.[10] And in May 2001, this resulted in rotating outages for consumers who were dependent on the three major California state investor-owned utilities (IOUs). In this case, I use the word *dependent* quite literally: Power brown-outs and black-outs can be life threatening in the air-conditioned deserts of southern California during the scorching summer months.

Skilling feared re-regulation, but the energy chaos was clearly a consequence of the widespread deregulation that California had embraced in 1994—the first state in the nation to do so—and had taken the lead in pursuing, ostensibly to help consumers by introducing competition.[11]

Deregulation broke apart what traditionally had been a vertically integrated industry, in which utility companies generated, transmitted, and distributed power. In the wake of deregulation, firms would specialize in one of these several activities. Each would then deal with one type of risk and set its ask price accordingly for the targeted service it provided. The danger for the consumer, of course, was that costs would go up at each disaggregated stage and that savings through increased competition would not materialize. As it turned out, this was exactly what happened—and on a grand scale. A much larger number of actors were involved in the chain from energy production (or purchase) and retail, and each of them built in a healthy margin for itself. Between the spring of 1999 and early 2000, consumers saw an eightfold increase in electricity costs, apparently through the natural workings of the market (that is, without any fraudulent activity).

California Governor Gray Davis tried to solve the crisis by negotiating long-term contracts with the utilities. At the time, the long-term contracts were popular with the public and seemed like the lesser of two evils. However, the energy ultimately delivered under those contracts turned out to have been grossly overpriced.

Therefore, as implied earlier, California sued the energy-trading firms for alleged price gouging. This created a judicial risk that compounded the growing regulatory risk—that prices would be capped. And although Enron's chosen candidate—Patrick Wood III—recently had been named the head of the Federal Energy Regulatory Commission (FERC), Enron feared with ample justification that the growing turmoil might lead to a reversal of what years of patient and costly lobbying had managed to secure. (Ultimately, FERC did indeed impose price caps.)

In the face of mounting public fury, Enron displayed an astounding degree of insensitivity. During a conference call with analysts, for example, Jeffrey Skilling told an ill-conceived joke: "What's the difference between California and the *Titanic*? Answer: At least when the *Titanic* went down, the lights were on."

During a hearing before the Senate Commerce Committee in February 2002, Democratic Senator Barbara Boxer of California took Skilling on: "We also hear from Enron traders—that's T-R-A-D-E-R-S—that Enron jammed transmission lines, used futures and derivatives to, according to California State Senator Joe Dunn, possibly buy and sell the same electricity 15 times in an effort to inflate prices. And as you answer these questions, I hope that you will realize that at the time you were making jokes about California, we were realizing that energy is a necessity, not a luxury."

A little more than 2 months after this exchange—in May 2002—a correspondence between Enron and several law firms about the energy-trading strategies used by the company were made public, clarifying the role that Enron had played in the California crisis. What the memos revealed was a mix of strategies, all aimed at raising Enron's profit and most leading to artificially inflated retail prices and therefore hurting Californian consumers.

Enron's techniques were various with varying degrees of deviousness. Some took advantage of the unintended consequences of deregulating a deregulated industry. Some exploited the fact that Cal-ISO was grossly understaffed and had no jurisdiction beyond California's borders. Some were designed to outmaneuver and outsmart the IOUs. Some appear to have been based on outright fraud (or in the tame language of the Cal-ISO tariff, "gaming").

The relationship between California and Enron that emerges from these documents is something like that between a population of farmers and a neighboring group of nomadic raiders. Occasionally, in lean times, the raiders can be helpful by selling to the farmers what they have stolen elsewhere. Far more often, the raiders are a nuisance, raising anxieties and siphoning off limited resources. And every once in a while, they are outright dangerous.

Most of the time, however, the nomads live within the letter (if not the spirit) of the law. The release of these exchanges between Enron and its lawyers led to an immediate outcry on the part of California legislators—in Sacramento and in Washington—that California had been gouged by Enron and that there were now clearly identified "guilty" parties. Senator Boxer, for example, declared that the documents "confirm what I've been saying for months, that Enron manipulated the California energy market and needs to be held accountable. It is high time we see some indictments handed down in this case."[12]

In fact, there was almost no chance that the top Enron brass would wind up in shackles because of these offensive memoranda. The correspondence may have been a "smoking gun," but firing that particular gun was not a capital offense. Indeed, the penalties specified in the Cal-ISO tariff for the kinds of mischief and misdeeds that Enron engaged in are fines and suspensions.

I raise this point because it illustrates a pattern that investors need to understand. Every time so-called damning evidence about Enron is revealed, what is *also* revealed is the vast gulf between what the public views as reprehensible and what the business world views as "business as usual." The farmers and the nomads, even though they live in close proximity, cannot begin to understand each other because their value systems are so different. The amazing increase in the percentage of the American public that is directly involved in investing has led to a similar cultural clash. We invest in businesses and demand that they make money for us. Then we are *shocked* to discover that the companies in which we are investing are not exactly rushing to seize the moral high ground. For their part, the corporations feel like they are being invaded by an alien life form. They long for Granddad's day—or perhaps Great-Granddad's day—when corporations could do what they wanted, and the public be damned.

Factor 5: Buying Time with Derivatives

As a result of the various causes just outlined, the price of Enron's stock plunged, and this plunge, in turn, triggered a series of events that spelled the company's doom. I mentioned in Chapter 1 that up to a certain point in time, the curve of Enron's stock price and that of the Nasdaq Index were strikingly similar. This means that when Enron's stock started dropping, it was not alone in that plight—in fact, far from it. All across the high-tech landscape, companies were sagging. But the sags were particularly scary for Enron when these victims included companies in which Enron had invested heavily.

For example, Enron had put large sums into Avici, a networking company that was a competitor of Cisco Systems. In October 2000, Enron spun off its so-called New Power Company. Both companies turned out to be an investor's nightmare, with the New Power Company's stock price dropping catastrophically shortly after its initial public offering (IPO). By the second quarter of 2001, Avici was managing to lose $11.5 million on gross revenues of $21.4 million, with its stock price sagging appropriately.

I mentioned also that Enron's stock price held up about 6 months longer than did those of most firms listed on the Nasdaq. In other words, there was a brief window of time within which Enron's stock price was still rising while most other technology stocks had already initiated their descent. This would have been a good thing, in most circumstances. But cash-strapped Enron soon found itself tempted to regard its own stock as an asset to which it had easy and reliable access.

A firm is forbidden to capitalize on its own stock—period. This was a prohibition that Sherron Watkins, Enron's whistleblower, would remind legislators of pointedly and repeatedly throughout the Senate hearings. "Under generally accepted accounting principles," the Powers Report agreed, "a company is generally precluded from recognizing an increase in value of its own stock (including forward contracts) as income. Enron sought to use what it viewed as this 'trapped' or 'embedded' value."[13]

However, there is a back-door tactic. Instruments known as *derivatives* provide a way to evade such prohibitions as long as some distance is maintained between the derivative and its underlying product. Treating Enron's stock as the *underlying* product rather than the product itself allowed the company to take advantage of the fact that its stock was still rising in a nose-diving market.

Once again, Enron was not the only company playing this game. When Bernard Ebbers resigned as WorldCom's president and CEO, Andy Kessler of the *Wall Street Journal* wrote Ebbers' corporate obituary. "Mr. Ebbers," Kessler wrote pithily, "went on a buying binge using his inflated stock as currency."[14] However, the investor's peril is clear in both cases (and all the others that have come to light): When a company begins depending on its own derivatives, *watch out!*

Factor 6: Hooked on a Bull Market

Of course, Enron's managers knew that the scheme underlying the company's partnerships, the "special-purpose entities," could only work if Enron's stock remained pumped up to artificially high levels. At the same time, they knew they had little choice: They needed to reach a level of capitalization that was much higher than that which they had already achieved, but this would be difficult to pull off without hard assets. (This is the dark side of being asset-light, as discussed in Chapter 1.)

Several researchers reviewed the figures in real time and concluded that Enron was going nowhere. Investment manager Jim Chanos, for one, calculated that Enron's return on capital was 7 percent, whereas its cost of capital was more than 10 percent. Based on numbers such as these, Chanos decided that a contrarian strategy would *have* to succeed sooner or later with Enron. Said Chanos to *Barron's* Jonathan R. Laing, "We could see the partnerships becoming insolvent and this in turn causing a financial death spiral for the parent. We knew we were right when Skilling quit the company in August. In our opinion, he saw that Enron's declining stock price meant the game was over for Enron."[15]

I wish I could report that Enron's managers were alone in betting that the bull market would last forever. They were not. In April 2002, Vivendi Universal—a French media and utility conglomerate—revealed that in 2001 it had sold "put options" on tens of millions of its own shares, with the premiums being used to finance its executive stock option plan. This was not wise. If the stock price falls, the seller of a put option loses the difference between the current price and the so-called strike price (most often the stock price at the time the option is granted).

Something similar happened in the telecommunications industry—this time not for financing stock option plans but for growth by acquisition. France Télécom, Deutsche Telekom, and Telecom Italia used puts on their own stock for that purpose, making acquisitions with a mix of cash and stock. Sellers were given puts as insurance against a possible decline in the price of the stock they were offered as payment. *New York Times* correspondent Suzanne Kapner comments, "While shares were heading higher, the options seemed like a smart move. Now that share prices have sunk to a fraction of their former levels and the telecommunications companies tend to be short on cash, companies face the dismal prospect of having to buy their shares or those of another company—buying out a partner, for instance—often at a premium to the market price. If these options are exercised, and most come due in the next year or two (2003 or 2004), that could add millions in liabilities to companies already struggling under heavy debt. And this could cause their credit ratings to suffer, making borrowings more expensive."[16]

Enron's strategy only worked in a bull market. But guess what else only works in a bull market? The equities component of your 401(k) plan, all executive stock option plans, and all index funds. And in contrast, the technique known as *short selling* (betting against the market) only works when things are headed downhill. The key point: Sooner or later, any strategy that assumes that prices only move in one direction will fail.

LESSON FOR INVESTORS

To the extent possible, learn about the culture of the company in which you propose to invest. If you would like to see evidence of a moral compass, can you find it? How much do you like the CEO's sense of humor?

Look for the line between entrepreneurship and buccaneering. Is there a sensible plan for growth, or will this group embark on any adventure to help the numbers?

Look at the types and levels of senior-executive compensation. How are the top personnel getting paid, and how much? Do you think it is appropriate?

What kinds of friends does the company have, and how much does the company's success depend on those friendships? It is nice to have friends in high places, of course. But even well-placed friends cannot distort a market indefinitely—nor can they resist a tide of public opinion that is rising against a given corporation or sector.

Beware the market maker who has no frame of reference. When you set out to do it all, the chances of model risk and market abuse go up significantly. Projecting forwards, for example, is fraught with perils and temptations.

Be realistic about business values. At the risk of seeming to contradict myself, doing business is not like going to church. You and I, as investors, place extraordinary demands on companies to perform and produce great numbers. This often leads to behaviors that you and I might consider slippery but which fall well within the letter of the law.

Make friends with a contrarian. There *were* people who figured out that "Bad Enron" could not go on indefinitely. Some of those people head up funds (*contrarian funds*) that do very nicely. Consider including a contrarian in your portfolio.

The escalator goes in both directions. The market goes up, and it goes down. Any strategy that assumes steady up or steady down is bound to lose.

Stock Options: The War Between Management and Shareholders

In 2000, the cost of stock options was nearly 10 percent of profits, demonstrating that such expenses can be substantial. For 2001, the value will be even higher. If stock option expenses are ignored, profits may be misrepresented. Moreover, stock options can directly affect shareholders, because when options are exercised, new shares are issued and shareholders' existing holdings are diluted.

—STANDARD & POOR'S, May 14, 2002

In the aftermath of the Enron debacle, many companies have found that stock options—who gets them and how they are accounted for—have emerged as a main bone of contention between shareholders and management. Briefly stated, stock options were invented as a way to align the interests of professional managers with those of their stockholders. Senior executives are given the option to buy stock at a given price. If the price of that stock goes up over time—the theory goes—the option holder gets an additional form of compensation, which is (theoretically) tied to his or her good stewardship of the company's fortunes.

Stock options are defined in the following terms in Statement 123 of the Financial Accounting Standards Board (FASB): "Stock-based employee compensation plans. Those plans include all arrangements by which employees receive shares of stock or other equity instruments of the employer or the employer incurs liabilities to employees in amounts based on the price of the employer's stock. Examples are stock purchase plans, stock options, restricted stock, and stock appreciation rights."[1]

Stock options allow firms to avoid treating as compensation a large amount of remuneration being paid to corporate officers that would otherwise be expensed from reported earnings. (See the section on earnings below.) They also allow the company to take what can amount to substantial tax deductions.

I recently came across an excellent summary of the evolution of the stock option by the *Washington Post*'s Steven Pearlstein. Here is part of what Pearlstein wrote:

> Ten years ago, Harvard University professor Michael Jensen co-authored an influential study that concluded that the pay of top executives was unrelated to the performance of their companies' stock. Jensen studied the period 1974 through 1988, during much of which stock prices, adjusted for inflation, stagnated. He concluded that as long as corporations continued to pay their leaders as if they were bureaucrats, the self-interest of those executives would remain fundamentally different from that of their shareholders. By then, Wall Street had already come to a similar conclusion. . . .A new era of shareholder-focused capitalism was born, and with it, a new favored instrument for getting executives to behave more like owners than bureaucrats—the stock option.[2]

The climate that Pearlstein describes led to a shift away from salaries and bonuses in executive compensation, with the purpose of better aligning executive pay with the financial and stock performance of the company.

There are two problems with this, however. First, executives may be tempted to manipulate the price of the stock upward to realize gains on their options. (Less stewardship, more shenanigans.) And second, as Standard & Poor's has observed, stock options cost real money, which has not always shown up in the corporate accounts. Read the next annual report of the companies in which you hold stock. If they announce proudly that they have been "expensing stock options" for years, good for them—and good for you. The inflated representation of earnings that characterized the 1990s is due in part to companies ignoring the fact that stock options are a mode of compensation that taps their earnings.

How, exactly, do options work? Traditionally, a company's earnings have been distributed as dividends to shareholders and as compensation to entrepreneurs. Stock options blur the distinction between the entrepreneur (the sharecropper in a share system) and the investor or capitalist (the shareholder in a share system). They introduce a type of compensation that, because it reflects capital gains, remunerates entrepreneurs in a way that mimics the share allocation that is due to investors. Through stock options, corporate officers are compensated as if they were investors in the company. This, of course, is in addition to the salaries (rent on time passed working) they earn as employees of the company and the bonuses (share in capital growth) they earn in their capacity of entrepreneurs.

To cast this arrangement in its worst light, it is as if the arrangement allocated two parts out of three for the investor in the form of dividends and one part out of three for the entrepreneur in the form of a bonus and then again one part out of three for the entrepreneur in the form of stock options. This wording highlights the source of the trouble: We have now allocated four parts out of three. How can this be? Well, mainly through smoke and mirrors. One favorite smoke-and-mirrors approach is to make the investor's two parts out of three *appear* to be two parts out of three but actually be less than this. This particular approach has been called out and faulted by Federal Reserve Chairman Alan Greenspan, among many others.

The Low-Down on Earnings

Earnings are a corporation's revenues minus the costs of running the firm. This sounds straightforward, but of course, it is never quite that easy. Earnings can be considered either after or before some specific accounting items have been taken into account. The word *earnings* used without any qualification refers to "as-reported earnings" or "reported net income"—that is, after taxes and interest income have been accounted for. *Pretax earnings* are "earnings before interest and taxes," shortened as EBIT.

Earnings of various kinds are calculated through the following steps:

Operating revenues
– cost of goods sold
– selling, general, and administrative expenses
– depreciation expense
_____

Total: **Earnings before interest and taxes (EBIT)**
+ interest income (expense)
– amortization expense
+ dividend income
+ royalty income
+ pension gains (costs)
_____

Total: **Income before taxes**
– taxes
_____

Total: **Reported net income (as-reported earnings)**
+ discontinued operations
+ cumulative effect of accounting changes
+ extraordinary items
_____

Total: **Net income**

We will return to these calculations when we discuss Standard & Poor's new definition of *core earnings* in Chapter 10 on what I call—politely—*aggressive accounting.*

Alternative Uses for Earnings

There are a number of ways a company's earnings can be allocated. Earnings can be distributed as dividends to shareholders, used to retire debt, reinvested as capital to the company, invested in acquisitions, used to buy back outstanding shares of stock, or used as extra compensation for executives.

The last option—increased executive compensation—is rarely discussed, although in the aftermath of the Enron debacle the spotlight fell on a number of companies (Tyco International, WorldCom, Adelphia, and others) where a nonnegligible portion of earnings ended up, in one form or other, as extra compensation for executives.

Chapter 4—on the subject of sharing capital growth—introduced the notion that distributing earnings as dividends is one common way of assigning earnings within a share system, the other method being compensating the entrepreneurs who are the active agents of capital appreciation. All other uses depart from the essence of the share system and therefore require justification.

There are at least three justifiable alternative uses for earnings, apart from distributing them as dividends and entrepreneur compensation. These are reinvestment in the company, acquisitions, and the retirement of corporate debt. Let's look at each of these alternative uses and then at a few uses that are harder to justify.

Reinvestment versus Acquisition

Growth by acquisition is commonly regarded as a legitimate and laudable use of corporate earnings. However, it is not as straightforward as it may sound. Michael Perry, the chief executive officer (CEO) of IndyMac Bank in Pasadena, California (a company the author has been associated with), considers growth by acquisition a fashionable but problematic strategy. In his view, breakeven on return on investment (ROI) when earnings are reinjected into the company is achieved at the 15 percent level. With an acquisition, however, breakeven level needs to exceed 25 percent ROI.

Perry deplores the fact that reinvestment within the company itself is penalized compared with investment through acquisition. Specifically, well-intentioned but failed internal innovations do not get the benefit of the generous write-offs that are allowed in the context of mergers and acquisitions. Perry gives the example of a strategy that would call for his bank opening 100 new branches in underprivileged neighborhoods. An alternative strategy would be to acquire 100 new branches through an acquisition. Both strategies entail risk and could fail. However, the financial consequences of the "internal" failure (opening 100 new branches) would be far greater than the financial consequences of a failed acquisition.

In Chapter 2 I cautioned investors to keep an eye out for circumstances in which well-intended regulations lead to economic distortions, which lead, in turn, to shenanigans. This is another of those situations.

Retirement of Debt

In the traditional perspective, the retirement of debt is not controversial because it restores the autonomy of the entrepreneur by diminishing his or her dependence on creditors. And from the shareholder's perspective, retirement of debt is an absolute priority because the entrepreneur pays rent on debt—is being burdened with cash flows of a fixed amount—whether capital appreciates or not. Debt, therefore, is a threat to the shareholder's interest. In cases of insolvency, creditors' claims on corporate assets take precedence over shareholders' claims.

Because the American tax system treats interest cash flows as tax-deductible, corporations are tacitly encouraged to get into debt. In some sectors, such as the banking industry, firms have their debt levels strictly limited by the industry's overseers. In these sectors, therefore, retirement of debt is a less legitimate use for earnings.

While the tax system encourages debt, rating agencies pull in the other direction, applying pressure to rein in debt. Rating agencies discourage excessive debt by making credit increasingly costly for companies when their debt rises compared with their total capital. Why? Because when a company's debt-to-total-capital ratio rises too high, it may pose an excessive risk to its counterparties. (I will explore the rating agencies in greater depth in Chapter 13.) The downgrading of the company's credit rating makes any additional debt more costly. Effectively, a corporation's drop in rating advises prospective counterparties that the interest rate they charge for new credit should include a premium reflecting the increased credit risk (risk of default).

Which is better, reinvestment, or retirement of debt? Of course, there is no single right answer. But neither of these two uses of earnings *hurts* shareholders, and in the right circumstances, each can benefit shareholders, sometimes in a significant way.

Share Buyback and Executive Compensation

Two other possible uses for earnings are buying back shares and distributing earnings among corporate officers as compensation. There was a turning point in the late 1990s when, for the first time, companies began devoting a larger part of their earnings to repurchasing their own shares than to granting dividends to shareholders.[3] What happened to lead to this result, and how should we investors respond to it?

The capitalist system allocates entrepreneurs their share in the company's capital growth by distributing a portion of earnings as compensation of corporate officers. Traditionally, investors receive their part of the deal as dividends. What share buybacks achieve is a channeling of earnings in such way that investors will be remunerated in capital gains rather than in dividends. Share buybacks substitute capital gains for dividends as the investors' share.

Share buyback plans and executive compensation are linked through the company's executive stock option plan. They are interconnected and to some degree mutually offsetting: Stock option plans cause dilution in earnings per share; share buyback plans increase earnings per share.

Agency costs is the phrase used commonly when referring to corporate governance processes where the interests of management and shareholders diverge. As Jeremy Siegel notes:

> One might question why management would not employ assets in a way to maximize shareholder value. The reason is that there exists a conflict between the goal of the shareholders, which is to increase the price of the shares, and the goals of management, which are prestige, control of markets, and other objectives. Economists recognize the conflict between the goals of managers and shareholders as *agency costs*, and these costs are inherent in every corporate structure where ownership is separated from management.[4]

This assumes, of course, that the main goal of shareholders is to see the price of shares rise. As noted in previous chapters, this runs counter to the view expressed by Robert Shiller that the "reliable return attributable to dividends, not the less predictable portion arising from capital gains, is the main reason why stocks have on average been such good investments historically."[5]

In a March 2002 talk, Federal Reserve Chairman Alan Greenspan made reference to the diminishing role of shareholders in the definition of corporate goals. "By law," Greenspan said, "shareholders own our corporations and, ideally, corporate managers should be working on behalf of shareholders to allocate business resources to their optimum use. But as our economy has grown, and our business units have become ever larger, de facto shareholder control has diminished: Ownership has become more dispersed and few shareholders have sufficient stakes to individually influence the choice of boards of directors or chief executive officers. The vast majority of corporate share ownership is for investment, not to achieve operating control of a company."[6]

Greenspan argues that the power balance between entrepreneurs and investors has shifted in recent years away from the investor and toward the entrepreneur. The fact that the role of "investor" has become more widespread in recent years—with one American household out of two now being an investor in public companies—is a contributor to that shift in the power balance. With a much broader base of "owners" to deal with, it is far easier for management to divide and conquer.

There is an obvious exception—the institutional investor. Institutional investors hold large blocs of shares and therefore wield more power than individual investors—and they are in a better position to act on their unhappiness. In the aftermath of the Enron debacle, institutional investors have become increasingly vocal, and they have found an articulate and outspoken representative in Sarah Teslik, executive director of the Council of Institutional Investors. Asked whether she favored jail time as well as fines for any Enron executive or board member found to have broken the law, Teslik expressed the council's strong opinion: "It is probably the single easiest, cheapest reform that could occur to make corporate boards do their job."

In more measured terms, Bill Gross, manager of the world's largest bond fund, PIMCO, wrote as follows in an open letter to corporate executives about General Electric's short-term debt instruments policy (*commercial paper*): "I want management to focus not on their options, but on mine and that of other investors. We have the option to buy or not to buy your securities. And that option should be based not just on the increasingly revealing financial statistics that have had to be dragged kicking and screaming out of the bowels of corporate back offices, but on the investor-friendly/investor-honest/investor-first attitudes of management."[7]

The impact of agency costs is most often downplayed. In Chapter 4 I noted that a larger share of capital growth for the entrepreneur means a smaller one for the investor, and vice versa. Both parties, entrepreneurs and shareholders, want to see the pie get bigger. And when it comes to divvying up the pie, each wants the biggest possible piece.

Stock Options as Compensation

So far I haven't talked much about the third party that's more or less present when the pie is divvied up—the wage-earners. Corporations compensate investors for their contributions in capital through the securities they own: shares and corporate bonds. Wage earners are paid rent on the work time they contribute to the company. Their payment is prorated on the time spent working, not on the profit the company makes because of that work. *Bonuses*, by contrast, constitute compensation that respects the principles of a share system. Bonuses are prorated on the company's capital growth, to which the employee has contributed personally. The same applies to traditional piece-work compensation. Some argue—and I tend to agree—that bonuses constitute the "normal" way for entrepreneurs to get their share of capital growth.

A company's officers are paid a wage in their capacity as a corporate employee. In addition, they are being paid bonuses—often quite handsome bonuses—as a reward for entrepreneurship. Stock options are above and beyond wages and bonuses. At some point we investors have to ask, *How much is enough? How much is too much?*

Figures compiled by Massachusetts-based Clark/Bardes Consulting indicate that in 1995, 41 percent of a chief executive officer's (CEO's) total pay was wages, 17 percent was bonuses, and 42 percent was long-term incentives, primarily stock options. By 2001, wages had dropped to 18 percent of the total; bonuses still represented 17 percent, and long-term incentives had surged to 65 percent! Meanwhile, the comprehensive figure for the CEO's compensation had nearly tripled: The median CEO pay package was slightly over $1 million in 1995 and had grown to $2.85 million by 2001. Stock option compensation on its own had grown by more than 425 percent.[8]

According to a Federal Reserve Board publication, in 1998, among the 144 largest corporations in the Standard & Poor's (S&P) 500, shares resulting from the company's stock options plan represented 6.2 percent of the outstanding stock. This figure was up from 4.47 percent in 1994—nearly a 50 percent increase.[9]

In the 1990s, stock options were the main reason for two notable trends: (1) the dramatic increase in corporate officers' income and (2) the widening gap in compensation between rank-and-file employees and top management. For "star" executives, companies introduced so-called megagrants (or jumbo grants) of stock options representing more than eight times the executive's salary and bonus. In a survey of corporations released in March 2002, pay consultant William M. Mercer, Inc., found that 28 percent allocated megagrants of options.[10]

Repricing of Stock Options

In the backlash that took place at the beginning of the new millennium, and with the sickening drop in the major stock indices, executives saw the incentive of stock options vanish. The companies' response? In many cases, it has been shameful. Many have simply repriced the options at a lower strike price, short-circuiting the single principle that supports stock options—that they constitute an incentive for employees to beat a specific target. The reset at a lower level amounts to starting all over from downgraded expectations.

Think about this. Isn't this sufficient proof, in and of itself, to refute the notion that the interests of stock-option holders can be truly aligned with those of shareholders? Shareholders *lose* when the stock price dips below what they paid for the stock. (In fact, shareholders lose whenever the stock price fails to exceed what they have paid for the stock and the brokers' fees.) Thus the alleged "alignment" between the interests of stock-option beneficiaries and shareholders exists *only when the stock price goes up.*

To revert to the terms of Chapter 4, with stock price variation, the shareholder participates in a chance of gain and in a risk of loss, whereas the holder of a stock option participates only in the chance of gain. If recipients of stock options exercise them and then keep the stock, of course, they become ordinary shareholders. In other words, they have traded a certain gain for a combination of chance of gain and a risk of loss. In the unreasonable world of stock options, this seems like a (relatively) reasonable approach.

However, if the firm has a policy of repricing stock options, stock-option beneficiaries gain when the stock price goes up and *again when it comes down.* This is very different and a much better deal than what the ordinary shareholder is ever offered.

The previously quoted Michael Perry, CEO of IndyMac Bank, admits that repricing is a mistake (at best): "In retrospect, the one major error I've made was in repricing options in 1998 after the company suffered a major setback. This should never happen!"

Several commentators have observed, acidly, that given the far-ranging decision-making power that CEOs possess within the current corporate context, these senior officers are in a position to push levers that effectively enable them to determine their own compensation. Yes, there may be some uncomfortable conversations with the corporation's compensation committee, but these most likely will happen after the fact.

"CEOs have taken to using profits to buy back shares of the company stock rather than pay dividends," remarks Andrew Tobias in his witty *The Only Investment Guide You'll Ever Need*. "What they won't tell you is that the bulk of their own compensation comes from stock options—so they have little interest in paying out cash that could be used to boost the stock price."[11]

Burton G. Malkiel, in *A Random Walk Down Wall Street,* observes that "larger appreciation benefits the managers by enhancing the value of their stock options, whereas larger dividends go into the pockets of current shareholders. From the 1940s until the 1970s, earnings and dividends grew at about the same rate. During the last decades of the twentieth century, however, earnings have been growing much faster than dividends."[12]

William Miller, a mutual fund manager whose $11 billion Legg Mason Value Trust has beaten the S&P 500 Stock Index for 11 years in a row, stresses that stock option plans can be manipulated by corporate officers to the detriment of shareholders. In particular, it is in the interest of CEOs to drive a stock price lower over short periods if those coincide with the time when new stock options are being granted. CEOs are similarly in a position to start boosting the stock price just ahead of the time when they plan to sell shares.[13]

Here is an example of what Miller has in mind, in this case at Computer Associates:

> Federal authorities are trying to determine whether Computer Associates International, Inc., wrongly booked over $500 million in revenue in its 1998 and 1999 fiscal years as part of a scheme to enrich the company's senior managers. . . . Rising revenue was an important part of the logic that propelled Computer Associates shares on an upward arc in the 1990s, as the company appeared to be growing faster than rivals in selling software to big corporate customers. In May 1998, because the shares had reached a trigger price of $55.13 and stayed there for a sustained period of time, the company's three top managers . . . received a special incentive stock award then valued at $1 billion. Today, the stock trades at about $18. Now, investigators want to know why the company overstated its revenue for the period immediately preceding and following the stock grants.[14]

Digging Deeper: The Value of a Stock Option

Most stock options have a maximum term of 10 years. As a rule, the stock option is issued *at the money,* meaning that the strike price that needs to be exceeded for there to be a profit is the most recent price of the stock. Statement 123 stipulates, "Most fixed stock option plans—the most common type of stock compensation plan—have no intrinsic value at grant date." The *intrinsic value* of a *call* option is the difference between current price and strike price. Thus, if a stock option is assigned today, its *strike* or *exercise price* typically will be that of yesterday's market close, and its intrinsic value is whatever movement has taken place on the stock price today since the market opened.

With the passage of time, a stock option either gets "in the money" as a result of a rise in the stock price—in which case there is a profit to be made by exercising the option—or it gets "out of the money" with the stock price dropping below the strike level, in which case the option is worthless. As is the case with all types of options, there is no risk associated with a stock option for its beneficiary: There is a chance of gain but no risk of loss because chance of gain and risk of loss have been split, and the owner of the option has paid its *writer* (or seller) a premium compensating the latter for taking the full risk of loss.

When the *call* option is "in the money," the net gain for the holder is the difference between the current price of the stock and the strike price (the intrinsic value of the option) minus the premium initially paid for the *call* to its writer minus the interest that would have accrued on the premium over the time period between the purchase of the call and its exercise—had it been invested at a risk-free rate. In the case of a stock option, the premium and the accrued interest can be ignored: The stock option was granted by the company, and no premium therefore was disbursed by its beneficiary, and because there was no premium paid, there was automatically no loss of a potential interest cash flow.

The bottom line: Because the company granted the stock option to its employee, it is the company that pays a premium and incurs a loss on a potential interest cash flow.

Losing Money with Stock Options

When I say that there is no risk of loss for the beneficiary of stock options, I mean that because this is a call option, the grantee will not lose any money if the stock price drops below the exercise price and the option is not exercised. Obvious, right? If you have an option to sell your house next week at a loss and you are under no particular pressure to sell, you don't sell. You don't "exercise your option."

It is possible to lose money with stock options, but you have to work at it. If you hold onto the stock after you exercise your option, for example, and then the stock price falls below the exercise price, you lose. These losses also can be leveraged—multiplied—by borrowing the cash needed to exercise the options. It is also possible to pay tax on realized gains and then lose the money when the stock price falls.

The press has reported disaster stories of these types,[15] especially in the case of WorldCom stock. In a number of instances, stock-option beneficiaries exercised their options, kept the stock, and paid for the exercise of the option and the tax owed from a margin account with the broker. A *margin account,* like those held by traders on financial markets, is (for all practical purposes) a loan guaranteed by the stock being used as collateral for the loan. There will be *margin calls* if the stock price drops and the stock ceases to be of sufficient value to guarantee the loan.

The bone of contention in this issue is whether it was the brokerage house—WorldCom's advisor for its stock-option plan, Salomon Smith Barney—that concocted this particular recipe for disaster or it was a response by the brokerage to the employees' expression of greed. Of course, each party blames the other, and the truth probably lies somewhere in between.

A likely scenario for what happened would be something like this: Employees who left WorldCom were given up to 1 year after their departure to exercise their stock options. Joe Doe (for example) left WorldCom nearly 1 year ago and decides that it is time to exercise his options. World-Com's stock price is still rising, though, and Joe feels that holding onto the stock might be a good idea. Therefore, instead of selling the stock and pocketing the capital gains, Joe looks into ways to both exercise his options *and* keep the stock.

Joe has not got the cash he would need to simply buy the stock outright, but a helpful Salomon Smith Barney's broker suggests that he create a margin account (a loan) using the stock as collateral. By keeping the stock for 1 year, Joe will benefit from the more favorable tax treatment afforded to long-term capital gains. In addition, the margin calls (money due) on the loan are interest-rate cash flows and therefore are tax-deductible.

Now WorldCom's stock price starts to fall. Joe starts to get worried. He has borrowed money to buy an asset that is declining in value. He needs to keep coming up with real money to service his margin account. He has to hope that the once-mighty WorldCom stock will come bouncing back. But it doesn't. In fact, it keeps sinking. Each news story about WorldCom is worse than the last.

In the press treatment of stories such as this, the consistent theme is that this is all Joe's fault—a combination of his greed and his poor judgment.

When you think about it, however, Joe's behavior at the outset of this scenario is perfectly reasonable. After all, who wants to sell a stock that is riding the up escalator?

The Tax Treatment of Stock Options

An additional worry that arises—or *should* arise—when one is both exercising a stock option and holding onto the stock arises from the tax treatment of these maneuvers. At the time most stock options are granted, the benefits that may result from them are uncertain (at best). In these circumstances, where all gains are still hypothetical, the Internal Revenue Service (IRS) says that there is no immediate need for taxation. (As a general principle, the IRS refrains from raising money in the form of taxes that it is just going to have to give back someday.) Of course, the element of uncertainty would be removed if stock options were issued "in the money"—that is, if they had an *intrinsic* value at the time of issue. For example, if today I am offered a stock option at the $25 level and yesterday's *close* price was $27, there exists from inception a gain: the $2 I would make by exercising the option right away. Guess what? Such a gain is taxable.

The intrinsic value of the option at the time it is exercised is considered by the IRS as income for *alternative minimum tax* (AMT) purposes. The reason is obvious: The intrinsic value is a realized gain. The price at which the stock-option beneficiary ultimately sells the stock is of no concern to the IRS.

Then there's the company perspective on the tax issue. The difference between the stock price when the option gets exercised and the option's strike price (the option's *intrinsic* value) is tax-deductible for the company granting stock options. One of the two main reasons why Enron only paid corporate tax once over the 1996–2000 period was because of this particular tax deduction. [The other grew out of matching employees' contributions with company stock in 401(k) plans, as explained in Chapter 14.]

As Tracy Byrnes noted in the *Wall Street Journal Online*, "Now let's think about this. Companies are not required to report an expense for these things, yet they get a huge tax deduction for them. So the larger the spread between the exercise price and the market price, the fatter the company's tax deduction."[16]

In a later column she added, "If the exercise price was 15 cents and the employee exercised at $5 . . . the company gets its $4.85 tax deduction. If the stock subsequently falls to $1, the company does not have to adjust a thing."[17]

"It's no wonder," Byrnes wrote in her first column, "that Cisco and Microsoft rarely pay corporate taxes. In 2000, Lucent had a $1 billion 'tax benefit from employee stock options.' You have to wonder, without this gratis tax benefit, would stock options have taken off at all?"

The answer to this last question is "yes." In addition to the tax incentive, stock options allow firms to avoid recording large compensation expenditures *under that label*, which would otherwise have to be deducted from reported earnings. Stock options thus have a double positive effect for a corporation. The paradox is that the tax deduction is justified by the fact that the profit through exercising stock options is regarded as compensation paid by the company. At the same time, it is not expensed as compensation that would materialize as a reduction of pretax earnings. In other words, the tax deduction is very difficult to justify.

A bill introduced in the Senate by Michigan Democrat Carl Levin and Arizona Republican John McCain in February 2002 would require corporations to deduct compensation through stock options from their pretax earnings. This would not affect the tax deduction that stock options currently allow; instead, it would merely stipulate that in order for the tax deduction to apply, the stock option would have to be expensed. As another sponsor of the bill, Republican Senator Peter Fitzgerald (of Illinois), declared: "The bill does not reduce earnings. It reduces what companies are reporting as earnings."

Share Buybacks: An Antidote

When corporate officers exercise their stock options, they cause a dilution of earnings per share. A share buyback strategy counters that dilution. Let me explain how.

Stock options are not allocated on shares of stock available on the open market prior to their exercise. As a rule, grantees of stock options exercise their options when the stock price is substantially higher than the strike price they were offered. Let's say stock options were granted with a strike (or exercise) price $16 and the current stock price is $25. The grantee exercises to realize the $9 trapped profit, meaning that he or she purchases the stock from the company for the $16 strike price.

The company *does not* acquire shares on the open market to meet this demand; instead, it uses its standing authority to issue new stock (assuming that shareholders have previously granted this authority). Thus the option is exercised on *new* shares specially issued for the occasion. Does this matter to the average investor? Absolutely. This creation of shares for the sole purpose of meeting the requirements of stock options dilutes earnings per share (EPS) because it adds shares to the existing equity pool. (The same pie henceforth will be divided into more pieces; therefore, your existing piece is necessarily worth less.) Recent studies suggest that dilution due to outstanding stock options may lower the value of a stock by between 2 and 4 percent.

How does reducing EPS hurt the average investor? Not necessarily in the way you might think—that is, by reducing the dividend stream. As we have already seen, there is almost no dividend stream to be reduced in the case of many contemporary corporations. No, the real impact is indirect. A majority of investors make their decision to buy on the basis of the EPS ratio. A lower ratio is likely to mean a reduced pool of potential buyers and an enlarged pool of potential sellers. This shifts the power balance between buyers and sellers in favor of sellers, which results in lower prices and therefore diminishes the likelihood of capital gains. The same device that is supposed to lead to capital gains therefore can serve as a drag on those gains.

When the stock price rises, a stock-option plan tends to create a rising number of outstanding shares. (People cash in.) One way to counter this negative effect is by retiring an equal quantity of outstanding stock through other means. One such method is through channeling earnings to stock repurchase, either from the open market or through alternative methods such as a Dutch auction or fixed-price tender offers (although these have become less popular in recent years). Stock buybacks, in other words, can be used in conjunction with an executive stock option plan as a way for compensating for dilution as it occurs. Microsoft and Dell are among the firms that have a systematic policy of doing so.

Share buybacks also can be used as a stand-alone method for raising earnings per share, benefiting shareholders who are counting on capital gains. Of course, this particular use for earnings needs to be assessed compared with alternative uses. In their challenging *Expectations Investing: Reading Stock Prices for Better Returns*, Alfred Rappaport and Michael

Mauboussin emphasize that stock repurchase does not automatically raise earnings per share. It all depends on the current price of the stock: For a share buyback plan to be effective, the stock needs to be undervalued within the corporation's global financial context. As an illustration, Rappaport and Mauboussin show that in each particular configuration of a company's circumstances, there is a stock price beyond which share buyback actually *lowers* the EPS ratio.[18]

The same authors stress that in the case of an undervalued share price, stock buyback is an effective method for passing earnings back to shareholders—and more specifically, for transmitting value from sellers of the stock to its current owners: "One of the surest ways for a company's managers to create value for its continuing shareholders is to repurchase stock from shareholders who do not accept management's more optimistic view. . . . Then wealth transfers from exiting shareholders to continuing shareholders."[19]

Another benefit of share buyback lies in the tax perspective: "[A] tax advantage to buybacks is deferral. Shareholders can choose to retain rather than tender their stock and defer tax payments until they sell. Thus buybacks are more advantageous than dividends not only because of the lower tax *rate*, but also because of the discretionary *timing* for incurring the tax liability."[20]

Michael Perry, IndyMac Bank's CEO, considers that, contrary to habit, share buyback should not be driven by stock price but should instead reflect a company's current economic circumstances. If a corporation's activity sector is cyclic—as is the mortgage industry—share repurchase should be used to expand or contract global equity, reflecting what part of the cycle the company is currently in.

In March 2002, Allan Greenspan commented on share repurchase plans:

> Prior to the past several decades, earnings forecasts were not nearly so important a factor in assessing the value of corporations. In fact, I do not recall price-to-earnings ratios as a prominent statistic in the 1950s. Instead, investors tended to value stocks on the basis of their dividend yields. Since the early 1980s, however, corporations increasingly have been paying out cash to shareholders in the form of share repurchases rather than dividends. The marginal individual tax rate on dividends, with rare exceptions, has always been higher than the marginal tax rate on capital gains that repurchases create by raising per share earnings through share reduction. But, until the early 1980s, share repurchases were frowned upon by the Securities and Exchange Commission, and companies that repurchased

shares took the risk of being investigated for price manipulation. In 1982, the SEC gave companies a safe harbor to conduct share repurchases without risk of investigation. This action prompted a marked shift toward repurchases in lieu of dividends to avail shareholders of a lower tax rate on their cash receipts. More recently, a desire to manage shareholder dilution from the rising incidence of employee stock options has also spurred repurchases."[21]

In other words, share repurchase plans are not (usually) blatant attempts at stock price manipulation. Instead, they are merely another reflection of the preferential tax treatment enjoyed by capital gains over dividends.

Stock Options in Financial Statements

Because the employee is not charged for the premium of the stock option, it is reasonable to assume that someone else is. And since it is the company that grants the stock options, it might seem reasonable to assume that it is the company that takes this hit. In this case, wouldn't it be reasonable to require companies to display consolidated figures for stock-options allocation in their financial reports? Sure. Does it happen? Not often enough! And why not? In part because of a 1994 phenomenon known as the "Rally in the Valley."

Here's what happened, according to a recent report of past events by *Wall Street Journal*'s Greg Hitt and Jacob M. Schlesinger:

By the early 1990s, there were sophisticated new methods available for projecting the long-term value of stock-option grants. . . . And so, the FASB voted in April 1993 to require companies to treat options as an expense, based on the estimated future value of those options. The vote produced a political tsunami that started in Silicon Valley. . . . In 1994, thousands of high-tech workers gathered in northern California for a raucous pro-options demonstration called the "Rally in the Valley," sporting T-shirts and placards with such slogans as "Stop FASB!" and "Federal Accounting Stops Business." The new accounting rule would "destroy the high-tech industry," warned the head of the American Electronics Association. The high-tech sector circulated studies predicting that corporate profits would fall by 50 percent and that capital would dry up as a result of the new rule. . . . The Clinton administration weighed in against the FASB. So did institutional-investor groups, who said the rule change would muddy financial statements. A non-binding resolution opposing the FASB rule change passed the Senate by a vote of 88 to 9. . . . By the end of 1994, the FASB withdrew the rule, deciding instead that companies would have to disclose the value of their options only in a footnote in their annual reports."[22]

Once burned, bureaucrats are doubly fearful of fire. As a result, the FASB directions on how to account for stock options in financial reports are notably low key on the issue, "recommending" that the company mentions an aggregated figure for the opportunity cost of giving away the premium on the stock options it grants and requiring nothing more than that the cash is mentioned "pro forma" in the financial report's footnotes.

Tracy Byrnes again has an amusing analogy for the FASB's position: "'Well, we'd like you home at 10:00 P.M., but if you want to stay out until 2:00 A.M., that's fine too, just let us know.' 'Gee, I don't know, Mom.'"[23] As a consequence of this wishy-washy guidance, most companies choose to stay out until 2:00 A.M. In fact, when Enron filed for bankruptcy at the end of 2001, only two firms among the S&P 500—Boeing Co. and Winn-Dixie Stores, Inc.—had chosen to expense stock options in their financial reports. The expense is progressively amortized in equal amounts over the lifetime of the option.

This is exactly what the FASB's Statement 123 says on the subject:

> This Statement defines a *fair value based method* of accounting for an employee stock option or similar equity instrument and encourages all entities to adopt that method of accounting for all of their employee stock compensation plans. However, it also allows an entity to continue to measure compensation cost for those plans using the *intrinsic value based method* of accounting prescribed by APB [Accounting Principles Board] Opinion No. 25, *Accounting for Stock Issued to Employees.* The fair value based method is preferable to the Opinion 25 method.[24]

The *intrinsic-value method* of APB Opinion No. 25 is defined this way: "Under the intrinsic value based method, compensation cost is the excess, if any, of the quoted market price of the stock at grant date or other measurement date over the amount an employee must pay to acquire the stock." The value of the option is here simply the option's "intrinsic value": the difference—if positive—between the current price and "the quoted market price of the stock at grant date." It therefore assumes—contrary to common opinion nowadays—that an option at the money (with current price equal to strike price) is valueless. If this were the case, the grantee of a stock option facing grant date would be indifferent as to whether to keep it or dispose of it. That employees as a rule keep their stock options suggests that they—at least intuitively—disagree with APB Opinion No. 25.

The *fair-value method* is defined this way in Statement 123: "For stock options, fair value is determined using an option-pricing model that takes into account the stock price at the grant date, the exercise price, the expected life of the option, the volatility of the underlying stock and the expected dividends on it, and the risk-free interest rate over the expected life of the option."

The fair value of an option in Statement 123 is therefore the current standard way of option pricing (the Black-Scholes pricing method); it holds in particular that an option at the money still has a value: the price of the premium that would need to be paid to purchase it.

Greenspan: Expense Them!

The most influential proponent of expensing stock options in terms of their actual value is Federal Reserve Board Chairman Alan Greenspan. Over the years, he has repeatedly condemned the widespread corporate practice of not deducting a company's stock-options cost from its reported earnings. Greenspan mentioned his objections back in 1994 at the time of the "Rally in the Valley" and has reiterated them repeatedly in the wake of the Enron debacle. In his February 2002 testimony before the House Financial Services Committee, for example, Greenspan stated that the use of options as compensation was part of an effort by corporations "to try to game the accounting system in a manner to create the perception of short-term earnings growth which would be confused with long-term earnings growth."

Greenspan made additional comments a month later in his talk at New York University's Stern School of Business:

> In principle, stock-option grants, properly constructed, can be highly effective in aligning corporate officers' incentives with those of shareholders. Regrettably, the current accounting for options has created some perverse effects on the quality of corporate disclosures that, arguably, is further complicating the evaluation of earnings and hence diminishing the effectiveness of published income statements in supporting good corporate governance. The failure to include the value of most stock-option grants as employee compensation and, hence, to subtract them from pretax profits,

has increased reported earnings and presumably stock prices. . . . Expensing is only a bookkeeping transaction. Nothing real is changed in the actual operations or cash flow of the corporation. If investors are dissuaded by lower reported earnings as a result of expensing, it means only that they were less informed than they should have been. Capital employed on the basis of misinformation is likely to be capital misused."[25]

Institutional investors have held consistently over the years a pro-stock-option position, fighting to keep them from being expensed in pretax earnings. This position has changed dramatically in the wake of Enron's demise. In March 2002, for example, the Council of Institutional Investors, an influential coalition of pension funds, endowments, and investment houses, "voted overwhelmingly to reverse its mid-1990s position and endorsed the expensing of options. 'We recognize the downside of options more,' said Sarah Teslik, the group's executive director. 'They turn companies into Ponzi schemes,' she added."[26]

Exactly. As explained in Chapter 5, an obsessive focus on earnings rather than on dividends helps turn firms into Ponzi schemes, and this pressure takes many, many forms.

Standard & Poor's Weighs In

As we wrap up this chapter, let's revisit the issue of earnings, introduced earlier. In May 2002, Standard & Poor's released a very interesting report entitled, "Measures of Corporate Earnings." In it, the rating agency offered a new definition for *operating earnings* that it chose to call "core earnings." Standard & Poor's "core earnings" have the following definition:

> Core Earnings focus on a company's ongoing operations. They should include all the revenues and costs associated with those operations and exclude revenues or costs that arise in other parts of the business, such as unrealized gains or losses from hedging activities. Items that reflect ongoing operations include compensation of employees, expenditures for materials and supplies, and depreciation of capital equipment used in production. Items that are not related to operations include litigation settlements, expenses related to mergers or acquisitions, and costs related to financing. These revenues or expenses are important and may be significant, but they are not representative of the company's core operations.[27]

Under this definition, stock options would be expensed automatically. Tellingly, Standard & Poor's did not offer much of an explanation as to *why* this should be the case. No doubt, they took it to be self-evident: "All parts of employee compensation, including stock options, should be included in Core Earnings."

It added: "Standard & Poor's intends to compile and report options-adjusted Core Earnings for its indices and its company coverage universe." Therefore, this looks like the wave of the future, and it is not necessarily a kind wave for many U.S. corporations. General Electric Co., for example—the largest company in the S&P 500—advertised earnings of $1.41 per share in 2001. Under the core earnings calculation, this figure would have been reduced to $1.11. This happens in both the "Old Economy" and the "New Economy." In the fiscal year 2001, Cisco Systems, Inc., reported a loss of 14 cents in earnings per share; under the new standards, the loss would have been 35 cents.

The *Wall Street Journal* was unenthusiastic about the proposed new standard. So too were the spokespersons of the companies who were brave enough to offer comments. No matter, reform was in the air, and the Standard & Poor's standard seemed to be a good one. Pat McConnell, an accounting analyst at Bear Stearns & Co., remarked that in light of the fact that Standard & Poor's itself will use its new standards, "the market will have no choice but to follow them to some extent." And this is exactly what happened; in the following weeks, Coca-Cola, General Electric, and Procter and Gamble announced that they would expense stock options, and in August, the leading financial firms followed suit. Only Intel among the leading blue chips voiced a dissenting viewpoint.

In one fundamental way, then, the matter of expensing or not expensing stock options has been settled. Standard & Poor's has spoken, and I say that it is for the good.

Stock Options at Enron

Let's bring the stock-options story home to roost with our recurrent poster child: Enron. According to Karen Demme, a spokeswoman at Enron, about 60 percent of the company's employees held stock options. This created a somewhat bizarre climate around the halls and offices: "Television sets in the elevators at Enron carried financial news stations that told employees how well the company stock was doing, letting them compute just how wealthy they would be if they could exercise their options before they reached the next floor."[28]

Generous? No. Self-interested. According to Bear Stearns & Co., Enron's operating profit for 2000 would have been 8 percent lower if the company had not granted $155 million worth of stock options. And Enron was not the only company in this circumstance. "Oracle's operating income," reported the *Wall Street Journal*, "was $933 million higher for 2001 than if it had given employees cash instead of options. Not counting options as an expense boosted Citigroup's operating income for the year by $919 million."[29]

In February 2002, Jeffrey Skilling discussed stock options before the Senate Commerce Committee. "There are cases where you can use equity to impact your income statement," he pointed out. "And the most . . . egregious, or the one that's used by every corporation in the world, is executive stock options. And as a matter of fact, I think FASB tried to change that, and you introduced legislation in 1994 to keep that exemption. And essentially what you do is you issue stock options to reduce compensation expense and therefore increase your profitability."

There it was in a nutshell: Reduce compensation *expense*—but not executive compensation, of course!—and increase your profitability. And note Skilling's pointed reference to the 1994 legislation that kept FASB from initiating reforms. *Who was it*, Skilling was asking, *that allowed companies to capitalize on their stock price? Who was it that didn't have the intestinal fortitude to blow the whistle in 1994?* Well, the Congress, of course.

Senator Carl Levin, the Michigan Democrat mentioned earlier, was already arguing strenuously that forcing corporations to expense stock options would be a salutary development. "Stock options," he declared accurately, "were a driving force behind management decisions at Enron that focused on increasing Enron's stock price rather than solid growth of the company."[30] Investors to Congress: *Better late than never.*

Compensation for Services Rendered

Many stocks rise as the larger economy expands. Sometimes this explains away most or all of the stock's appreciation. There is little room left in the equation for brilliant management, which is the rationale for stock options.

Alan Greenspan made the same point at a May 2002 conference at the Federal Reserve Bank of Atlanta:

One problem is that stock options, as currently structured, often provide only a loose link between compensation and successful management. A company's share price, and hence the value of related options, is heavily influenced by economy-wide forces—that is, by changes in interest rates, inflation, and myriad other forces wholly unrelated to the success or failure of a particular corporate strategy. There have been more than a few dismaying examples of CEOs who nearly drove their companies to the wall and presided over a significant fall in the price of the companies' stock *relative* to that of their competitors and the stock market overall. They, nonetheless, reaped large rewards because the strong performance of the stock market as a whole dragged the prices of the forlorn companies' stocks along with it.[31]

This bias could be removed through peer evaluation, that is, comparing a company's stock price with the overall performance of its economic sector.[32] Alfred Rappaport proposes something of the kind:

Look for the first companies that adopt indexed option programs, which link exercise prices to movements in either an industry index or a broader market index like [the] S&P 500. These programs align the interests of managers and shareholders seeking *superior* returns in bull and bear markets alike. Indexed option programs have the support of a growing chorus of institutional investors, but management continues to view them as too risky an incentive.[33]

The goal should be to reward executives for improvements in the company's results that are truly of their making. The global economy is beyond their reach, but so also are changes in the company's financial circumstances that occur before they have had any chance to affect them. Some observers, myself included, think that corporate officers cannot have any real influence on their company's performance in the first 3 to 5 years of their employment. It is like turning an ocean liner: It takes a lot of time and running room.

LESSONS FOR THE INVESTOR

Retirement of debt is a legitimate use for earnings. Debt—which creates costs that live independent of operating results—is a threat to the investor. Remember that creditors hold a rightful priority over shareholders if the corporation becomes insolvent.

The tax system is shareholder-unfriendly. Oh, I know I've said it before, but it's time to say it again. Among many other offenses, it is far too lenient regarding corporate debt.

Stock options are almost always bad for the investor. Through stock options, corporate officers get the benefit of having made advances of capital to the company without actually having contributed any capital. The compensation they are getting in this way is being transferred to them from investors. Stock-option plans involve misappropriation of corporate profit from shareholders, pure and simple.

Think kindly of the company that expenses its stock options. Thanks to public pressure and the new Standard & Poor's definitions, Boeing and Winn-Dixie will no longer be so lonely in expensing their options.

Dump the company that reprices its stock options. Repricing makes a mockery of the principle that stock options constitute a managerial incentive that is aligned with the shareholders' interest. Similarly, watch out for the Microsoft gambit, whereby the corporation simply ignores outstanding grants and replaces them all with new ones with a lower strike price. Good for them; bad for you.

Money can be lost—even large amounts—after stock options are exercised. But do not lose a lot of sleep over this one. Greed is the most common cause. If you exercise stock options, sell the stock to realize the capital gains.

Do not borrow money to buy stock. Remember that the lowest value for a share of stock is *zero*. This is much lower than the loan you are taking.

Understand the tax implications of exercising your stock options. The "alternative minimum tax" applies to the difference between the stock price at the time the stock option is exercised and the initial strike price—*not* to the stock price when the shares are ultimately sold.

Pick your moment. If you believe—for whatever reason—that the price of the stock may still rise, do not exercise your option. Wait. Above all, however, never exercise your option and *then* wait. If you do, you have replaced your certain gain with a chance of gain combined with a risk of loss.

Do not get fooled by bogus share-buyback programs. A share-buyback policy that simply aims at countering dilution of earnings per share is of no benefit to the investor. It simply restores the status quo ante that an executive stock option plan has upset. And by the way, a share-buyback policy is beneficial to the investor if the stock is undervalued. Otherwise, it can even be detrimental to your interest.

Keep an eye out for the first indexed options programs. This is one of Alfred Rappaport's good ideas: Make sure that the stock-option program that your money supports links option exercise prices to broader market indicators—meaning that they have a frame of reference for judging executive performance.

C H A P T E R

Wretched Excess

Where were the directors? I can understand when you've got a company doing extraordinarily well and beating its peers, and you feel some anxiety about retaining top people, but when a company is stumbling terribly, I don't understand cutting deals for people. We're not about class warfare but about everyone having the chance to move up, so this isn't just a business issue, it's also a social issue.

—Roger A. Enrico, CEO of PepsiCo[1]

And how do you feel about that and the employees, one of which wrote me recently—had $330,000 in his 401(k) account, his entire life savings, worked many years for your company, lives in the state of North Dakota. That $330,000 is now worth $1700. You still have most of your $66 million. That family has lost their life savings. How do we reconcile that? How is it that the people at the top got

wealthy and the people at the bottom got broke?
. . . But it occurs to me that, at least from those of
us who view Enron, if one were to make a similar
comparison, in the Titanic, the captain went down
with the ship. And Enron looks to me like the
captain first gave himself and his friends a bonus,
then lowered himself and the top folks down the
lifeboat, and then hollered up and said, "By the
way, everything is going to be just fine."

—SENATOR BYRON DORGAN, Democrat of North Dakota,
questioning Enron's former CEO Jeffrey Skilling[2]

The Enron's debacle triggered intense public indignation about executive compensation. There appeared to be three aspects to that indignation. The first was the sheer size of the dollars involved. The second had to do with how much license top executives had in the exercise of their daily duties to divert large amounts of money—measured in the millions or even tens of millions of dollars at a time—into bonuses or other types of personal financial advantage. The third derived from what Senator Dorgan captured in his *Titanic* analogy: Executives seemed to be emerging unscathed from the consequences of their own bad decisions, whereas employees and shareholders were left to bear the full burden of the company's demise.

Let's look at each of these in turn, with a particular focus on Enron and similar companies, and then look at the broader arena of executive compensation and perks.

Do you know how much *your* portfolio companies' chief executive officers (CEOs) are paid? I suspect that it is a relatively small percentage of individual investors that reads the fine print in financial statements to find out exactly how much top executives are being paid. In a second, much larger group of investors—those who invest through a financial advisor or through mutual or index funds—I suspect that there are very few who search out this fine print. (They do not even *get* the annual reports under normal circumstances.) And finally, there are those investors who are shareholders only in the context of their 401(k)s, most of whom restrict their investment decisions to the allocation and reallocation of funds within their plan.

In other words, although many thousands of people held stock in Enron, most of them were in the second and third categories of investors just defined. For the most part, they had no clear notion before the Enron affair of how much the company's senior executives were being paid. Many first heard about high levels of executive compensation on the same day that they heard about the life-shattering losses suffered by Enron employees with the collapse of their 401(k)s.

The second facet of public indignation, as noted, derives from the public's "discovery" of exactly how much freedom Enron's top executives had to divert huge sums of money in directions that would benefit them personally. Obviously, these huge cash flows could have been used in ways that would have benefited shareholders—retiring company debt, acquiring strong companies, repurchasing company stock, or making judicious reinvestments in the company.

One example of management taking good care of itself was Enron's so-called Performance Unit Plan, a program that gave executives cash bonuses "if Enron's total shareholder return—a combination of dividends and the increase in the stock price—ranked sixth or greater compared with a number of alternative investments." Under the terms of this plan, Enron's top executives received payments amounting to millions of dollars. CEO Kenneth Lay got a cool $10.6 million in 2001 under the terms of this plan.

There were lots of slugs of cash sloshing around on the Enron boat. Among the first big slugs to make the news were the commission fees earned by Chief Financial Officer (CFO) Andrew Fastow and his aides—extra compensation for running those notorious partnerships. Fastow is known to have "earned" a fee of about $23 million on the LJM1 partnership and about $22 million on LJM2. Michael J. Kopper and William D. Dodson together "earned" a fee of something like $10.5 million. When the press started investigating Enron's earlier dealings, it soon became clear that these payments were not anything unusual. One Rebecca Mark was granted a $54 million bonus when the deal was struck on what became the calamitous Dabhol project in India; a certain Joe Sutton made $42 million on the same deal. The justification for those extravagant bonuses on deals that turned out to be giant money losers was that at the time these deals were struck, they were marked to market and therefore would appear in Enron's next financial statement as huge money makers.

A similar case, although far away from Enron, involved Peter A. Boneparth, president of the Jones Apparel Company, a clothing and footwear company in Philadelphia. The story was reported in the *New York*

Times by Gretchen Morgenson. Boneparth's contract stated that if shareholders did not approve a costly stock-option provision (see Chapter 8), he would receive the equivalent of a $1.5 million share grant in cash. Thomas D. Stern, managing director of Chieftain Capital, Jones's largest shareholder, had this to say: "Peter is a capable executive, but he hasn't proven he can create value for the Jones shareholders. To award him $35 million in options and guarantee him $10 million in compensation, after nine months at Jones, is egregious. It appears that this company is continuing to be run more for the management than for the shareholders. This is unacceptable."[3]

Kudos to Mr. Stern for a clear statement of the obvious. Should corporate earnings be diverted from shareholders simply because management can get away with it? Of course not.

A third facet of the public's indignation about executive compensation derives from what Senator Byron Dorgan captured in his *Titanic* analogy. Not only do corporate executives get to poke holes below the waterline— or at least watch what happen as a result of larger economic troubles—they also get the opportunity to loot the ship before it goes down. In the case of Enron, the awarding of retention bonuses was particularly offensive. At a time when the company was publicly claiming that no additional cash could be found to relieve some of the hurt and the misery inflicted on ordinary employees, executives were being courted with wads of cash. "Enron paid a total of $55 million," a *Wall Street Journal* reporter noted, "or an average of $110,000 apiece to about 500 employees at all levels who were considered critical to its survival."[4] This "average" was somewhat misleading, in that a single executive was allocated $5 million of the $55 million just to keep that individual around for *an additional 90 days*.

Sometimes it is worth running these kinds of numbers through the lens of everyday reality. Let's assume that your average elementary school teacher earns $50,000 a year—this is probably on the high end—and works for 40 years (perhaps also optimistic). He or she therefore earns a *total* of $2 million over a working lifetime. Now look again at that $5 million retention bonus—paid to someone *in addition to* all the other sorts of compensation known to corporate America just to keep that critically important executive on the sinking ship's deck for an extra 3 months.

Of course, retention bonuses aren't uncommon when a company files under Chapter 11 of the federal bankruptcy code. They are part of a bigger picture—a way to give the wounded corporation the best possible shot at surviving while it reorganizes. However, the public tended to think along the lines of Salon.com's Jake Tepper, who argued that ". . . [senior management's] performance during Enron's meltdown casts some doubt on some of those executives' managerial worth."[4] When Enron proposed to create a $5 million emergency fund for 4500 laid-off employees, Lowell Peterson—a lawyer representing 20 former employees—noted that the size of this proposed emergency fund matched exactly that notorious $5 million retention bonus.

The sentiment of the public was aptly reflected in whistleblower Sherron Watkins' comments at a House hearing in February 2002: "Some of the amounts I find shocking for 90 days' retention. And I do not believe that it was in the best interests of creditors to—yes, we should retain certain people, but I don't think they needed to be paid three and four times their base salary to stay for 90 days. And I think it is an insult to the 4000 people that were let go with $4000 checks that there are a handful of people—more than a handful—that were paid $600,000, a million five, two million—$450,000—I mean, gargantuan sums of money to agree to stay at Enron for 90 days. I am appalled by that list."

These big sums are unpalatable to the public in good times; they are obnoxious in bad times. It makes it seem that there are lifeboats only for the first-class passengers. "Although American Express Co. last year suffered from a spate of bad news that depressed its financial performance," the *Wall Street Journal* recently reported, "Chief Executive Kenneth Chenault's compensation, excluding option grants, more than doubled to almost $14.5 million. . . . In its filing with the Securities and Exchange Commission, the company's board noted that American Express 'did not meet its long-term financial targets.'"[5]

Recall the comments of PepsiCo's CEO Roger A. Enrico cited at the beginning of this chapter: "When a company is stumbling terribly, I don't understand cutting deals for people."

I will do a little stating of the obvious myself: Excessive compensation of a company's executives is an unwarranted transfer to entrepreneurs of the capital growth that rightfully belongs to shareholders. A study published in August 2002 revealed that the CEOs of the 23 companies then under Securities and Exchange Commission (SEC) investigation were paid 70 percent more than the average CEO of a large U.S. company.[6]

As an investor, you need to *object* to this excessive compensation. (It is *your* money.) Go looking for it in either the corporation's printed or online version of its annual report. Look in the "Footnotes"—almost always a good place to go rummaging—as well as under "Certain Transactions" and "Other Compensation." It has to be there somewhere because companies are *required* to report it.

No Down Escalator?

In earlier chapters I referred to the myth of the stock that can only ride an up escalator. I pointed out that there is *always* a down escalator somewhere out there in the future. Not so with executive compensation, which tends to ride the up escalator pretty consistently.

Throughout the 1990s, salaries for top executives escalated effectively without restraint, in large part through the stock-option component. Competition for skilled executives, particularly in the high-tech sector, was ferocious. Investors were asleep at the switch, happy with their 20 percent returns. In good times, the "winner takes all" mentality is acceptable (or is at least ignored).

Carol Hymowitz, writing in the *Wall Street Journal,* explicitly linked the upward trend in executive compensation in the 1990s to the dot-com craze: "The special-deals mentality in some executive suites marks the culmination of a decade of runaway executive pay. Throughout the 1990s, executive compensation packages soared, and many top executives won guarantees of big rewards whether or not they succeeded. Directors at many companies agreed to the lucrative packages, convinced they were necessary to keep executives from jumping to high-tech start-ups."[7]

However, when the economy went into recession in late 2000, it proved to be very difficult to get those extraordinary compensation levels back down to earth. Hey, we have all been there: Once you attain a certain standard of living, it becomes your birthright—something that should not be withdrawn from you. (This is also tied up, in murky ways, with the notion that wealth is a badge of honor—an award for moral rectitude—and that its loss is a character failure.)

Neal Gabler, the author of *Life the Movie: How Entertainment Conquered Reality*, sees this all as a sign of "celebritization" of wealth: "In a society where celebrity was suddenly considered the most exalted state one could achieve," he writes, "the rich discovered that a large fortune and an extravagant lifestyle would bring media attention. . . . Now that celebrity had become a source of power, previously obscure titans of industry, from Lee Iacocca to Donald Trump, began bidding for stardom, too. In fact, the business world practically demanded it. This chase for recognition was the personal equivalent to botox economics—the idea that a corporate balance sheet must look good rather than actually be good."[8]

For these and other reasons, executive compensation levels seem to possess an in-built braking mechanism. In fact, instead of going down in hard times, they tend to go up. In March 2002, for example, FleetBoston announced a new compensation package for its CEO—a package that was promptly denounced as outrageous in light of the bank's faltering performance. FleetBoston huffed that its CEO's package was simply being aligned with that of the competition and was less than 75 percent of the average for the CEOs of the top 15 U.S. banks.

Such peer comparisons are standard practice, by the way. You can always find somebody up the ladder to point at.

To be fair, figures released in March 2002 seemed to suggest that top-level compensation seemed to be dropping somewhat, with the economy mired in a full-fledged recession. A survey by New York–based compensation consultant William M. Mercer covering 100 major U.S. corporations showed that while corporate profits fell from 2000 to 2001 by a median 13 percent, CEOs' direct compensation fell by a median 10.2 percent, to $2.16 million. This drop in compensation was meaningful, given that it was the first such decline in 12 years. Of course, one could make the case that CEO compensation should have dropped by the same 13 percent that corporation profits did. One could even make the case that they should have dropped by *more*, given that (1) these CEOs start from a very high base indeed, (2) they have been calling the shots, and (3) they have been well rewarded in the fat times. And, as you will see, many are getting paid in lots of other interesting ways.

Even More Compensation

Companies like to take care of their executives while they are active contributors. They also like to take care of them in their retirement—apparently concerned that their retired CEOs and other senior executives might have to lower their standard of living after they have left the company. Many therefore take steps to ensure that their retired top corporate officers are not constrained by the "decency" caps that govern "qualified" retirement plans. They provide them with additional "nonqualified" pensions—in most cases taking advantage of the delayed taxation benefits of *deferred compensation.*

What does this mean? It means that in 2002, you and I could not contribute more than $11,000 to our 401(k) plans, which are considered qualified plans. The purpose of this limit was to ensure that a 401(k) was truly a retirement vehicle rather than a tax-dodging device.

This is not the case with the kinds of nonqualified plans that are offered to top corporate officers and which take a variety of forms. However, one constant is that firms use these plans to minimize the payment of taxes— on both the executive's benefits and on their own contributions. And the *best* formula, from a company's standpoint, is one that allows the company in the end to reclaim the *entirety* of its contributions. Such plans do exist, mainly because there are tax loopholes to be taken advantage of.

On their deferred compensation, Enron executives were guaranteed a minimum annual return of 12 percent at a time when the 10-year Treasury Note yield was fluctuating in the 5 to 6 percent range. Even this extraordinary yield paled in comparison with the income obtained by so-called friends of Enron, mainly Houston-based cronies who routinely enjoyed a 15 percent return on very short-term loans. "Often," as some friends of Enron told David Barboza of the *New York Times,* "the deals were done near the end of financial reporting periods to meet Wall Street's expectations."[9]

Is this outright fraud? No. Is it just another example of entrepreneurial creativity? Well, no, not exactly that either. These stunts lie somewhere in the gray area, shading toward the unethical. They certainly do not pass the sniff test.

What else do the members of America's corporate elite have going for them? One special treat is the split-dollar deferred death-benefits plan, whereby the plain-vanilla life insurance contract is modified and put to very clever use. Here's the formal definition of the plan: "Split-dollar is usually an arrangement between an employer and employee, in which the parties agree to share (or 'split') the obligation to make premium payments on a life insurance policy, and share (or 'split') the rights and benefit under the policy."[10]

Several variations on this theme are in use today. The most common arrangement is the *equity variation,* under the terms of which, on the death of the employee, the company that contributed to the split-dollar plan recovers an amount equal to the premiums paid by it, whereas the employee's beneficiary receives the cash surrender value that is in excess of the premiums paid. Taxwise, the plan is extremely favorable. As a book devoted to deferred compensation structures observes, "If the employee establishes an irrevocable life insurance trust ('ILIT') which acquires the policy on the employee's life, and the trust is properly structured, the death benefit payable under the split-dollar arrangement can escape estate tax on the death of the employee, and then escape estate tax again on the death of the employee's spouse."[11] This is a very nice way to shelter assets and even skip a generation of taxation!

At Enron, Kenneth L. Lay enjoyed his own $12 million split-dollar life insurance policy and also had the benefit of a second policy in a similar amount for his wife and himself. Jeffrey K. Skilling had an $8 million split-dollar life insurance policy. "The assets in those policies are protected from (Enron's) creditors," as the *Wall Street Journal* reported. "The policies aren't assets of Enron, and the policies are secure from creditors who sue the executives personally."[12] Is it possible that this was one of the appeals of these policies in the first place? We investors need to ask these kinds of questions.

The magic of the split-dollar arrangement resides in the splitting of premium payments between employee and employer. Legal, yes, but does it pass the "in the intention of the Congress" standard? Probably not. Advantage is clearly being taken of an unintended consequence of the logic of life insurance.

The same applies to the so-called janitor life insurance (also known as *company-owned life insurance,* or COLI). It had never occurred to lawmakers that anybody but the bereaved would want to benefit from a deceased person's life insurance. Gradually, though, firms realized that life insurance provides a useful corporate tax shelter. In some cases, employees are not even advised by their employer that they have had life insurance policies taken out on them. In such cases, presumably, executive peace of mind is not the main objective.

Eventually, most of the tax loopholes that lie behind these kinds of sweetheart deals get closed. One such loophole was eliminated in the early days of March 2002. It had allowed a company, for tax purposes, to treat the deferred compensation of an executive as a financial hedge to its own business—the business in question being that of paying an executive's deferred compensation.

Confusing? Of course. To understand the scheme, you need to understand the concept of a *hedge.* The purpose of a hedge is to remove some financial risk by neutralizing it with risk of an opposite nature. You take a hedge on a financial product by taking a market position whose price is likely to move in the opposite direction from that of your original product. Products whose prices move in synch are said to be *correlated;* if they move in opposite directions, they are said to be *anticorrelated.* The perfect hedge is obtained using the one product that is perfectly anticorrelated with the risky one. Since no two products are perfectly identical, their price changes are not likely to be identical; therefore, their mutually canceling out can only be realized if their difference in responsiveness is fully taken into consideration.

Let's look at an example of a hedging strategy: sale of an all-electric cars. We can agree that electric cars are increasingly popular when the price of fuel rises. However, what if you are making electric cars, and the price of fuel plummets?

In order to hedge the sale of its electric cars, Acme, Inc., will take a short position on the fuel markets—for instance, by buying a put on oil prices, which means that Acme will make a profit if oil prices drop. This will lessen its possible losses in sales of electric cars if fuel prices drop. Matching the short position in oil in exact proportion to the amount by which sales of electric cars drop will be the perfect hedge. Should the match be perfect, Acme will be able to lock a profit at a particular level. If oil prices drop, Acme loses on the sales of its electric cars, but its put on oil prices gets in the money in the exact same amount. Conversely, if the price of oil rises, the put is out of the money, but the sales of electric cars compensate for unrealized gains on oil price.

The whole notion of hedging an executive's deferred compensation seems ludicrous on the face of it because the burden is (1) self-inflected, (2) tax-advantaged, and (3) not exactly crucial to the running of the business. As it happened, the government was not amused. Assistant Secretary of the Treasury Mark Weinberger, who focuses on tax policy, observed that it was "improper to use the hedge rules to get full tax deferral on deferred executive compensation." He called resorting to the hedge interpretation a "back door to obtain a favorable treatment for deferred compensation that Congress never intended."[13]

Such schemes offering extra compensation for executives create a two-tiered system in which rank-and-file employees take a hit in bad times and executives have relatively little to fear even from the company's demise. This kind of setup has become associated with Enron but appears to be far more widespread than anyone knew.

And for Dessert, Some Perks

Now let's make a quick tour of some additional executive perquisites, more commonly known as *perks,* both at Enron and elsewhere. Perks exist in a variety of guises—the nonqualified executive-only retirement packages outlined earlier, guaranteed returns on investment, loans with below-market interest rates, company-paid taxes, fringe benefits, and so on.

Enron's CEO Kenneth L. Lay got a nice deal. He was given a $7.5 million credit line by the company that could be repaid in company stock (often obtained at discounted price through stock options). Jeffrey K. Skilling, Enron's CEO between Lay's two terms in office, was granted a $2 million loan. Repayments would have been waived if he had stayed with the company until December 31, 2001; he actually resigned on August 14, 2001. But no matter, the *thought* was there.

Everything is relative, of course. The news that emerged from World-Com made Enron seem positively stingy toward its key officers. In March 2002, it was reported that Bernard J. Ebbers, then WorldCom's CEO, had the benefit of a line of credit of *$408.2 million* using his WorldCom stock as collateral. "The company generously agreed to lend Ebbers all the money he needed to cover his debts," reported the *Washington Post*, "and to lend it to him at a bargain rate—about 2.15 percent. That is less than half the prime rate charged by banks, which is [currently] 4.75 percent, and well below what he could borrow the money for from any brokerage house. That's what it costs WorldCom to borrow, company officials say, so it's only fair to charge the chairman the same rate. It's not fair to stockholders, however."[14]

And in the same month it became clear that the Rigas family, which controlled Adelphia Communications, had borrowed at least $1 billion in loans that were guaranteed by the company.[15]

What else? At Enron, Lay's personal use of a corporate jet in 2000 was valued $300,000. At Qwest Communications International, Inc., CEO Joseph P. Nacchio had criticized US West's CEO for flying on a private jet. He then traded the company's $5 million plane in for another one worth $20 million, which he then used to fly home on weekends.

Cause for Hope?

Perhaps I sound angry about these kinds of wretched excesses. Well, I am, and I suspect that I am not alone.

A story from a May 5, 2002, edition of the *Wall Street Journal* hints at a possible turning of the tide. Entitled "Shareholder Activists Win Big Ones on Votes at EMC, Mentor Graphics. Investors Approve Resolutions Management Opposed Concerning Independence of Directors, Stock Options," the story details a highly unusual occurrence: a shareholder revolt against management:

In a sign of increased shareholder activism following widespread corporate accounting scandals and concern over outsized executive pay, investors in two companies—EMC Corp. and Mentor Graphics Corp.—approved shareholder resolutions opposed by management. Typically, such measures are defeated, often by a wide margin. . . . The votes could provide encouragement to advocates of corporate good governance, which has been getting increased attention as a result of numerous disclosures of questionable practices and the sharp slide in many stocks in the past year, especially technology issues. Indeed, Peter Clapman, senior vice president and chief counsel for corporate governance at TIAA-CREF, a big institutional investor that sponsored the Mentor Graphics resolution, said the vote on the stock-option measure sends a "clarion call" for action by regulators.

Investors, both institutional and individual, are *angry*. "This really drives home the way executives treated a public corporation like their own cash cow," commented Harvard Law School Professor Elizabeth Warren. "They looked for any excuse to pay themselves."[16] And by extension, they weren't looking for excuses to pay shareholders.

Excessive compensation of a company's executives is *wrong*; it expropriates the investment of the people who make the enterprise possible. And, I would argue, it has ominous implications for our larger society. Simply put, there is a widening gulf between the wages of rank-and-file employees and the compensation of top executives, including salaries, bonuses, stock options, and other financial rewards. Peter F. Drucker has pointed to this widening gulf: "J. P. Morgan, no enemy of wealth, once said that a reasonable ratio of management pay to that of the average worker would be 20 to 1. But in U.S. business today it is 500 to 1." Average total pay, including stock options, for CEOs of America's largest companies rose past $15 million in 2000.

Yes, our democracy rests on the foundations of private property, individualism, and opportunism. However, it also rests on *fairness*—the vague but real conviction on the part of the majority that things are being divvied up in ways that are appropriate and balanced and that effective safeguards are in place to prevent abuses.

As we have seen, those safeguards were limited and late to the party; now there are signs that they may be put in place.

LESSONS FOR THE INVESTOR

Figure out who is getting paid what. This is the main lesson of this chapter. Get comfortable reading the fine print in the annual report. If you do not like what you are reading, write a letter to every member of the board of directors of the offending company and tell them exactly what you think.

If you are not involved, get involved. If you are an indirect investor—say, through mutual funds or a 401(k)—you can still take a look at the policies of the companies in which your money is invested.

Do not buy the stock of a company that allocates excessive executive compensation. If the company cheats on shareholders in this way, it probably does so in many other ways as well.

Aggressive Accounting

In the last few years, the reliability of earnings reports has dramatically decreased.

—STANDARD & POOR'S, May 14, 2002[1]

Accounting and *aggressive* are not normally two words that travel together. As the old saying goes, *Finance is playing the game; accounting is keeping score*. However, as explained in Chapter 2, the old rules have changed, and today we have to deal with the reality of aggressive accounting.

What makes accounting *aggressive*? Simply put, it is a systematic disdain for the spirit of financial reporting. In aggressive accounting, the principal concern of the auditor is not producing an accurate picture of a company's financial circumstances but rather painting the most favorable portrait that can be generated without actually breaking any rules.

Well, this is one kind of challenge in an established industry, such as steel or potato chips, where the rules are well known. However, it is a wholly different challenge when the company being audited is venturing out into new territory. "In a new industry," Henny Sender of the *Wall Street Journal* observed, "it is difficult to say what is conservative and what is aggressive accounting without the say-so of rule makers."[2] Both the audited and the auditor have to make a lot of judgment calls—a situation that ought to evoke conservatism but doesn't always.

Reporting Styles: The Menu

When you look at an accounting firm's product, you need to understand exactly what you are looking at. (No, they are not all the same.) There are a number of different styles for reporting financial results. I will quote Standard & Poor's definitions of a few of the most important.

- *As-reported earnings* are earnings including all charges except those related to discontinued operations, the impact of cumulative accounting changes, and extraordinary items, as defined by Generally Accepted Accounting Principles (GAAP). This is the traditional earnings measure and has a long history, having been used for the S&P 500 and company analyses for decades.

- *Operating earnings*: This measure focuses on the earnings from a company's principal operations, with the goal of making the numbers comparable across different time periods. Operating earnings are usually considered to be as-reported earnings with some charges reversed to exclude corporate or one-time expenses. . . . The use of this measure seems to come from internal management controls used when a business unit manager is not responsible for managing corporate level costs."[3]

Of a third style of reporting—*pro forma*—Standard & Poor's says the following: "Originally, the use of the term *pro forma* meant a special analysis of a major change, such as a merger, where adjustments were made for an 'as if' review. In such cases, pro forma measures are very useful. However, the specific items being considered in an 'as if' review must be clear. In some recent cases, 'as if' has come to mean 'as if the company didn't have to cover proper expenses.' In the most extreme cases, pro forma is nicknamed EBBS, or 'earnings before bad stuff.' Such abuses notwithstanding, pro forma earnings do have a place and should be used for special analyses of potential changes in a corporation. In such cases, pro forma earnings are defined for the particular analysis."

Pro forma, therefore, is an *informal* approach to reporting financial results. Firms that are leery of the connotations of the pro forma label often resort to alternative wordings, such as "cash earnings" or "operating earnings." However, what is common to all these phrases is that they refer to financial reports that do not have any guarantees behind them. Financial reports that are prepared using what are called *generally accepted accounting principles* (GAAP) are required by law to be accurate, truthful, and complete.[4] Other kinds of financial reports are not.

Commenting recently on the term *pro forma,* the Securities and Exchange Commission (SEC) concluded that the term "has no defined meaning and no unified characteristics." However, nothing precludes a company from communicating pro-forma statements to shareholders. According to the SEC, "There is no prohibition preventing public companies from publishing interpretations of their results." Nevertheless, says the SEC, "'pro forma' financials . . . should be viewed with appropriate and healthy skepticism."

Pro-forma information often can be deceptive. In particular, it can suggest the presence of profits where in fact only losses can be documented. In a March 2002 editorial on his firm's Web site, PIMCO's head, Bill Gross, referred to "the deceptive and sometimes illegal information disseminated by some of our New Age corporate elite. *The Economist* in a February 23 issue reported that the companies in the Nasdaq 100 for the first three quarters of 2001 reported combined losses to the SEC of nearly $82 billion, while at the same time promoting profits of $20 billion to their stockholders. *The Economist* explained the discrepancy by the companies' use of generally accepted accounting principles for regulators, and the distinctly more favorable New Age 'pro forma' accounting for owners of their shares. Charles Ponzi would undoubtedly have approved."[5]

Why do corporations release pro-forma statements? In many cases, it is because these allow the omission of information that would not fit well into the generally rosy picture that they are trying to promote. "They may assume that a proposed transaction that benefits the company has actually occurred," warns the SEC, or "may only address one component of a company financial results."

As financial writer Andrew Tobias has pointed out, "Annual reports are organized very simply. The good news is contained up front in the president's message and ensuing text; the bad news is contained in the footnotes to the financial statement."[6] Therefore, think of pro formas as being the happy talk up front; your job, as an investor, is to root out the footnotes.

Where's the Truth?

To be fair, some companies issue pro-forma reports because they are genuinely convinced that GAAP-compliant information distorts the picture and fails to convey the actual circumstances of the company. An interesting article in the *Wall Street Journal* tells the story of why IBM felt strongly that its own style of reporting was more truthful than the formats generally called for by the SEC.[7]

The story is revealing. Both in 1999 and in 2001, "Big Blue" used gains from selling assets to offset ordinary expenses rather than following the convention of listing the gains separately as "nonoperating income," "other general expenses," or some similar category. In IBM's 1999 financial reports, for example, the $2.7 billion in gains the firm realized from the sale of its Global Network business to AT&T Corp. were included under "sales, general and administrative." This was odd: "Sales, general and administrative," in the minds of SEC members and of most accountants, refers to such expenses as salaries, advertising, rent, and travel costs. How does the sale of an entire business show up here?

IBM claimed that its itemization of the sale of Global Network under "sales, general and administrative" was both compliant with accounting guidelines and consistent with what the company had done in the past. The difficulty the SEC saw with such an interpretation was that in several public statements IBM had seemed to imply that it had lowered its operating costs through tight expense controls on items such as salaries, advertising, rent, and travel when, in fact, this was not the case.

In December 1999, the SEC released its *Staff Accounting Bulletin 101*, which included the following provision: "Gains or losses from the sale of assets should be reported as 'other general expenses' pursuant to Regulation S-X, Article 5-03 (b) (6). Any material item should be stated separately." According to the *Wall Street Journal*, "SEC staffers referred to the provision as 'the IBM footnote.'"

However, "Big Blue" was neither impressed nor intimidated. It regarded the SEC's pronouncement as one opinion among many, with no particular binding authority. To a certain extent, the company was correct in this belief. As a rule, corporations go along with the SEC's rulings because they do not want to be compelled to restate their results. Cooperating with the SEC minimizes the chances that this will happen. In this case, however, IBM's spokesperson declared that since 1994, the company had included gains and losses from asset sales, licensing of intellectual property, and real estate sales under the "services, general and administrative" line. IBM considers such gains as a normal ongoing part of doing business, he explained, and believes that they properly belong in that category.

The issue clearly revolves around the definition of *normal*. Should this mean normal for what most businesses would include in "services, general and administrative" or normal for how IBM would treat this category? The *Wall Street Journal* seemed to come down on the former side of the argument, quoting Charles Mulford, an accounting professor at the Georgia Institute of Technology, as saying that *normally* means items that most companies would include in "services, general and administrative," not items that a particular company defines as its normal practice.

IBM continued to maintain that this was a matter of interpretation—or perhaps a balance-of-power issue—in which the SEC should not necessarily be granted the upper hand. However, as IBM was well aware, the case bore a close resemblance to another ongoing battle between the SEC and a recalcitrant company. And as IBM also was aware, in that case the SEC moved forcefully against Trump Hotels & Casino Resorts.

On January 16, 2002, the SEC issued a press release entitled "SEC Brings First Pro Forma Financial Reporting Case. Trump Hotels Charged with Issuing Misleading Earnings Release." Referring to Trump Hotels' earnings release for the third quarter of 1999, the SEC found that "the release cited pro forma figures to tout the Company's purportedly positive results of operations but failed to disclose that those results were primarily attributable to an unusual one-time gain rather than to operations." In summary, the SEC noted that "although neither the earnings release nor the accompanying financial data used the term *pro forma,* the net income and EPS figures used in the release were pro forma numbers because they differed from such figures calculated in conformity with GAAP by excluding the one-time charge."

Going a large step further, the SEC concluded that "the earnings release was fraudulent because it created the false and misleading impression that the Company had exceeded earnings expectations primarily through operational improvements, when in fact it had not. . . . In fact, had the one-time gain been excluded from the quarterly pro forma results as well as the one-time charge, those results would have reflected a decline in revenues and net income and would have failed to meet analysts' expectations."

Obviously, declining to play by the SEC's rules entails certain risks. However, it is entirely plausible that a company could decide that the benefits derived from keeping the analysts happy would outweigh the likely consequences of actions by an angry SEC. If so, they might knowingly put out bad numbers—and we investors would have to deal with those numbers.

Hiding the Bad News: Off the Balance Sheet

The corporate balance sheet is supposed to present a true picture of a company's assets and liabilities, which are supposed to balance (that is, equal each other). Over time, however, and by general consensus, certain items have migrated off most corporate balance sheets on the assumption that they do not belong there because they will not have a near-term impact on the company's financial results. When you hear the phrase *off-balance-sheet items,* this is what is being referred to.

Like what, for example? One example is lease agreements, at least in the case where there is no buy-out option at the end of the lease, and therefore the corporation cannot be said to own the item. A second is pensions assets and liabilities, which technically belong to the company's employees, not to the company itself. A third is what is called "joint ventures and affiliates." When these go off the balance sheet, they are accounted for through the *equity method,* whereby the company's risk is through holding their stock. (Otherwise, their results would be consolidated with the parent company.) A fourth is "special-purpose entities." These are essentially used for the securing of assets, as well as for hedging the company's investments.

I have already steered you toward the footnotes to the annual report more than once. I will do so again here: Off-balance-sheet items generally can be found in the footnotes, which come after the cash-flow statement.

Why is this interesting? In part because Enron (and other corporate miscreants) have recently *made* it interesting. Enron's partnerships (of various legal statuses) were used to hide very risky assets from scrutiny. If and when they incurred losses, those losses would appear incurred only by them and would not show up on Enron's financial reports. The point is that an off-balance-sheet item can do material financial damage to a company, even though the previous five years' annual reports may have made scant mention of this peril.

Fair Value: The Elusive Holy Grail

Any accounting of a company's financial health eventually gets into the murky realm of assigning value to assets. This is easier said than done, of course, especially when it comes to such things as derivative instruments on the balance sheet.

A fair price for a seller could be defined as the highest bid that the seller can find on the market so that if a party buys from you at that price, he or she will not easily find on the market an opportunity to resell at a higher price. Conversely, a fair price for a buyer means that no one can easily find a lower offer on the market.

In other words, a fair price is the common market price. Defining a fair price for a financial product is called *marking it to market,* a concept we looked at in earlier chapters. The price used to mark an equity to market is the price currently quoted in the auction area, either as an ask proposed by a potential seller or as a bid proposed by a potential buyer. Commonly, marking an equity to market means pegging its price at midspread between ask and bid.

Fair value is at the center of Financial Accounting Standard Board (FASB) Statement No. 133, the regulation that the FASB implemented in 2002 after a 3-year delay. It introduced mark-to-market valuation of derivative instruments in financial reporting as assets and liabilities on the balance sheet.

We saw earlier why it might be a good idea to mark to market a financial instrument. For instance, its *book value* (original cost minus depreciation) may be severely outdated: It may reflect a different period in time, when the asset was either more highly or less prized than it is today. A possible alternative to book value is, *How much is it worth right now?*—in the context of a secondary market where the product could be traded—and *How much would a third party be prepared to pay for it?*

This is something like a liquidation value: "Let's imagine that we need to sell it all right now; how much would we get?"

However, all such thinking is by its nature inadequate. How can we *know* how much we would get if we are not truly selling? How do you *simulate* selling right now in today's market conditions without actually doing so?

In the case of equities that are traded on exchanges, market prices do offer a reasonable indicator, especially in the case of small volumes. However, when it comes to valuing a large block of shares, things get trickier.

First, there is the issue of slippage, mentioned earlier: If I chose to sell this large slug of stock, how much would my own transactions move the market price unfavorably against me? And second, there is the issue of the *frequency* of trading: How old is the last actual transaction? Yes, that last price may have been a good one, from a seller's point of view, but is that price still available to the next market?

As a footnote, it is worth remembering that markets can swoon or even get extinguished. This happened, for example, to the French real estate market, which came to a near standstill in the mid-1990s. The banks that held all the mortgages on these properties were left more or less in the dark: What were they worth? When the market finally came back to life and transactions started occurring—at greatly reduced price levels—the banks dutifully marked to market and only then realized the horrendous extent of their losses.

The Land of Make-Believe

Thus equities and real estate—reasonably tangible assets with reasonably active markets—can be tough to put a value on. Even tougher to value is a product for which no market yet exists.

This was the case with Enron's dark fiberoptic cable, the unused capacity in the high-speed broadband telecommunications network that Enron built in January 2000. How does an auditor value *that*? Absent a current market, the auditor assumes a plausible date for when the existing infrastructure will get "lit," and the value of the deal is then discounted over the number of years involved.

Again, the difficulty is obvious: There are simply too many wild guesses involved, too many mutually dependent variables to be considered. However, Enron—aided and abetted by its aggressive accountants—took this a huge step further by booking the entire value of a contract up front and then recording variations from those expectations in subsequent years. This simply stacks guess upon guess. As an article in the *Washington Post* explained:

> Douglas R. Carmichael, a professor of accountancy at the City University of New York's Baruch College, said the type of 'mark-to-market' accounting used by Enron—recognizing the whole value of a multi-year contract at its beginning and then recording any gains or losses in value over time as the market dictated—is appropriate only when there is a ready market for such a contract, as there is for oil. If there's not an active and ready

market, Carmichael added, assigning values and recognizing revenue up front 'gets arbitrary.'[8]

Enron's approach to marking to market also was scrutinized in a *Houston Chronicle* article that made a heroic effort to untangle Enron's financial reports. Read this following passage carefully:

> As the years rolled by and Enron began losing (or occasionally winning) on long-term contracts, the difference between its original estimate and reality had to be put into the income statement. To find out how much of Enron's income was 'real,' and how much was mark-to-market adjustments, one would need to look at two pages on Enron's [2000] annual report that are 13 pages apart. On the 51st page is a chart showing 'income (loss) before interest, minority interests and income taxes,' known to financial experts as EBIT, earnings before interest and taxes. It divides the income between Enron's business segments, such as wholesale services, broadband, etc. But it makes no distinctions between regular income and mark-to-market. Back on page 38, in a footnote, is this sentence: 'The income before interest, taxes and certain unallocated expenses arising from price risk management activities for 2000 was $1,899 million.' 'Price risk management' is Enron-speak for mark-to-market. One must take that $1.9 billion back to page 51 and subtract it from the total earnings of the various divisions. Excluding Enron's pipelines and power plants, which don't use mark-to-market, it looks like Enron's other divisions had earnings before interest and taxes of $1.8 billion. So, excluding the pipelines and power plants division, Enron doesn't seem to have a penny of income without mark-to-market."[9]

Enron's approach to marking to market its financial positions was described by Jeffrey K. Skilling in a company seminar in 2000, a time when he was Enron's chief operating officer. In the following excerpt, Skilling first reads a question and then comments:

> Can you respond to the *Wall Street Journal* article claiming that we booked more mark-to-market income than we had in earnings for the second quarter and that but for mark-to-market, we would have had a loss in the second quarter. Is that correct?
> For those of you who didn't see it, there was an article in the Texas section of the *Wall Street Journal*, and I think it was about a week and a half ago that was talking about the accounting methodology used by energy merchant companies. And one of the comments they had in there was that we had more mark-to-market income than we had total earnings. So, if we

didn't have mark-to-market income, we would have had a loss for the quarter. As a matter of fact, that's correct, but that's a little bit like saying, if General Motors didn't sell any cars last quarter, they would have lost money. It's the exact same analogy. It is just totally, totally without merit. We mark-to-market our positions. And what that means is at the end of every day, we determine what the value of all of our purchases and the value of all of our sales are, we subtract them, and we figure out how much money we made that day. We don't only do it every day, we do it every quarter, and we do it every year, and that's how we recognize income. So every time we sell natural gas, typically, there's a contract attached to that, and that contract has some period of liquidation, but at the time the contract is entered into and signed, that's when we recognize the income, and that is the appropriate way to account for this business.

Well, yeah, but . . . ! The real question to ask is, *How likely is it that those extravagant amounts of cash will ever materialize?* If there is little chance that they will, then the company lives in a land of make-believe. Vast amounts of cash that may never materialize are more important than actual cash because—however fantastic they might be—they show up as earnings on the financial reports.

In this land of make-believe, lots of nutty things happen. Here's one: You can trade a little bit of real cash for a whole lot of funny money. In the following example, it cost Enron a mere $50 million of true cash to buy a $1.3 billion worth of paper money: "Eli Lilly and Co., the Indianapolis pharmaceutical manufacturer, signed a $1.3 billion contract in February 2001 turning all its energy requirements over to Enron for 15 years. But Enron paid Eli Lilly $50 million up front to win the deal, according to a former senior executive of Enron. Eli Lilly spokesman Ed West confirmed that Enron had made an advance payment but would not disclose the amount for business confidentiality reasons. 'We looked at it as Enron backing up their words with cash,' he said."[10]

Good Hiding Places

As investors, we need to train ourselves to look for the good hiding places— that is, the places where a corporation and its aggressive accountants might choose to play games with the numbers. Based on recent experience, here are a few such hiding places:

"Gain on Sale": Present Value of Future Profits

Under this heading may be calculated the present value of some future "locked" profits, as with annuities. Says Jim Chanos of the contrarian Ursus Partners hedge fund, "It has been our experience that gain-on-sale accounting creates an irresistible temptation on the part of managements heavily incentivized with options and heavy stock ownership to create earnings out of thin air."[11] Well stated.

"Charges": Massaging the One-Time-Only

"Charges" are, in principle, a way to account for one-time-only financial incidents; in actuality, they often offer a get-out-of-jail-free card for bad investments. The SEC's recommendation on charges is that "when a company purports to announce earnings before 'unusual or nonrecurring transactions,' it should describe the particular transactions and the kind of transactions that are omitted, and apply the methodology described when presenting purportedly comparable information about other periods."[12]

Again, a relevant comment from the press: "[WorldCom] may be too ambitious in taking one-time charges against its earnings—like improperly masking operating losses as one-time charges that might make its operating results appear stronger than they really are." [13]

"Other Revenues"

One-shot gains are often used to compensate for losses in other divisions of a corporation.

Footnotes: Drowning Perks in Legalese

In principle, footnotes provide a way of accounting for subsidiary issues. We have seen, however, that under current FASB guidelines, stock options—a major item of executive compensation—are mentioned only in footnotes.

Footnotes often offer management an easy way to render a financial issue fully opaque; this applies in particular to excessive executive compensation and perks. As PIMCO's manager, Bill Gross, once observed, "In the investment world, there are countless ways to deceive, starting with Charles Ponzi and winding all the way down to the seemingly innocuous footnote to a financial statement that hints at, but doesn't really disclose, what is going on."

Adelphia's peculiar predicament—the astronomical loans taken against the company by its founders, the Rigas family—were first revealed in a footnote. According to the *New York Times*:

> The disclosure of the debt was made in the company's earnings news release, in a footnote near the end. It said that 'certain subsidiaries of the company are co-borrowers with certain companies owned by the Rigas family' for borrowing of up to $5.63 billion. As of the end of last year, it said, $2.284 billion had been borrowed by the Rigas entities and was not shown on Adelphia's balance sheet, even though the company would be liable if the money were not repaid. It added that more information would be disclosed in the company's annual report to the Securities and Exchange Commission, which is scheduled to be filed by next week."[14]

I'll say again, at the risk of redundancy: This was a breathtaking abuse of privilege and an amazingly bald-faced effort to minimize the scope of the abuse.

"Certain Transactions," "Other Compensation"

Be aware that the "certain transactions" and "other compensation" items are likely to refer to loans granted to executives at preferential interest rates or to disavowed loans at the corporation's expense.

"Goodwill": The Extravagant Price of Blunders

A classic accounting textbook defines *goodwill* as "an intangible value attached to a business evidenced by the ability to earn larger net income per dollar of investment than that earned by competitors in the same industry. The ability to produce superior profits is a valuable resource of a business. Normally, companies record goodwill only at the time of purchase and then only at the price paid for it. The Home Depot has labeled its goodwill 'cost in excess of the fair value of net assets acquired.'"[15] These same authors also define goodwill as the value of a "favorable reputation and earnings potential acquired in a merger."[16]

For all practical purposes, goodwill refers in acquisitions to the premium that was paid shareholders to entice them into the acquisition process. This is the aspect that Standard & Poor's is emphasizing in its own definition: "Goodwill represents the difference between the price paid for an acquisition and the fair market value of identifiable assets of the acquisition."[17]

In other words, goodwill may simply be the price paid for poor judgment. This was the implication of a comment about the demise of Global Crossing: "The ending was gruesome. When Global Crossing filed for bankruptcy in January, it listed assets of $22.4 billion and liabilities of $12.4 billion. At first blush that might look like $10 billion in value, but most of the assets were worthless goodwill from overpaying for all those acquisitions."[18]

A write-off for goodwill also can offer an easy way out for colossal errors of judgment in the past. Referring to a change in the accounting method for goodwill applicable to 2001 financial results (FASB 142), Shawn Young reported in the *Wall Street Journal:*

> Qwest's charge stems from a change in rules set by the federal agency that has put pressure on companies to write off in a lump sum goodwill assets that have fallen in value. In this case, the write-down reflects the fallen value of Qwest, which merged with the former US West in 2000. The new rules also will allow the company to stop making deductions from earnings of about $900 million a year for amortizing its goodwill costs. . . . Many companies are facing huge goodwill write-downs after paying large premiums for acquisitions, many of which turned out to be speculative, during the technology frenzy of the late 1990s. Indeed, WorldCom expects to take a charge of $15 billion to $20 billion and last week AOL Time Warner said it would take a $54 billion goodwill write-down.[19]

Targeted by the SEC

Does the cavalry ever come to the aid of the hapless investor? Yes, indeed. In May 2002, the SEC identified a number of practices in the aggressive-accounting category and announced that it would be scrutinizing these practices. Among them were

Revenue recognition. The SEC has especially in mind *round-tripping,* meaning double counting of transactions between companies. For obvious reasons, this is also known as *corporate back scratching.*

Quality of earnings. Some companies improve their balance sheets "by simply changing accounting methodology and not disclosing it." For example, an asset that used to be depreciated over 5 years is now depreciated over 10 years. SEC to corporate sector: Cut it out.

Acquisitions. Companies that have acquired others may be tempted to report improved overall earnings that actually only reflect the good health of the acquisitions.

Netting. One-time gains are improperly netted against operating expenses, making operating earnings appear better than they really are.[20]

These are not new practices, nor is the SEC new to the game of scrutinizing them. It is fair to say, however, that the *scope* and *scale* of abuses in these and similar realms in recent years have been unprecedented. Most likely, the regulators have been spurred to a new standard of scrutiny. And this is all to the good.

LESSONS FOR INVESTORS

You are not being paranoid; they are ganging up on you. Corporate executives have lots of incentives—and lots of leeway—to "cook the books" and make their earnings look better than they actually are. Their aggressive accountants have as much leeway or more and may feel compelled to conspire with the executives to protect the account.

Not all reporting styles are meaningful. Beware the pro forma and similar kinds of accounting. These are often management's way of putting its best foot forward. In other words, they may be nonsense.

Look for off-the-balance-sheet items. What are they, and why are they off the balance sheet?

If there is no established market, be doubly cautious about the numbers. I mentioned a version of this in Chapter 7, but it is worth reiterating: If your company is creating a market and then assigning a long-term value to that market, clamp your hand on your wallet.

Look for the hiding places. There are lots of entries in standard financial reports—starting with goodwill—where strange stuff happens and odd numbers squirt out. Train yourself to look for these words and phrases, and read carefully when you find them.

11

Massaging Financial Reports

In a nascent industry with few financial conventions, both Wall Street and companies such as Global Crossing focused on revenue growth as the arbiter of the firms' financial health.

—DENNIS K. BERMAN in *The Wall Street Journal*[1]

Imagine that you are an investor in a fast-moving technology-intensive company. (If you have gotten this far in this book, you probably are, or have been, and/or hope to be in the future.) Assume, too, that you are an *involved* investor. You read your annual report and quarterlies carefully, you keep an eye on the company through its Web site, and you follow the company and its industry through the financial press and trade publications.

Do you think that you would develop a true picture of the economic value of the company in which you are investing?

Don't be too quick to answer "yes." First of all, developing an accurate picture of *any* complex organization is extremely difficult, even if its leaders are trying their hardest to help you get it right.

And what if they are *not* trying to be helpful?

In financial circles, there is a pretty solid consensus that if management wants to hide from the shareholder what's really going on, it can. In fact, this is one of the principal lessons of the Enron mess. A lot of very savvy people were taken in.

However, there is something of a silver lining here. In the wake of Enron and similar fiascoes, self-policing has kicked in. Companies are trying harder to get it right and to convey it in accessible terms. And equally important, the Securities and Exchange Commission (SEC) has lurched into action and has started to crack down on delinquent companies.

This is belated, but it is all to the good. This chapter looks at financial reports—what's in them and how they are massaged. My hope is that this chapter will be less important as self-policing and the SEC have their combined effect, but only time will tell. Meanwhile, the self-interested investor should be aware of where we have come from and—to some extent—where we still are today.

Financial Reports and Reporting

Let's start with the basics. A corporation's financial statements are the balance sheet, income statement, statement of stockholders' equity, statement of cash flows, and explanatory notes that accompany the financial statements. They can be found in a corporation's quarterly and annual reports (10-Q and 10-K filings). They are public information and are easily accessible. You can almost always find them at the individual corporation's Web site; they are also available through the SEC's EDGAR database: *www.sec.gov/edgar/searchedgar/webusers.html.*

A general principle when reading financial statements is as follows: *The closer you are to the top, the more reliable is the information.* Why? Because the material up at or near the top is relatively unprocessed and unfiltered, and unprocessed financial data are more trustworthy. Every line down the page you go allows for the introduction of more interpretation, wishful thinking, and even wild speculation about the future.

A second general principle—and it pains me to write it—is as follows: *It is all about earnings.* Unfortunately, this principle has acquired a new and negative connotation in recent years. As noted in previous chapters, in the past, the price of a stock reflected the present value of the future cash flows that the shareholder would receive from the company—in other words, the present value of the dividends to come over the years. Now that dividends are nearly extinct, though, a stock's value derives mainly from its presumed power to generate capital gains: the difference between the price of the stock tomorrow compared with today's price.

With capital gains having replaced dividends, companies started focusing on earnings, which can be considered the ghosts of departed dividends. Today, earnings—real, projected, and imaginary—mainly dictate the movement of stocks. Companies that understand this turn become *earnings-obsessed.*

And of course, Enron was one of those companies.

Enron's Financial Statements: Accurate but Incomplete

One of the basic problems with financial statements is that they look so *authoritative.* The numbers all line up neatly, and—if you check the math—they all add up, too. Plus they have been printed or posted on a Web site maintained by the SEC, so they *must* be accurate, right?

Yes and no. For all their authoritative appearance, the numbers in financial statements are simply a *representation* of reality. They can be an accurate or an inaccurate representation. They can accurately represent a reality that is now 6 months old—a century in Internet time. They can accurately represent a piece of the picture but mislead by omitting other relevant parts of the picture.

Jeffrey Skilling regarded Enron's financial statements as truthful. He said so at a hearing of the Senate Commerce Committee:

> SKILLING: I believe the financial statements were an accurate representation of my understanding of the financial condition of the company. And I'd like to address—as you brought up, I would like to address one of those issues. There's been a lot in the press, and I think your question suggests that there is some issue of hiding debt, that the use of off-balance-sheet or special-purpose entities had its intent in hiding debt. And all I can do is I can refer you to page 78 of the year 2000 10-K. There's a section that's called "Unconsolidated Equity Affiliates." "Unconsolidated Equity Affiliates" would be partnerships and special-purpose entities that were not consolidated into Enron's balance sheet.

There's a two-page description of the earnings that were appropriate or associated with those vehicles. And on the second page it shows the full . . .

SENATOR ALLEN: All right, let me interrupt . . .

SKILLING: . . .balance sheet. I'm—Senator, please—the . . .

SENATOR ALLEN: I just want . . .

SKILLING: This chart shows exactly—exactly what the total amount of the outstanding liabilities were that were nonconsolidated liabilities. So the whole issue of hiding debt, it's not—it was in the 10-K. Anyone reading the 10-K would have a hard time missing this page.

SENATOR ALLEN: Okay, thank you, Mr. Skilling. A lot of people must have missed it. Now (laughter). . . .

Enron's financial reports were certainly detailed, and they were accurate, as far as they went. Nevertheless, critical pieces were omitted from the reports in what appears to have been a systematic pattern of strategic omission.

Each of the following paragraphs keys off one such piece. The quoted passages are from an excellent article by Dan Feldstein of the *Houston Chronicle*.[2]

Leverage: Debt versus Equity Interest in Affiliates

Enron indeed listed several such affiliates, from Azurix to Whitewing. But the prose was obscure and the note only showed what Enron had put into the companies, not its possible debt exposure, said analyst John Olson of Sanders Morris Harris. By showing its equity interest in the partnership, but not the debt, Enron had not spelled out the relationship between the two, known as "leverage."

This is a consequence of accounting for partnerships ("special-purpose entities") through the *equity method* rather than consolidating their results with those of the parent company. Arthur A., the anonymous Web commentator at *www.eraider.com* explains this: "Most observers have called the Special Purpose Entities a form of off-balance-sheet financing, in which Enron engages in transactions that it somehow doesn't even record on its balance sheet. That would be illegal. Rather, Enron put them on the balance sheet, in plain sight for everyone to see, but just in a place that few people think to look. Enron had a choice in how to record the investment in and activities of the SPEs: It could consolidate them, or use the 'equity method.' Consolidating them meant that the assets of an SPE become the assets of Enron, its liabilities become Enron's liabilities, and so forth. Enron certainly didn't want to do this, since it sought to avoid the SPE liabilities in the first place. In contrast, the equity method allows a firm merely to add the shareholders' equity of a subsidiary or affiliate (such as the SPEs) to its own. This way, Enron wouldn't care about the revenues and expenses or assets and liabilities of the SPEs."

This is extremely complicated and probably down to a level of detail that most readers of this book will not need to master. But you get the idea: Enron found a "legitimate" way to represent its subsidiaries and affiliates that created a very misleading picture.

Missing: Debt

"Enron was doing leveraged buyouts with recourse to itself. This debt should have been fully disclosed in the footnotes of the minority interests," Olson said.

Missing: "Commitments and Contingencies"

The collateral could have been shown in "commitments and contingencies" in the balance statement. It isn't. It also could have been in the footnote discussing earnings per share.

Missing: "Contingent Stock Obligations"

If Enron stock faced the possibility of being diluted by new shares issued for the partnership, experts say, stockholders should have been warned under "contingent stock obligations." It wasn't. Things got even more confusing from there, analysts said. In some deals, the potential stock obligation simply wasn't included in dilution calculations. But in others, Enron actually acted as if the stock had already been issued, including it in the total of outstanding shares. This effectively boosted Enron's equity, making the company appear less dangerously leveraged, Olson said.

Peter Eavis produced a detailed analysis of Enron's "contingent stock obligations" after the second 2001 restatement:

In its 2000 annual report, Enron included some disclosure of the 55 million shares connected with LJM2. It reads: "At December 31, 2000, Enron had derivative instruments on 54.8 million shares of Enron common stock." . . .But these derivatives-linked shares don't show up where they should in the annual report: in the table that breaks out the difference between the basic and diluted share counts.[3]

Conflicts of Interest: Only Part of the Story

Analysts' final complaint is that they should have been told, explicitly, that Enron chief financial officer Andrew Fastow was also an officer in some partnerships and stood to make a lot of money from them. In Enron's annual report, under the footnote for related party transactions, it says, "Enron entered into transactions with limited partnerships whose general partner's managing member is a senior officer of Enron." That could have been any one of thousands of vice presidents, the analysts said. It was the CFO. But one disclosure *was* more explicit—in the company's 1999 proxy, page 26, "Certain Transactions": "In June, 1999, Enron entered into a series of transactions involving a third party and LJM Cayman, L.P. ('LJM1'). . . . Andrew S. Fastow, Executive Vice President and Chief Financial Officer of Enron, is the managing member of LJM1's general partner. The general partner of LJM1 is entitled to receive a percentage of the profits of LJM1 in excess of the general partner's proportion of the total capital contributed to LJM1, depending upon the performance of the investments made by LJM1." That's actually pretty clear.[4]

The Uses of Opacity: The Impenetrability of Enron's Financial Reports

Because parts that would make the whole picture emerge were missing, Enron's financial reports were considered opaque by the experts. "We're pretty good at deciphering footnotes and other disclosures," Jim Chanos of contrarian Ursus Partners hedge fund commented, "but these [Enron] reports left us scratching our heads."[5]

Arthur A. remarks: "Many smart analysts have spent years trying to understand Enron's finances, and it was their nosy questions about a $1.2 billion charge to shareholders' equity in its third quarter earnings release in mid-October that started the company down its fateful path. As those questions boiled over, and Enron claims it got religion on disclosing everything to investors, it issued its sole official public document explaining its position—and few analysts could understand even that disclosure. I've been through last week's 8-K filing several times and have only the most superficial idea of what took place."[6]

"Earnings Management": Enron's Marketable Skill

The often ambiguous use of marking to market of financial positions in order to boost earnings was discussed at length in Chapter 10. However, there are lots of other tools available to the earnings-obsessed corporation. For example, one technique that can be used to boost cash flows in an acquisition process is the acceleration of payments in the acquired company before the merger. In this way, cash flows are artificially deflated in the preacquisition period and artificially inflated in the postacquisition period.

An article in the *Wall Street Journal* explained how Tyco International, Ltd., played this particular game:

> Executives at a large electronics company acquired by Tyco International, Ltd., took action to accelerate certain payments, at Tyco's request, to boost Tyco's cash flow after the deal closed, according to internal e-mails at the acquired company. Tyco critics have said the Bermuda-based conglomerate routinely forces companies it acquires to prepay expenses and lower their earnings and cash flow just before they are melded into Tyco. . . . The electronics company, Raychem Corp., was bought by Tyco in August 1999 in a cash-and-stock deal valued at about $3 billion. About three weeks before the deal closed, then-Raychem Treasurer Lars Larsen told financial staffers in an e-mail that "Tyco would like to maximize cash outflow from Raychem before the acquisition closes." He followed up a few days later with another e-mail, saying that at "Tyco's request," Raychem was planning to pay all bills due to suppliers "whether they are due or not." . . . The action, he estimated, would consume between $55 million and $60 million of cash. . . . He added: "The purpose of this effort is, at Tyco's request, to cause cash flows to be negative in the 'old' Raychem, and more positive in the new company."[7]

Over time, Enron developed a highly marketable expertise in earnings management. The energy-trading company would proselytize and train other companies in its self-styled brinkmanship—and of course, they willingly went along with it. David Barboza explained how in a *New York Times* article:

> But Enron did not just find creative ways to manage its own cash flow and profits. It marketed that expertise to other major corporations, including AT&T, Eli Lilly & Company, Owens-Illinois, Lockheed Martin and Qwest Communications. . . . Enron and a customer might, for instance, agree to swap telecommunications services, use shell corporations or take advan-

tage of accounting loopholes to improve each other's balance sheet or income statement, former Enron officials said. . . . Former Enron employees who marketed the services said that their mission was clear: to sell a form of "structured finance" that could accelerate a customer's earnings or otherwise dress up the corporate books. "Ultimately, that was my job—to help companies make earnings," said one former executive of Enron's broadband services unit. . . . "This was one of the secrets of Enron."[8]

Massaging Cash Flow

Cash flow is classically regarded as a more reliable figure than earnings mainly because of the difficulties involved in fabricating cash flow. Unfortunately, however, cash flow is *not* immune to manipulation. *Cash swaps* and other types of *round-tripping* amount to a form of barter whereby companies exchange the same product in the same amount to inflate volume. Such maneuvers allow the massaging of cash flow:

> At Global Crossing, the company traded capacity with other fiber optics companies. In reality, almost nothing happened, but both companies involved in a swap were able to report revenue without offsetting expenses. They treated their purchases as capital investments. So the companies reported profits and operating cash flows. Global Crossing was careful to structure the transactions so that the money it spent would not show up in its cash flow number.[9]

And here's an example of a cash swap at WorldCom:

> In February 1999, WorldCom entered into a complex transaction with Electronic Data Systems. . . . Under that deal, E.D.S. agreed to buy as much as $8.5 billion of communications services from WorldCom over 10 years. WorldCom, in turn, said it would hire E.D.S. to oversee its billing and other basic services, agreeing to pay E.D.S. as much as $7 billion in the same period. E.D.S. also agreed to buy a WorldCom unit for $1.6 billion, taking on more than 12,000 WorldCom employees. The question for analysts is how each company booked the nearly equal amounts of revenue from the deal. . . . Mr. Ebbers . . . [declared about] the E.D.S. deal . . . that some analysts' characterization of it as a 'cash swap' was 'ridiculous.'[10]

Ebbers, of course, left his position as WorldCom's chief executive officer (CEO) in April 2002 and, as of this writing, is squarely in the crosshairs of federal investigators. However, his offhanded comment raises a legitimate question: *Was this a real deal or a shell game?*

Let's take a down-home example to explore the point. Let's say that you and I make a swap: I give you my Andy Warhol lithograph for your pure-breed puppy. Per our agreement, no cash changes hands; it is pure barter (so far).

You decide that you want to insure your newly acquired Warhol litho against theft. Meanwhile, I decide to insure myself against the liability of my sharp-toothed puppy biting a passerby. Your policy premium is $25 per year; mine is $325. Thus the exchange creates for me an additional expense of $300 per year. I issue my financial report, and suddenly, the deal is no longer barter but a "concurrent transaction."

This is exactly what Tom Siebel, CEO of Siebel Systems, Inc., does. Here's the story as reported by the *Wall Street Journal:*

> Siebel Systems, Inc., a company developing software automating corporations' sales and telemarketing operations, reported in 2001 $1.065 billion in total software licenses. During that year its revenue from "cash swaps" with its suppliers increased more than sixfold, even as the company's total software sales fell 4 percent. Siebel's swap deals accounted for $76.4 million, or 7.2 percent, of its total software license revenue in 2001, up from just $11.6 million, or 1 percent, in the previous year. Chief Executive Officer Tom Siebel defends his company's accounting techniques of what he calls "concurrent transactions."[11]

When earnings became an issue at Enron, the emphasis was switched from earnings to cash flow: "At an emergency meeting in October," the *New York Times* reported, "two top executives, Mark A. Frevert and Greg Whalley, said that the trading desk had to change its accounting practices because the company was perilously short of cash. Until then . . . the desk had focused on generating reportable net income. It structured deals to that end—sometimes at the expense of generating immediate cash, and in the process sometimes inflating the value of trades. Mark Frevert said, 'Before, cash flow wasn't important, it was always earnings.' A manager on the trading desk who attended the meeting said, 'Now we were going to have to have a whole new paradigm.'"[12]

The point, again, is that although cash flow is a *relatively* good barometer of fiscal health, it can be manipulated. And when the earnings-obsessed corporation gets into deep trouble, it most likely *will* be manipulated.

Massaging Figures for the Quarterlies

One safe and effective way to manipulate information is to manipulate the company's operations. In other words, as a senior manager, you do (or do not do) certain things in the time period that is about to be reported on. If you see a hole in the numbers, you take operational steps to plug that hole.

Bill Gross, manager of the PIMCO family of mutual funds, suspected General Electric of engaging in just these sorts of practices: "In the past year," the *Wall Street Journal* reported, "Mr. Gross has been increasingly suspicious of GE and how the company has managed to just barely beat earnings expectations for many quarters. 'What you keep hearing behind the scenes is they're selling corporate securities to book profits before each quarter ends,' Mr. Gross claims. 'Everyone on Wall Street knows GE plays games; it's totally legal but just another example of how companies aren't coming clean with investors.'"[13] And, of course, GE is not alone. Fannie Mae, Freddie Mac, Hershey Foods Corp., Pfizer, Inc., Starbucks Corp. and Wal-Mart Stores, Inc., are among the companies that have consistently met or beat estimates by a couple of cents for the nine quarters leading to the first quarter of 2002.

Enron, too, has been accused of pre-report maneuvering: "According to . . . former Enron executives, the goal of the company's off-balance-sheet partnerships was to help Enron quickly make deals that lowered its debt or generated earnings and cash flows. Often, they said, the deals were done near the end of financial reporting periods to meet Wall Street's expectations. 'This allowed us to have someone else buy assets, and we could play around with the assets,' said a current Enron executive with knowledge of the deals."[14]

Insider Trading: One Way of Taking the Corporation's Pulse

Through these and other accounting devices, Enron's executives massaged the earnings that would be reported in their quarterly and annual reports in such way that the stock price movements would become almost entirely predictable. One more time: Enron had a group of managers with major stock options who came up with—and then wielded—a bunch of levers that enable them to manipulate the price of their stock. Well, guess what happened next? Insider trading—and on a massive scale. Top-ranking executives would buy stock before the release of craftily engineered good news and sell before the bad news that was sometimes unavoidable.

Let's define terms. Most investors take the phrase *insider trading* to be synonymous with *illegal trading*. However, insider trading, according to the SEC, comprises both legal and illegal activities. The legal version of insider trader occurs when corporate insiders buy or sell stock in their own company. There is nothing wrong with this per se, but since the potential for abuse exists—both on the sell and the buy sides—these trades must be reported to the SEC.

Illegal insider trading, according to the SEC, refers to "buying or selling a security, in breach of a fiduciary duty or other relationship of trust and confidence, while in possession of material, nonpublic information about the security." The definition of illegal insider trading violations also extends to insiders who give stock-trading tips to outsiders and the outsiders who act on those tips.

Although insiders are not supposed to buy and sell based on inside information—and can be punished severely for doing so—it is well known that, in fact, they do. Therefore—in a perverse twist of financial logic—insider trading can be regarded as a highly reliable source of information about a company's health.

However, isn't this information difficult to obtain? Not really. The press and financial Web sites report routinely on insider trading, and investors should use this information (skeptically and judiciously) in their decision making about personal trades. The SEC, too, keeps records of insider trader filings, and these are public records. Be careful when relying on SEC information, though, because there are many questions about the currency (that is, the up-to-date-ness) and reliability of the information available through the SEC channel.

The Enron filings with the SEC are a case in point, especially those of Enron's CEO, Kenneth Lay. Reporting of insider trading to the SEC takes place with the filing of Form 4, which must be submitted no later than the tenth day of the month following the insider's trades. This by itself may represent a considerable delay in the release to the public of time-sensitive information. The bigger problem, however, lies elsewhere. According to regulations in effect since 1991—and not changed until the spring of 2002—if company executives sold their shares not on the open market but as part of a transaction internal to the company [for instance, to repay a company loan or to reallocate money within a 401(k) plan], they had a choice of either filing the monthly Form 4 or filing instead the annual Form 5. This form needs to be submitted to the SEC *not later than the forty-fifth day after the end of the fiscal year.*

See the problem? The public was rightfully incensed to find out belatedly, through SEC Form 4 filings, that Lay had been trading large blocks of Enron stock throughout the fall of 2001. In fact, over the period November 1, 2000, to August 2001, Lay was selling blocks of 1000 to 4000 shares almost every day. At the time, of course, he was conveying upbeat comments to employees about the company stock, then quoted at $27 a share. For instance, on September 26, in an electronic forum with Enron officers, Lay encouraged employees to *buy*: "Talk up the stock and talk positively about Enron to your family and friends." Meanwhile, Lay was selling heavily.

The public indignation took on a new dimension when it was discovered through Form 5 releases in February 2002 that Lay *also* had sold $70 million worth of stock through internal company transactions. According to the *Wall Street Journal*, "former Enron Corp. Chairman Kenneth Lay sold $70.1 million of stock back to the company between February and October of last year. . . . The stock sales are disclosed in a Securities and Exchange Commission proxy filing. . . . The stock sales detailed in the report include 20 transactions governing 1.77 million shares of stock. From a high price of $78.79 a share in February 2001, Mr. Lay continued to sell stock as the price fell to $15.40 a share for the final disclosed transaction on Oct. 26."[15] As Allan Sloan observed in the *Washington Post*: "You can bet that Enron's stockholders, creditors and especially employees would have dearly loved to know that the company's leader was selling, regardless of who was buying."[16]

Why was Lay selling Enron stock? A spokesperson speaking on his behalf had a ready explanation: Because Enron's stock price was falling, and because this stock was used as collateral on an account he had, the more the price dropped, the more shares he had to sell to meet margin calls. All along, and deep in his heart, though—the spokesperson emphasized—Lay *never doubted* that Enron's stock would come back strong.

So was the selling due to the logic of finance or driven by Lay's self-interest? It's hard to tell, because in either case Lay would have acted just the same.

Enron's Version of "Full Disclosure"

In January 2000, Jeffrey McMahon—then Enron's treasurer—made a presentation to the rating agencies. His goal was to communicate the message that Enron's stock was underrated. The problem he faced was that there were a number of "misperceptions" about Enron floating around out there. He called them "myths," which he then tried to dispel:

MYTH: There are massive amounts of debt that is not included in Enron's credit profile.

FACT: The inclusion of all obligations (without adjustment for non-recourse) does not materially change the financial profile of Enron.

MYTH: Management does not communicate its true financial position to the investor community or the rating agencies.

FACT: Management is extremely accessible to anyone willing to take the time to understand its credit—banks, institutional investors, rating agencies.

MYTH: Enron dealmakers worldwide aggressively pursuing new business lines bind the company without centralized approval and control.

FACT: Risk and assessment controls policy requires the approval of Enron Corp. senior management and the board of directors to bind the company.[17]

Orwellian, isn't it? I personally find it hard to imagine talking to a fairly hard-nosed bunch of analysts and telling them *the exact opposite of the truth*. As we have all learned, however, many of us to our sorrow, McMahon's "myths" were facts, and his "facts" were myths.

This again raises the issue of corporate culture, cited in previous chapters. Enron was known for the "smart" tone of its conference calls. Its managers were getting away with murder, they knew it, and they were proud of it. And right up until the end, the best defense is sometimes a great offense. I noted at the outset of this chapter that two good trends are now well underway: increased SEC scrutiny and a new wave of corporate self-policing. The *New York Times* recently reported an example of the latter, which may serve as a helpful antidote to much of what has been laid out in preceding pages: "A success story in building confidence comes from AmeriCredit, an automobile loan company in Fort Worth. Five years ago, its chief financial officer, Daniel E. Berce, recognized the complexity of his business and set out to make it easier for investors to understand. AmeriCredit began broadcasting conference calls on the Internet, making extra financial data available online and building an investor relations department to explain the numbers."[18]

Of course, Mr. Berce's story can only be as good as AmeriCredit's numbers (which we will assume to be accurate). However, it is these kinds of confidence-building measures that are going to be needed—from corporate headquarters across the nation—before investors will be willing to return to a market that has bruised them badly.

LESSONS FOR THE INVESTOR

In financial statements, top is better, bottom is worse. The closer the information is to the beginning of the statement, the less processed and more trustworthy the information is likely to be.

It is all about earnings. This used to be a good thing, back in the days when earnings translated into dividends. Now it tends to be a bad thing because earnings-obsessed companies are tempted to defend and manipulate their stock prices—driven by the prospect of capital gains—in all sorts of seamy ways.

When it is not all about earnings, worry about the new focus of attention. As soon as corporate executives started focusing on the once-reliable cash-flow numbers, those numbers started getting less reliable.

The quantitative is often qualitative. Do not be wowed by columns of numbers that line up and then add up. They are being used to paint a certain kind of picture. You, as the investor, have to figure out how accurate that picture really is. Is it timely? Is it comprehensive?

Watch out for corporate viruses. When a company learns a bad trick—such as Enron's version of "earnings management"—they tend to teach it to other companies. Bad practices thereby get exported.

Keep your eye on insider trading. Especially the legal kind, which is all you are likely to find out about in time to act. What do the Form 4s and Form 5s tell you about senior management's confidence in their company?

Apply the sniff test. Your gut feeling or intuition about a company is not a bad method of assessment. An overly aggressive tone in a conference call to investors, for example, can be a bad omen.

Don't cut 'em any slack. If you find out that one of the company's claims cannot be trusted, don't believe any of its claims.

12

Reading (or Ignoring) Analysts' Recommendations

But, as we can see from recent history, long-term earnings forecasts of brokerage-based securities analysts, on average, have been persistently overly optimistic. . . . The persistence of the bias year after year suggests that it more likely results, at least in part, from the proclivity of firms that sell securities to retain and promote analysts with an optimistic inclination. Moreover, the bias apparently has been especially large when the brokerage firm issuing the forecast also serves as an underwriter for the company's securities.

—ALAN GREENSPAN, Federal Reserve Board chairman[1]

During the dot-com bubble, several research analysts—for example, Merrill Lynch's Henry Blodget and Salomon Smith Barneys's Jack B. Grubman, became the financial equivalent of pop stars. Not that their jobs at that time were particularly demanding: When they recommended a buy, the bubble meant that the stock almost always went up, and the analysts looked ever smarter. It was a virtuous circle: More "wins" meant more money coming in, which meant more wins.

Then things started to go wrong. The same star analysts told investors that a given company was a strong buy at $100 a share—even as the bubble was bursting, and these stocks were starting to collapse. Mysteriously, the analysts sent out the same "buy" signals again when the stock dropped to $50 and when it hit $10. In some cases, they remained just as bullish when the stock slid to under a dollar a share.

Were they simply optimists, as Greenspan's quote implies? Or was something else at work here?

The Role of Analysts

Let's imagine that you have a portfolio containing, say, 20 stocks. Reading all the stuff that these 20 companies crank out could be nearly a full-time occupation. Add to this the kind of homework I outlined in Chapter 11— tracking Forms 4 and 5 on the Securities and Exchange Commission's (SEC's) Web site, reading the financial and trade press, scouring the companies' Web sites for small but telling clues, and so on—and it is clear that keeping an eye on your 20 companies is an unmanageable task.

Thus it is somewhat reassuring to investors that there are financial institutions out there that hire experts whose job it is to scrutinize the corporate financial statements filed with the SEC, summarize the data in concise and helpful ways, and then issue buy/sell recommendations.

Why only "somewhat reassuring"? Well, aside from the "optimism quotient," there are at least two questions that we need to raise about the work of the research analysts who study companies' financial reports and advise investors. The first is, *How good are they at arriving at a valid conclusion about a company's future performance based on a mixture of number crunching and insiders' opinions?* And the second is, *Once they have developed a personal opinion about a company's stock, what is the likelihood that the public will get a full and unsanitized version of that opinion?*

How good are they? Simply put, the answer is that the analysts' track record was decent until the mid-1990s and has become abysmally poor in recent years.

And will you get the full story? At least before the fall of Enron, the likelihood that the public would be offered an unfettered expression of the analysts' opinion was close to nil.

Research analysts came under the spotlight after they quite unanimously failed to send sell signals during the collapse of the dot-com speculative bubble. An investigation led at Merrill Lynch by the New York State Attorney General's office revealed that researchers were aware of the sinking companies' financial situation, but—under pressure from the investment bank departments within their own brokerage houses—remained bullish in order to stay on good terms with their client firms. The attorney general's investigation revealed sometimes extensive negotiating about rating between research analysts and executives from the corporations being researched.

It had been a source of pride for research analysts that an academic study covering the period 1985–1996 had shown that their stronger recommendations had beaten the market indices by an average 4.13 percent. The same group of academicians found, however, that for the year 2000, investors following the stronger recommendations would have underperformed the market by a staggering 31.2 percent. Even more embarrassing, a portfolio of the worst stocks (in the professional estimation of research analysts in 2000) would have overperformed the market by 49 percent. One of the authors of the report made the following startling conclusion: "While we can't say that the poor 2000 showing is necessarily a result of increased analyst involvement in investment banking, our findings should certainly add to the current debate over the usefulness of analysts' stock recommendations to investors."[2]

As we saw in Chapter 11, it sometimes takes a disaster to create some forward motion. I suspect that this will be the case here. The combination of the profession's current efforts to self-police and the investigation led by the office of the New York State Attorney General (see below) should lead in the future to more reliable buy and sell recommendations. Clearly, though, the reform process will need to be assessed over a period of at least a year, and preferably several, before it can be deemed to be a success.

The Conflict of Interest Between Research and Investment Banking

In June 2001, New York State Attorney General Eliot Spitzer initiated an investigation of Merrill Lynch, prompted by a case that had ended in arbitration. Trying to preempt the attorney general's conclusions that were due in April 2002, the National Association of Securities Dealers (NASD), in conjunction with the New York Stock Exchange (NYSE), came up with their own recommendations in February. These came in the form of a proposal addressed to the SEC for new rules that would apply to the members of the NASD. Interestingly enough, their report was entitled, "Research Analysts' Conflicts of Interest."

One month later, in March 2002, Merrill Lynch announced that it was immediately implementing its own new rules. A spontaneous leap into self-policing? Probably not, in light of the fact that in the following month, Attorney General Spitzer won a court order that, as a first step, compelled Merrill Lynch to overhaul its approaches to research on companies that also were its investment banking clients. The order was in conformance with New York's General Business Law and, in particular, the Martin Act (GBL Article 23-A), relative to stock recommendations issued by research analysts. On April 25, 2002, SEC Chairman Harvey Pitt announced that the SEC was initiating its own formal investigation into alleged conflicts of interest among Wall Street research analysts.

Reading NASD's February recommendations alongside the 38-page New York court order, it is perfectly clear that NASD was fully aware not only of what the New York attorney general was investigating but also of what he was about to conclude. And what Spitzer managed to document during his 10-month inquiry was pretty astounding. The report ended with these words, which should be chilling to all investors who have counted on firms like Merrill all these years:

> Contrary to the image of objectivity that Merrill Lynch has sought to cultivate for its research arm, the evidence shows that analysts knowingly compromised their honestly held beliefs regarding the merits of particular stocks and skewed the ratings they issued in order to promote the interests of Merrill Lynch's investment banking business, and that the analysts' involvement in that business netted them substantial monetary rewards. The investing public, of course, knew nothing of the inherent conflict of interest underlying the Merrill Lynch rating system, and was deprived of the analysts' honest opinions.[3]

The report hinted at the lack of cooperation that the investigators had encountered: "Some of the witnesses examined have displayed an implausible lack of recollection of key conversations and documents, even when they authored or received such document and it was placed before them. This lack of recollection often related to events and documents that one would be unlikely to forget. The credibility of these witnesses is consequently suspect."

Strangely enough, the financial press did not seem to realize right away the import and seriousness of Spitzer's court order. That there was actually only moderate commotion on the day—a simple mention in the press of a possible fine—might have been due to the other thing that was happening that day. David Duncan, who had been heading the Andersen team at Enron, agreed to plead guilty to obstruction of justice and serve as a government witness. This caught the media's attention, and deservedly so.

Thus it came as a shock to many when, on the following day, the New York State Attorney General's office announced that it was expanding its probe of possible conflicts of interest among Wall Street analysts to Goldman Sachs Group, Crédit Suisse First Boston (CSFB), Morgan Stanley, Lehman Brothers Holdings, the UBS PaineWebber unit of UBS AG, the Salomon Smith Barney unit of Citigroup, Lazard Freres, and Bear Sterns & Co.

That the next move in Spitzer's strategy involved CSFB came as no surprise to a gleeful Thomas Brown, a former research analyst at Donaldson, Lufkin & Jenrette Securities, acquired by CSFB in 2000. Immediately after the court order against Merrill Lynch was issued, Brown said in a statement that he had recently spoken with Mr. Spitzer about his being fired by DLJ in March 1998 because he had refused to issue positive research reports on companies that were current or prospective investment banking clients. In Brown's eye, the attorney general's investigation "should be fabulous news to anyone interested in restoring ethics to Wall Street equity research. . . . It must be terrible news to my former associates at Donaldson, Lufkin & Jenrette, now part of CSFB."

"I would be shocked," Brown added, "if DLJ and CSFB [are] not the target of this investigation, because there's too much good stuff there."[4]

No Chinese Wall Here

What Mr. Spitzer had uncovered was exactly how little independence the research team at Merrill Lynch had been granted by the investment bank. In theory, the separation between these two business units is ensured by a so-called Chinese wall—an "internal relationship barrier by which investment bankers are prevented from sharing with other firm employees material, non-public information received by the bankers from their publicly-traded company clients."

However, when asked about how his activity for the firm should be broken down, Merrill Lynch's "pop star" analyst Henry Blodget gave a surprising answer: "85 percent banking, 15 percent research." In November 2000, Merrill Lynch's Internet research team was asked to report on its contributions to investment banking during the year. Blodget replied that "(a) his group had been involved in over 52 completed or potential investment banking transactions; (b) the completed transactions had earned $115 million for the firm; and (c) more transactions would have been completed had not the 'market window for most Internet companies closed in June.'"

So much for the Chinese wall. And the problem was not that the investment bankers were sharing the information they were privy to with analysts but that the functions of "investment banker" and "research analyst" were more or less the same thing. They were often carried out by the same person.

Equally disturbing were the internal e-mails that were quoted in the court order. They showed that although the analysts often performed genuine appraisals of stock, they routinely saw their conclusions overruled by business considerations. A sell recommendation went into the corporate hopper and somehow came out a buy recommendation. The massaging of the information passed to investors was so blatant and offensive that one researcher exploded in frustration, writing in one e-mail that she did not "want to be a whore for . . . management." She added, "We are losing people money and I don't like it. John and Mary Smith are losing their retirement because we don't want Todd [Tappin, GoTo's CFO] to be mad at us."

At one point, Blodget himself got so exasperated that he threatened his superiors at Merrill Lynch that from then on he would release honest recommendations, whatever the pecuniary consequences: "The more I read of these," he stated, "the less willing I am to cut companies any slack, regardless of predictable temper-tantrums, threats, and/or relationship damage that are likely to follow. . . . If there are no new e-mails forthcoming from Andy [Melnick] on how the instructions below should be applied to sensitive banking clients/relations, we are going to just start calling the stocks (stocks, not companies) . . . like we see them, no matter what the ancillary business consequences are."

What are the underlying economics? Simple. Investment banks can make considerable amounts in fees from companies for which they underwrite stock and debt instruments. In Enron's case, according to First Call/Thomson Financial, the figure amounted to $323 million since 1986. Goldman Sachs, for example, earned $69 million of these fees; CSFB, $64 million; and Salomon Smith Barney, $61 million.[5] And note how evenly these fees were spread around!

One Conclusion, a Different Recommendation

The objectionable practices at Merrill Lynch were many and varied. Most notably, analysts would assign a firm a higher rating than it merited according to the conclusions they had reached in their research and the opinions they were expressing in conversations and e-mails. In one table in the court-order document, companies are mentioned with their ratings as published by Merrill Lynch's Internet research team (the scale is 1 for a strong buy, 5 for a sell) and comments from e-mail correspondence by analysts. It reads like this: 2–1—"such a piece of crap"; 1–1—"powder keg"; 1–1—"piece of junk"; etc. In other words, strong accumulate-buy recommendations for crap, junk, and powder kegs.

Another objectionable practice consisted of assigning a stock a rating and then never going back to that stock when it began to sink. This happened in two different ways: either by not modifying the rating while the stock price was plummeting or by ceasing coverage without any further explanation. About a mobile Internet access company called InfoSpace (to which I will return later), the court order reports, "Merrill Lynch initiated coverage of InfoSpace in December 1999 with a rating of 2–1 (accumulate-buy) and a price objective of $160. The stock then traded at $152.50. Shortly thereafter, Merrill Lynch upgraded the rating to 1–1. As of March 2, 2000, the price had reached $261, but thereafter the stock dropped steadily. Yet Merrill Lynch's Internet group maintained a 1–1 rating on the stock to December 10, 2000, when the price was $13.69. No sell rating was ever issued."

The office of New York's attorney general stressed that "as a matter of undisclosed, internal policy, no 'reduce' or 'sell' recommendations were issued, thereby converting a published five-point rating scale into a de facto three-point system. . . . Although Merrill Lynch's published rating system provided for 4s (reduce) and 5s (sell), the Internet group never used 4s or 5s."

If you never use the sell end of your spectrum, do you still have a spectrum? I would argue not.

Negotiating Recommendations with Company Representatives

Another objectionable practice was that of negotiating ratings with representatives of the company being appraised, often at the senior-management level. This, incidentally, was in direct and blatant violation of Merrill

Lynch's corporate policies. In one case, the chief executive officer (CEO) of a company "consented" to the downgrading of a recommendation because its immediate competitor would be downgraded simultaneously. This meant, in effect, that not one but *two* recommendations were being directly affected by the CEO of an "evaluated" firm.

These might be categorized as mortal sins; there also were venial sins. For example, the investment bankers encouraged analysts to boost a stock price to a level where—following in-house policy—research was allowed to be initiated, which typically was a minimum of $10 a share. Why? Because in exchange for investment banking work, the bankers had promised their clients that they would receive research coverage. Where's the harm in this? Well, it is in the initial ballooning of the price up to an undeserved level—something north of $10—and then telling investors to buy the inflated goods.

Three Sad Stories

As a cautionary tale, let me relate the sad stories of Henry Blodget at Merrill Lynch, Jack B. Grubman at Salomon Smith Barney, and Chung Wu at PaineWebber. The incident that kicked off Attorney General Spitzer's investigation of Merrill Lynch in the first place was an arbitration claim filed with the NYSE in March 2001. At that time, a Merrill Lynch investor claimed to have lost $500,000 when following Blodget's advice about Info-Space—the mobile Internet company mentioned earlier.[6] Merrill Lynch's ace broker had maintained the stock's 1–1 rating while the stock price was plummeting—all the way from $261 to $13.69.

The court order documented the context of that highly visible case in these terms:

> Merrill Lynch maintained a list of its highest recommended stocks, selected from all of the stocks Merrill Lynch covered—not just Internet stocks. To be selected for this list (the "Favored 15"), to which retail brokers and the public had access, a stock had to have a 1–1 rating. . . . Info-Space was on the "Favored 15" list from at least August 2000 until December 5, 2000, even though Blodget had acknowledged as early as July 2000 that the stock was a "powder keg" and that "many institutions" had raised "bad smell comments" about it, and in October had referred to it as a "piece of junk." . . . Oddly enough, Blodget was unaware that the

stock he had been covering for months carried the imprimatur of the "Favored 15." . . . When a broker eventually complained on October 20, 2000, about Blodget's price objective and rating of the stock, Blodget contacted a fellow analyst: "Can we please reset this stupid price target and rip this piece of junk off whatever list it's on. If you have to downgrade it, downgrade it." . . . InfoSpace however, was not removed from the "Favored 15" until December 5, 2000 . . . and was not downgraded until December 11, 2000.[7]

What had happened to the Merrill Lynch investor was that he had purchased InfoSpace shares for prices between $122 and $135. When a few months later the stock dropped to $60, he expressed to his broker his desire to sell his shares. At that point, his broker said to him, "No, stay in it because Blodget will issue a research report and the stock will go up based on that." Notwithstanding Blodget releasing his report in July, the stock went on falling. The investor finally sold his stock in December with the price down to $11 a share. Later on he found out that Merrill Lynch had been hired by InfoSpace to advise it on a deal with a gain for Merrill Lynch worth $17 million.[8]

In July 2001, Merrill Lynch settled the disagreement by paying the investor $400,000. At the time, a spokesman for Merrill Lynch declared that the "matter was resolved to avoid the expense and distraction of protracted litigation."

What happened at Salomon Smith Barney (Citigroup) in the case of Jack B. Grubman was different—involving as it did a dispute within the same firm between two brokers and one of its prominent analysts—but no less disheartening. Grubman, Salomon's star telecommunications analyst, was sued by two former brokers for having persisted in recommending WorldCom stock while its price was plummeting, leading to substantial losses in their customers' portfolios. Philip L. Spartis, one of the plaintiffs, was head of the WorldCom stock-option plan for Salomon; he had joined the firm in 1984 and had held WorldCom's account for Salomon since 1997. Spartis was helped in his task by Amy Jean Elias, a former insurance agent. Both were terminated by Salomon on March 1 for having abandoned their job.

In the lawsuit they initiated against Salomon, they claimed that Grubman's upbeat rating of WorldCom stock had persuaded them to recommend to their clients that they hold onto their shares while the stock price was falling. They maintained that their accounts had suffered mainly because of their own firm's flawed research.

Grubman is known to have continued recommending stock that had lost over 90 percent of its value. Why? Well, you cannot ignore the fact that over the years WorldCom had been a treasured client for Salomon in its investment banking activity. Since 1997, in fact, Salomon managed or comanaged all 16 offerings of public debt by WorldCom. Those deals, which raised $25 billion for the telecommunications giant, resulted in $75 million in fees for Salomon.

In the days that followed Spitzer's court order, Jacob Zamansky, the lawyer who had successfully sued Blodget, filed a similar suit against Grubman. This time the case involved a CBS video editor who had filed for personal bankruptcy after having lost about $455,000 in his investment portfolio. Zamansky was seeking $10 million in redress for his client.

I do not intend to pass judgment on the individuals in these two cases, who have been or will be judged in other venues. What seems clear and consistent across these two very different situations is that individuals making recommendations to investors are under intense pressures—at least some of which are not exerted in ways that help the investor. In fact, the investor is very likely to get hurt under circumstances like these.

The demise of Enron brought to light an even more extreme case of pressure being applied. In this case, as the *New York Times* reported, the pressure was applied in a different direction:

> The broker, Chung Wu, of PaineWebber's Houston office, sent a message to clients early on Aug. 21 [2001] warning that Enron's "financial situation is deteriorating" and that they should "take some money off the table." That afternoon, an Enron executive in charge of its stock option program sent a stern message to PaineWebber executives, including the Houston branch office manager. "Please handle this situation," the newly released message stated. "This is extremely disturbing to me." PaineWebber fired Mr. Wu less than three hours later. That evening, the firm retracted Mr. Wu's assessment of Enron's stock—then about $36—by sending his clients an optimistic report that Enron was "likely heading higher than lower from here on out." A few months later, the stock was worthless, and the company was in bankruptcy court.[9]

Analysts report that companies routinely stop communicating with them if they issue a sell recommendation. What can we conclude from all this? Well, to put it bluntly, we have to conclude that most research analysts are considered to be salespersons for the investment banking activity of their firm. If and when they depart from that role, they are punished, cut adrift, or both.

So How Good *Are* Analysts?

The editorials and commentaries in the press in the days following the release of Attorney General Spitzer's court order were mainly supportive of his action. The *New York Times* and *Washington Post* commentators, in particular, were enthusiastic. An article in the *Times* by Patrick McGeehan quoted David Pottruck, co-chief executive of Charles Schwab, as saying, "It's a little disheartening to see companies tout the depths of their wisdom and then put out research that is so incredibly flawed. This doesn't just hurt a company, it hurts our industry. No company, no matter what their business model, is immune from the dissatisfaction, mistrust and disappointment investors are feeling. We see it as investors' being angry." McGeehan added: "That rage has not yet registered with everyone on Wall Street."[10]

Quite true. In particular, it had not registered with the *Wall Street Journal*, the editorial pages of which are conservative (to put it mildly). The opinion pages of the April 12, 2002, edition included a two-barreled onslaught against Spitzer. One opinion piece, signed by James K. Glassman (associated with the equally conservative American Enterprise Institute), took the interesting tack that brokerage houses perform "strong analysis" only reluctantly. "New regulations," Glassman argued, "will inevitably load new costs onto firms and diminish their resources—not to mention their desire—to provide clients with strong analysis." Thus, insisting that firms rebuild their Chinese walls—or even follow their own internal guidelines to avoid conflicts of interest—was likely to *hurt* investors.

Later on in the same piece, Glassman reported the results of a study supporting the view that over the previous 10 years, analysts had done a remarkable job separating the winners from the losers on Wall Street:

> The proof is not in the anecdotes, but in the broad results. Fortunately, there's a study that looks at such results. A year ago, a group of four California economists—Brad Barber, Reuven Lehavy, Maureen McNichols and Brett Trueman—published in the peer-reviewed *Journal of Finance* the most extensive research on record of the performance of stock analysts. It showed that analysts do an exceptionally good job picking winners. The researchers examined "over 360,000 recommendations from 269 brokerage houses and 4340 analysts" between 1985 and 1996, classifying consensus rankings on individual stocks into five categories. They found that the highest-rated stocks produced average annual returns of 18.8 percent, while the lowest-rated returned just 5.8 percent. The market as a whole over this period returned an average of 14.5 percent. Mr. Barber

and his colleagues then controlled for "market risk, size, book-to-market, and price momentum effects" and concluded that a portfolio composed of "the most highly recommended stocks provides an average annual abnormal gross return of 4.13 percent, whereas a portfolio of the least favorably recommended ones yields an average annual abnormal return of negative 4.91 percent." In other words, an investor who bought the top-rated stocks and shorted the lowest-rated stocks would beat the market by about 9 percentage points a year. This performance can only be called astonishing.[11]

Unfortunately for Glassman's argument, the authors of the study he was quoting had updated it in 2000 and had come up with a notably different story. A press release from the Haas School of Business at the University of California at Berkeley—where two of the researchers were based—was entitled "Study Sheds Light on Value of Analysts' Stock Recommendations, Finds That 2000 Was Disaster."

Disaster? You be the judge. The researchers concluded that "the most highly recommended stocks in 2000 returned 31.2 percent less than the market, on average, while the least favorably recommended stocks gained almost 49 percent more than the market." As one of the authors of the report, Maureen McNichols, elaborated, "While we can't say that the poor 2000 showing is necessarily a result of increased analyst involvement in investment banking, our findings should certainly add to the current debate over the usefulness of analysts' stock recommendations to investors."

So what should we take away from this sequence of two studies? One possible conclusion—which I endorse—is that stock pickers tend to do great when the market is booming and most stocks are headed upward (for example, 1985–1996). They tend to do far less well when market conditions are rougher. This is not quite so obvious as it may sound and deserves more study—some of which might focus on Alan Greenspan's theory of optimism among analysts. Meanwhile, we investors need to note this pattern and apply appropriate doses of skepticism to what our analysts tell us.

Finding Solid Research

Or we can go find a new analyst. If you think about it, the problem with your current analyst—if you have one and if there *is* a problem in your case—is that he or she is paid by an entity (the brokerage house) that is beholden to someone else (the rated companies). One way to change this formula is to pay the analyst yourself and make sure that he or she is "beholden" only to you (and your fellow investors).

Recent years have seen a renaissance of independent equity research. Access to it is not necessarily expensive: The reports these firms offer on individual companies are billed in the $10 to $300 range. A report typically includes an examination of the stock price and the company's earnings targets. The company's structure is also analyzed, in terms of its appropriateness to the success of its business.

How do you assess the assessors? Start at their Web sites. They show a number of these independent operators and also assess each of these firms' hypothetical portfolio.[12]

Some of the independents had a good track record when assessing Enron. "Computrade Systems, Inc., and Alpha Equity Research, Inc., urged investors to sell Enron [in the spring of 2001]," reported the *Washington Post*, "when its shares still hovered in the $50 to $60 range, well below their $90 high but miles above the pennies they trade for [in April 2002]. Callard Asset Management told investors to sell on Aug. 14, the day the stock closed at $42.11 and one day before Goldman Sachs said buy."

Or, if you can satisfy yourself with ratings that derive simply from number crunching with no (or little) human filtering, try StockScouter at MSN Money. I do not particularly like to confess this, but in my experience, robots—with no deep issues related to emotion or compensation—can be more reliable than humans. Try *moneycentral.msn.com/investor/srs/srs-main.asp*.

So Where Does This Leave Us?

I mentioned earlier that two people went after Attorney General Spitzer in the April 12, 2002, edition of the *Wall Street Journal* after the court order resulting from Spitzer's investigation was issued. The second individual remains nameless because he or she was writing in an unsigned editorial. The editorial was entitled, "Buying and Selling," and focused on the specifics of Henry Blodget's case (described earlier).

Unlike Glassman's column, which dealt with the question of analysts' *talent*, the editorial addressed the issue of analysts' *truthfulness*. If I read it right, the editorialist more or less concludes that truthfulness is unimportant. On the subject of Blodget's disingenuousness—my word choice, and a kind one—the writer commented, "Big surprise."

Well, it *was* a surprise for many observers, including many investors who had placed their trust in Blodget and others like him. Brokerage houses offer their clients a double service—trading securities on their behalf and advising them in the process. New York's General Business Law, Section 352 (1), defines fraud as, among other things, "any device, scheme or artifice to defraud or obtain money by means of any false pretense, representation or promise. . . ." When a brokerage house defrauds its clients, that *is* a big surprise—or should be.

Comments such as the *Wall Street Journal*'s "Big surprise" have the same general odor as Enron's public utterances "before the fall." They are a mixture of arrogance, smugness, and condescension. The offending party offends, the public reacts with indignation, and the business community shrugs its shoulders: "We all knew that!" My own sense is that although the *Wall Street Journal*'s editorial writers may not yet recognize it, we have collectively crossed an ethical Rubicon. When enough individual investors have enough money in the game—a state we are in today despite a large-scale flight from the markets—a new ethical norm comes into play. There is no doubt in my mind that business—and business ethics—will have to change.

Too optimistic? Maybe. However, in May 2002, Merrill Lynch & Co. settled the charges resulting from the State of New York's findings that it had misled investors with its research. It agreed to pay $100 million to New York and several other states. According to the agreement, analysts would no longer be paid directly from investment banking revenues. In addition, Merrill Lynch would create a committee to monitor analysts' research and recommendations, and it also would monitor electronic communications between investment banking and research analysts.

No, it is not clear that Merrill Lynch got the point entirely. In its statement, the firm expressed its regret that "there were instances in which certain of our Internet sector research analysts expressed views that at certain points may have appeared inconsistent with Merrill Lynch's published recommendations." This is at least a little bit backwards, the way I read it. However, I still hold out hope that Merrill Lynch and its industry colleagues—under threat of $100 million judgments—will eventually get the horse before the cart.

LESSONS FOR THE INVESTOR

Who is working for whom? At least until the Enron wake-up call, research analysts with investment banks were essentially salespersons for the bank.

Two things can go wrong with the analysis. Your analyst may or may not get it right. Even if he or she gets it right, the analysis may not make it past interested parties elsewhere at the brokerage house. (This latter problem may be on the wane in light of some houses' highly publicized woes.)

Analysts tend to be good in good times and bad in bad times. It is like the old joke about banks: They only lend you money when you don't need it. When times get rough, you should get more skeptical about optimistic analyses. They are probably wrong.

Consider an independent. Independent researchers can be found through the following Web sites:

www.investars.com

www.thomsonfn.com

www.starmine.com

www.jaywalkinc.com

We are going to win ultimately. I believe that the widespread involvement of basically decent people in the publicly regulated markets eventually will force an improvement in ethical standards within those markets and in the various industries that surround them.

The Perils of Cliffs

Once upon a time, a company named Enron was a utility of sorts. It owned pipelines, and fuels flowed through them. It thought of itself as a utility and more or less behaved like one.

Then, in August 1999, Enron started trading contracts on future delivery of energy. A psychological shift accompanied the strategic shift. Enron began thinking of itself as a *financial* company. This was gratifying because it meant the company had moved into the fast lane—where the drama, excitement, and money were. Goodbye to the plodding old days of being a regulated utility; hello to the "Big Time."

One of the most successful divisions of Enron, it turns out, was a hedge fund called ECT Investments. "The hedge fund, the brainchild of Enron's former chief executive officer, Jeffrey Skilling, did quite well," according to a report in the *Wall Street Journal*, "averaging annual returns of more than 20 percent after it was launched in 1996. In that period, the Dow Jones Industrial Average had returns of 11 percent. The hedge fund's gains amounted to as much as 8 percent of Enron's overall earnings in recent years. . . ."[1]

However, the transformation to a financial company also meant that Enron became susceptible to all the fragilities to which financial companies are vulnerable. One of the most pernicious of these is the *confidence factor:* How much confidence do your clients and shareholders have in you today? How much will they have tomorrow? Absent a Three Mile Island–type disaster, the confidence factor does not vary much for a utility. However, it bounces all over the place for a high-flying financial company, especially if the main financial product that the company is trading in is its own stock.

The business depended in large part on the stock being constantly on the rise—or at least not losing value. The reason was leverage, which has the unpleasant capacity to go from positive to negative overnight. Enron was perched on the edge of what Standard & Poor's calls a "credit cliff," meaning that any drop in its credit rating would materialize in a deterioration of its debt, leading in no time to a further downgrading. Although Enron's financial health was an exercise in brinkmanship, what actually brought it down in just over 6 weeks was little more than a glitch, which on its own merits should have been survivable. The rest, as its former chief executive officer (CEO) would say, was only a "run on the bank."

Thus the point of this chapter is to help you, the investor, understand and recognize a credit cliff, as well as its equally daunting sibling, a rating cliff. I am confident that when you spot a company living on these cliffs, you will decide to stay away.

Enron and the Rating Agencies

On December 12, 2001, 10 days after Enron's official filing for Chapter 11 protection, Standard & Poor's issued on its Web-based and e-mail-driven *RatingsDirect* a commentary entitled, "Playing Out the Credit Cliff Dynamics," written by Solomon B. Samson. During that 10-day period, rating agencies, Moody's Investors Service in particular, had been accused of precipitating Enron's downfall. The press reported that the Houston energy-trading corporation had been drawn into a downward spiral once Moody's and Standard & Poor's had downgraded its debt.

On Friday, October 26, Enron CEO Kenneth Lay put in an urgent call to Secretary of Commerce Donald L. Evans. Evans was in St. Louis for the day and was not able to return Lay's call until the following Monday, October 29. According to James Dyke, a spokesperson for Evans, Lay "indicated that he would welcome any support the secretary thought appropriate" in dealing with the major rating agencies—and with Moody's Investors Service in particular, which had expressed its intention to downgrade Enron's credit rating.[2]

On November 28, 2001, Enron's smaller rival Dynegy, Inc.—in talks since October about a possible acquisition of Enron—canceled any further discussions, claiming in a bitter statement that the Houston energy-trading firm had misrepresented its own financial circumstances. The major credit rating agencies immediately downgraded Enron's bonds to "junk" status (we will see why below, in Samson's analysis). Four days later, on December 2, 2001, Enron filed for Chapter 11 status under the federal bankruptcy code.

Living on the Cliff Edge

The following month, in another commentary—this time signed by Clifford M. Griep, the rating agency's chief credit officer—Standard & Poor's announced a change in its rating policy. The reason, Standard & Poor's explained, was that in certain (unnamed) corporations, the "credit cliff" previously spotlighted by Solomon B. Samson was now materializing as a "rating cliff."

Griep's paper was entitled, "Credit Policy Update: Changes to Ratings Process Address Economic Conditions and Market Needs." This somewhat opaque title was clarified in the press release accompanying Griep's analysis: "S&P Comments on Changes to Credit Ratings Process, Says 'Triggers' Should Be Made Public."

To understand this significant step, we need to dig into Samson's December 2001 commentary. In that commentary, using Enron as his main example, Samson had explained that certain companies have their finance structured in such a way that embedded "triggers" can lead the credit rating of the company to suddenly plunge by several notches rather than degrade gracefully under financial pressure.

The introductory paragraphs in Samson's study had a somewhat defensive tone, as if Samson (and his company) were responding to some reproaches made in the preceding days about what some saw as a proactive role played by the rating agencies in precipitating Enron's demise. Samson wrote: "The credit cliff dynamic figured prominently in several recent severe credit downgrades—including the California utilities (PJ: Pacific Gas & Electric and Southern California Edison) and Enron Corp. Observers accustomed to gradual changes in credit quality questioned the wisdom of the original ratings, but in fact, it was merely the credit cliff dimension that played out."

Illustrations involving Enron figured prominently in Samson's analysis. Of the eight types of business configurations embedding credit cliffs,

Enron was mentioned in three: "Event-Specific Dependencies," "Confidence-Sensitive Entities," and "Rating Trigger Situations."

Moreover, as I will show, two other types of credit cliffs—"Capital-Intensive Entities" and "Structured Finance"—clearly applied to Enron as well.

Ratings and Why They Matter

To understand the concept of *credit* or *rating cliff*, it is important to grasp the role that rating agencies play in the economy and how their downgrading of Enron's debt affected the company in the days immediately preceding its Chapter 11 filing. A good place to start is with the credit of individual consumers.

Most people understand what a credit report is and how the information contained in it affects an individual's access to credit. As long as you are a conscientious borrower—meaning mainly that you pay a reasonable amount against your debt each month before the deadline—further credit will be extended to you on favorable terms. If you are not so conscientious, future credit will be complicated. You may be told that you can only get it at a higher rate, or you may be told you cannot get it at all.

Ever wondered who came up with the idea of working out these individual credit ratings? The answer is Fair, Isaac & Company, headquartered in San Rafael, California. Fair, Isaac has designed a complex method for assessing a person's financial history, which is summarized in something called a "FICO score," with values theoretically between 0 and 900 and effectively between 500 and 800.

This may sound somewhat remote to the average borrower, but this is absolutely not the case. Your personal FICO score—which already exists unless you have been living in a cave—can have an enormous impact on your financial life. For example, using figures borrowed from a *Los Angeles Times* article of March 2002, the same fixed 30-year mortgage could be obtained at a rate of 6.556 percent by a borrower with a FICO score in the 720 to 850 range, at a rate of 8.508 percent for a borrower in the 620 to 675 range, and at a rate of 11.164 percent for a borrower in the 500 to 560 range.[3] In other words, you will pay twice the interest if you have a shoddy FICO score.

This might seem to be a dirty trick to pay on the less affluent among us—who, after all, are more likely to miss some scheduled payments—but in fact, it objectively reflects the credit risk that lenders incur when lending to a "bad risk" consumer. Thus the pricing of debt includes what might be called *risk logic:* To the price paid by the less creditworthy for borrowing is added a premium that compensates for the additional risk involved. This is the equivalent of an insurance premium for the lender, offsetting the risk that the borrower will not be able to meet the terms of the outstanding debt.

Some advocates for the less affluent have argued that this is a vicious circle. Poor people have to borrow to get access to necessities—for example, housing, insurance, and transportation—for which rich people can pay cash. As a result of being compelled to pay an interest rate differentially higher than what the rich would pay, poor people are pretty likely to *stay* poor. In recognition of this self-fulfilling prophecy, the states of Washington, Utah, and Idaho recently have passed laws prohibiting insurers from using credit scores when setting rates for home and automobile insurance. Similar legislation restricting the use of credit scoring in one way or another is already on the books in more than 20 other states.

This brief sideways look at credit on the personal level helps set up the discussion of corporate credit that follows.

Rating Agencies and Corporate Credit Ratings

Standard & Poor's, Moody's Investors Service, and Fitch Ratings are the three "nationally recognized statistical ratings organizations," a label assigned by the Securities and Exchange Commission (SEC) that authorizes them (and *only* them) to come up with certain kinds of bond ratings.

Rating agencies deal with corporations in roughly the same way that credit-scoring companies do with consumers: They assess their creditworthiness and advise prospective lenders about the default risk that a corporation presents in its debt. They ask fairly predictable questions: What is the proportion of debt compared with revenue? How good has the company been in making the repayments associated with its debt?

By grading corporations, the rating agencies determine how much those companies will have to pay to gain access to additional credit on the markets. The grading system typically starts with AAA (pronounced "triple A") as it highest rating, typically applied to the debt instruments (bonds, bills, and notes) issued by the most trustworthy of governments. It typically drifts all the way down to D, the lowest grade, assigned to highly speculative "junk bonds" and similar products.

Just as in the case of consumer debt, the rating that is assigned to a particular company determines how much of an added premium will be built into loans to that company, compensating for the risk of default that the company presents. Thus, to give a simple-minded example, financial players will know that they can charge a "risk free" AAA counterparty 6 percent for a loan but that they need to charge a B counterparty 7.2 percent. Again, the 1.2 percent difference in interest rate reflects the increased default risk of a B rating compared with a rating of AAA and is a kind of insurance premium against the added risk. When you buy a junk bond, you get a relatively high return—a premium—for putting your money behind a venture with a relatively low rating.

Standard & Poor's assigns the AAA rating to government agencies (on the assumption that the federal government will never allow itself to default on its debt) through AA, A, BBB, BB, B, and so on down to D. "Junk" starts in the low Bs, and this is precisely the status that Standard & Poor's and Moody's assigned Enron in the aftermath of Dynegy canceling its prospective agreement to purchase the Enron corporation.

Indeed—as Standard & Poor's emphasized in its press releases following Enron's collapse—at no point had Standard & Poor's assigned Enron particularly high marks. In a news release dated December 6, 2001, Standard & Poor's, under the pen of Tanya Azarchs, reminded the public that "as a 'triple-B' category credit in a market that prefers very high credit, Enron frequently had to put up collateral to enter into trades with its counterparties, which were generally commercial and investment banks, utilities and other power companies."[4]

Thus corporate credit ratings are a big deal. Money is the lifeblood of business. By putting a price on money, the rating agencies have a lot to say about the cost of doing business: A low rating means hefty penalties for accessing the markets in search for new capital, and a high rating means highly favorable conditions.

Obvious, so far? What you may not know is that none of this is quite as hands off as you might expect. Provisions have been made that, within limits, allow companies to *negotiate* their grade with the rating agencies. They can provide the agencies with detailed nonpublic financial information—inaccessible to other analysts because of securities regulations—in an attempt to obtain either an initial assessment of their creditworthiness or an upgrading of their existing rating.[5]

This is just more evidence that the three rating agencies have enormous power over the fate of individual companies, especially those in less than stellar financial health. This amount of power residing in the hands of three private entities is an anomaly in the financial landscape, and—not surprisingly—there have been calls to see their number increased. For instance, in March 2002, Senator Jim Bunning (Republican, Kentucky), himself a former investment broker, said that we "obviously need more credit-rating agencies."

Others have drawn legislators' attention to the need for increased accountability on the part of entities with such far-ranging influence on the operation of the financial markets. As Senator Joseph I. Lieberman (Democrat, Connecticut), chairman of the Senate Governmental Affairs Committee, declared after a March 2002 hearing about the role played by the rating agencies in the Enron collapse, "They see themselves as private, but they're playing at least a quasi-governmental role in this unusual system that has built up where the laws give them the authority to decide where literally trillions of dollars can be invested or borrowed, depending whether they say this company is O.K. or not. And we hold them to no accountability. Congress ought to consider such legislation."

And I am sure that Congress will do so. On balance, though, I would argue that the rating agencies perform a crucial function, and they perform it well. One measure of this performance is that throughout the entire seamy unraveling of Enron and similar messes, the rating agencies have only been criticized for having played their rule thoroughly and consistently.

If you are going to get criticized, this is a good kind of criticism to get.

Back to the Cliffs

The principle underlying the notion of a credit cliff is what is called in mathematics a *nonlinearity*. A linear process is one in which a small change in the cause produces a small change in the effect and a large change in the cause leads to a large change in the effect. A car's accelerator and brakes, for example, are designed to govern linear processes. You want *gradual* in both cases.

A nonlinear process has *thresholds,* or jumping-off points, whereby a small change can induce considerable consequences or, conversely, a modification of wide amplitude in the cause only induces a small change in the effect. Nonlinear processes involve big leaps—and associated consequences—where you might not expect them. Nonlinearities can be associated with either good things or bad things. Among the bad things are such phenomena as vicious circles, chain reactions, and domino effects.

Looking to the world of options, for example, if the strike price of a call is $83, the small price change from $82.99 to $83.01 takes the option from "out of the money" to "in the money." Meanwhile, the much larger price movement from $25 to $82 does not make any difference: The option is "underwater" and stays there until that seemingly insignificant threshold at around $83 is reached.

Alternatively, looking to the physical world, if you pull on both ends of a rubber band, it gets longer and thinner. Within some limits, the process remains linear: An additional slight pull produces a limited thinning and expansion. There is an upper limit to the tension, however, above which the band snaps. It is the proverbial "straw that breaks the camel's back." The first 10,000 straws are bearable; the 10,001st is unbearable.

Perhaps it is now easier to see why, in the eyes of the rating agencies, a credit cliff translates pretty quickly into a rating cliff. The presence of a credit cliff means that the given company's credit risk is nonlinear. When pushed over an edge, the credit risk the company represents will amplify brutally, and the rating agencies may translate this sharp fall into a downgrade of more than one notch, depending on the translation system from credit risk into rating grade. The accident-proneness is even more dramatic if the company has been so foolhardy as to make its financial soundness hinge on a particular credit rating. Such was the case with Enron.

Nonlinearities can manifest themselves in the workings of a corporation, especially one that, like Enron, has enormous complexity woven in its fabric. On November 8, 2001, the day when Enron released its restatements, the *Houston Chronicle* cited a prescient analysis of the corporation's circumstances by Jeff Dietert of Houston-based Simmons & Co. International. "'If Enron doesn't move to calm investor fears, they could become a self-fulfilling prophecy,' . . . [Dietert] wrote in a research report. The vicious cycle potentially goes like this, he said: 'Fears drive down the stock, the lower prices force credit agencies to consider downgrades, potentially lower credit ratings force trading partners to reduce business with Enron, and Enron's ability to generate earnings and cash flow suffers.'"[6] This is an apt description of the rating cliff off of which Enron was soon to fall.

Samson's Cliffs

Earlier I mentioned that Standard & Poor's Solomon Samson produced an analysis spotlighting eight types of business configurations embedding credit cliffs, several of which Enron embodied. Let's look at several of these categories.

In his first category, "Event-Specific Dependencies," Samson discusses companies whose good health depends on the support of a stronger parent. "The credit rating for a weak company," he wrote, "ordinarily takes into account expected support of a stronger parent company—or parent company-to-be. Such was one of the bases for the 'BBB−' rating of Enron Corp. at the point following its widely disclosed problems: There was a signed agreement to be acquired by Dynegy, plus liquidity infusions from Dynegy and its affiliates to maintain Enron until consummation of the acquisition. When that agreement was renegotiated and ultimately abandoned, Enron's rating dropped to 'B−', 'CC', and 'D' in rapid succession. Even then, the ratings on Enron's Portland General Electric Co. subsidiary were kept at 'BBB+', reflecting continued confidence that its sale to Northwest Natural Gas Co. would still go through. The alternative scenario—getting embroiled in Enron's bankruptcy—obviously represents a serious credit cliff."

In his second category, "Confidence-Sensitive Entities," Samson pointed to companies whose main asset is their good reputation. Such companies are "confidence-sensitive," and—in case of a corporate disaster—the individual investor might be the last informed. "Whereas a manufacturing company can continue to make and market its products even while facing a financial crisis," he pointed out, "that may not be the case for a bank, insurance firm, or trading company. Any problem that erodes confidence in such financial institutions tends to lead to a downward spiral with severe consequences—the colloquial 'run on the bank.' Enron's problems related primarily to the actual and potential loss of trading business, as a result of loss of confidence by its counterparties (in the wake of disclosures of unusual financial and accounting practices). This alone explains the drastic rating consequences—a decline to 'B−' from 'BBB+.'"

"Run on the bank" refers to events that have tended to take place at the outset of the financial disturbances that ultimately tend to bring forth recessions and even depressions. This was before there was a Federal Reserve insuring the mutual guarantee of financial institutions. Clients of a local bank would hear a negative rumor about its financial health and "stampede" the bank in an effort to get their savings out. However, the stampede caused the very event that the rumors (often false) had hinted at. Because some of a bank's assets are almost always locked in relatively illiquid investments and therefore are not immediately available in cash, a stampeded bank can quickly get insolvent and be forced to fold.

"Run on the bank" was the phrase that Jeffrey Skilling, Enron's one-time chief executive officer (CEO), used in his testimony before the House Energy and Commerce Subcommittee on February 7, 2002: "a classic run on the bank," Skilling said. He returned to this interpretation of what precipitated Enron's downfall in his testimony before the Senate Consumers Affairs Subcommittee on February 26: "In the 1880s when there was a run on the bank, it was the bank that went under. What's happening now is that the banks can pull their money out of a company that is threatened. And if somebody . . . claim[s] [there is] an accounting fraud, it's tantamount . . . in the business world . . . to walking into a crowded theater and screaming 'Fire!'—everybody runs for the exits. When they set up the Federal Reserve Board . . . and deposit insurance [the intent] was to try to [prevent] runs on the bank. . . . We have it now automatically built into the contracts, material adverse change clauses, which means that if anything happens to the borrower, the bank can come in and pull their money back."

The following day, on February 27, Federal Reserve Chairman Alan Greenspan addressed the same issue of "confidence sensitivity" in his testimony before the House Committee on Financial Services. "As the recent events surrounding Enron have highlighted," Greenspan said, "a firm is inherently fragile if its value added emanates more from conceptual as distinct from physical assets. A physical asset, whether an office building or an automotive assembly plant, has the capability of producing goods even if the reputation of the managers of such facilities falls under a cloud. The rapidity of Enron's decline is an effective illustration of the vulnerability of a firm whose market value largely rests on capitalized reputation. The physical assets of such a firm comprise a small proportion of its asset base. Trust and reputation can vanish overnight. A factory cannot."[7]

In other words, companies with factories are that much less likely to make their way toward credit or ratings cliffs. Companies that rely on what Greenspan called a "capitalized reputation" are far more likely to wind up there.

Samson's third category of business configurations that embed credit cliffs was the "Rating Trigger Situation," which consists of companies that have linked their future fate to a particular level of credit rating. If and when their credit rating gets downgraded below that level by the rating agencies, this triggers a host of financial consequences. These, in turn, may lead the rating agencies to further downgrade the company's creditworthiness.

Samson wrote: "Particularly insidious are situations where the company has tied its fate to maintaining a certain rating. It is one thing for a company to agree to pay a higher rate of interest on certain debt issues, if its rating were to go down; this normally would not have an immediate dramatic impact. It is another thing to have credit 'puts' that require the company to retire large chunks of its financing or posting of new collateral against trading positions in the event of a downgrade. These can easily precipitate a liquidity crisis—and even default—as the result of just a single-notch downgrade. Also, as a result, any proposed downgrade would be followed quickly with additional rating changes, or it would have to be larger in the first place—or both. . . . And, yes, Enron also had such triggers aplenty—in both its trading contracts and its off-balance-sheet financings."

Six weeks before Enron's filing for Chapter 11 protection, Peter Eavis of TheStreet.com was analyzing one of Enron's rating triggers, which was embedded in the workings of the Whitewing Special Purpose Entity: "Something . . . has to happen before the trust investors can claim their money back. . . . Enron's credit rating must fall below investment grade. That looks to be a long shot, since its rating is currently three notches above subinvestment grade. But it is something the market will watch after Moody's said last week that it was putting Enron on review for a possible downgrade."[8] Eavis gets credit for having spotted one of the ticking time bombs in the shaky Enron structure.

In May 2002, under Solomon B. Samson's signature, Standard & Poor's released an investigation of companies from a "Rating Trigger Situations" perspective. The conclusions of the study were reassuring. Of 1000 large American and European companies investigated, only 23 (2.3 percent) seemed to have a built-in rating cliff, whereby a credit rating downgrade would trigger a further downgrade. Among the corporations exposed to the risk were energy companies Dynegy, Inc., Reliant Resources, Inc., and Williams Companies, Inc., as well as European entertainment and utility giant Vivendi Universal S.A.

Still More Cliffs

An additional type of trigger that Standard & Poor's Solomon did not cover but which proved to have a particularly perverse effect is one mentioned by the *Wall Street Journal* in a March 2002 article. In this scenario, the downgrading of a corporation by one of the rating agencies—as a response to a credit decline—leads another rating agency to downgrade the same company within its own rating system: "Earlier this month, Standard & Poor's lowered its credit rating on Chicago-based GATX Corp., which leases rail cars and aircraft. The reason? The company's access to the commercial-paper market was curtailed, due to a downgrade by rival Moody's, which cited concerns about volatility in the aircraft-leasing business."[9]

The peril associated with such a process cannot be overstated. It is easy to imagine a situation in which each downgrade by a rating agency triggers a further downgrade by either or both of the other two, pushing the company into a downward spiral not of its making, having been fueled by a single initiating event. This kind of effect is called a *positive-feedback loop,* whereby information about a recent change triggers a new change in the same direction. Note that in this context, *positive* is definitely *not* a synonym for *favorable;* in fact, positive-feedback loops tend to end in disaster. A *negative-feedback loop,* by contrast, is one in which information about a particular change triggers a change in the opposite direction, dampening the effect of the prior one. Fortunately, this is by far the more common kind of feedback loop.

The other types of business configurations mentioned by Samson in his "Playing Out the Credit Cliff Dynamics" as tending to embody either credit or rating cliffs were "Government-Support Dependencies," "Capital-Intensive Entities," "Structured Finance," "Insured Ratings," and "Catastrophe Bonds."

"Capital-Intensive Entities" and "Structured Finance" can be considered subsets of the "Confidence-Sensitive" categories. "Government-Support Dependencies" refers to companies that are implicitly supported by the government, meaning that, should they default on payment, there is an expectation that the federal government would move in to prevent insolvency. Of this category, Samson wrote: "Standard & Poor's assesses implicit government support—and regularly relies on such expected support to achieve ratings equal to or close to those of the government itself [meaning 'AAA']. In the rare instance that the government walks away from the entity in question, the result can be devastating. For example, . . . Standard & Poor's concluded that there was only a remote risk that the State of California would allow its troubled utilities to go under; the 'BBB−' rating reflected this conviction. However, when the needed support was not forthcoming—at least not in a timely fashion—the consequences were default for the two major utilities, Southern California Edison and Pacific Gas & Electric."

In the wider context of financial institutions, the "Government-Support Dependencies" (GSDs) credit cliff applies in particular to the "Government-

Sponsored Entities" (GSEs) of the mortgage industry, whose task it is to "promote home ownership." Fannie Mae (the Federal National Mortgage Association—FNMA—founded in 1938) and Freddie Mac (the Federal Home Loan Mortgage Corporation—FHLMC—founded in 1970) were once government entities but are not anymore. Their current status of "Government-Sponsored Entities" represents the rating agencies' view of them as a hybrid of government entity and public corporation. They embody, according to the *Wall Street Journal*, "an odd kind of corporate governance [for] an odd kind of company. Fan and Fred make private profits but with public risk."[10]

At the time they became public corporations, Fannie Mae and Freddie Mac kept their "AAA" rating, meaning that their debt is seen as being backed by a full government guarantee against credit default, just as is the case with Treasury debt instruments. This allows the GSEs to borrow at the lowest floating market rates. The assumption underlying their current "AAA" credit rating is that the government will never permit them to default in light of the decisive role they play in supporting the government's housing policies.

Earlier I mentioned that money is the lifeblood of business and that the availability of money is largely a phenomenon of credit ratings. A great deal of the GSEs' current business success can be assigned to their "AAA" rating. In recent years, their debt has been growing at an astounding annual rate of 25 percent. They have accumulated credit and prepayment risk obligations on that basis, worth—according to Moody's Investors Service—*$2.6 trillion* at the end of 2000.

Good business for them and with lots of salutary impacts on the housing markets. However, it is worth pointing out the dark side of that federal loan guarantee as well. Should either or both of the GSEs ever default, the cost to the taxpayer will be colossal.

Enron as a GSD

Samson's analysis of "Government-Support Dependencies" applied to some extent to Enron. Insofar as its foreign energy projects were concerned, Enron resorted extensively to the protection offered by two programs insuring American businesses against potential losses abroad: the Overseas Private

Investment Corporation (OPIC), which was owed $453 million when Enron filed for Chapter 11 protection, and the Export-Import Bank, which was due $512 million. OPIC and the Export-Import Bank have governmental status, and OPIC has a $4 billion reserve from the user fees U.S. businesses pay for its loans and insurance.

In the 1990s, Enron became OPIC's largest customer, with $3 billion in OPIC loan pledges. Enron's Cuiabá pipeline through Bolivia and Brazil— by most accounts, an environmentally dubious project at best—was only made possible when OPIC decided to back it. (No commercial bank was willing to do so.) In fact, as James V. Grimaldi wrote in the *Washington Post*, Enron and OPIC had developed "a symbiotic relationship. While Enron was seeking billions in OPIC loans and insurance, the company lobbied Congress to save OPIC from extinction."[11] Enron lobbied hard for OPIC at the time of its reauthorization votes in 1997 and 1999. In 1999, for example, Enron's Cuiabá lobbyist "led industry groups working Congress to save OPIC. Lay wrote every member of Congress in April seeking votes for OPIC reauthorization. The effort paid off, and, to celebrate, Enron executives joined trade groups to fete OPIC employees at a posh holiday party."

This was not a case of a company acting out of an urgent sense of public responsibility. In fact, Enron depended on the continued support of OPIC and the Export-Import Bank. Revenues from the Cuiabá pipeline represented nearly 15 percent of Enron's global income at the end of 1999. However, even this picture was not exactly as it seemed. "In an interview with academic researchers nine months ago [May 2001]," Grimaldi wrote, "Jeffrey K. Skilling, who then was chief operating officer, conceded that Enron 'had not earned compensatory rates of return' on investments in overseas power plants, waterworks and pipelines. Skilling said the projects had fueled an 'acrimonious debate' among executives about the wisdom of its heavy foreign investments." [12]

Of course, beginning in 1999 with the failure of Project Summer— detailed in Chapter 7—Enron no longer worried excessively about operating like a traditional utility. It was now a *financial* company. Support from OPIC and the Export-Import Bank was crucial, in the sense that Enron had started concentrating on pumping up the price of its stock, and window-dressing for its financial statements was of paramount importance.

"Insured Ratings," another of Samson's cliff-embodying business configurations, also applied to Enron: " An insured issue of even the weakest credit may be enhanced to the lofty level of the insurer. Accordingly, if it turned out that the insurance were not in force, the rating would drop pre-cipitously. For example, Hollywood Funding No. 5 and No. 6 were rated 'AAA' on the basis of a financial guarantee insurance policy; they dropped to 'CCC–' last February (2001) when the insurer, a subsidiary of AIG, Inc., contested the coverage."

Here's a typical "insurance-sensitive" scenario: A secondary-market mortgage company realizes that some of the loans it has purchased under the assumption that they are insurable turn out not to be. A double loss results. First, the bid to brokers has been overstated, and the price paid was too high. Second, because the loans are uninsurable, they will not qualify for securitization and may have to be redeemed on a so-many-cents-to-the-dollar basis.

Finally, in the category of "Catastrophe Bonds," Samson was examin-ing the specific case of companies whose fate depends on a low-probabil-ity event—such as an earthquake—*not* taking place. The problem here, of course, is that low-probability events *do* take place.

As Samson wrote: "Ratings for this relatively new genre of financing rely on the statistical remoteness of the occurrence of specific events, such as earthquakes or windstorms. Those bonds that refer to a single event clearly represent an 'everything-or-nothing' proposition. . . . For example, the Residential Re 2001 deal is intended to cover some of the losses of insurer USAA with respect to a Category Three or higher hurricane mak-ing landfall in certain geographies along the Eastern and Gulf coasts. The bonds will pay out 100 percent if no such hurricane occurs; were the storm to occur, the investors' principal is likely to be completely lost."

To Samson's list, I would add what I call "Loophole-Sensitive Entities," meaning a business configuration wherein the health of the business depends on a tax and/or legal loophole. The label certainly applies to Enron: The cap-italization of its partnerships was based on the "synthetic lease," enabling the company to claim simultaneously one favorable status for the sake of financial reporting and another for the purpose of reporting to the SEC.

True, when Standard & Poor's decided that real estate operations should not be reported under its definition of "core earnings" in the case of com-panies for whom real estate is not part of their core business, this reduced the potential impact of closing the synthetic-lease loophole. Should the syn-thetic-lease loophole be closed entirely, however, a considerable number of companies would have to report lower earnings and might well be looking at the cliff edge.

LESSONS FOR THE INVESTOR

A rating cliff in a company's financial structure makes it accident-prone. Stay away!

Look for companies that can clearly stand on their own two feet. Do not buy stock in a company whose good health depends on the support of a stronger parent. By the same logic, be wary of investing in a creaky parent company whose numbers are being rescued by the stellar performance of one or two divisions.

Do not buy stock in a company whose main asset is its good reputation. A company of this type is too confidence-sensitive. It there is an accident, you will not be able to run fast enough. The big players will find out and run away long before you can.

Do not buy stock in a company whose fate is linked to a particular credit rating. If corporate survival depends on hanging onto the current credit rating, the corporation is a cliff-hanger.

Do not buy stock in a company whose credit rating depends on the government's implicit support. It is nice to have friends in high places, but this is a shaky foundation for a business.

Do not buy stock in a company whose fate depends on a low-probability event not taking place. Low-probability events do happen, and—within reason—the companies in which you invest should be able to withstand one.

Do not buy stock in a company whose business depends on a legal or tax loophole. Yes, it sometimes takes a while, but loopholes eventually get spotlighted and closed.

14

Employees as Shareholders

*Ideally, the 401(k) should be a supplement to
a traditional pension plan, not a substitute.*

—KAREN FRIEDMAN, director of policy
strategy for the Pension Rights Center[1]

Most people's attention was first drawn to the Enron disaster because of
what happened to the retirement savings of Enron's personnel when the
company filed for bankruptcy. A large number of employees were involved,
and in many cases—because of the dramatic plunge in the value of Enron's
stock—their 401(k) accounts were effectively wiped out.

However, Enron's 401(k) plan was pretty much a "vanilla" plan. It had
no particular traps or complications. The scope of the disaster was the result
of so much of the collective value of the plan residing in Enron stock. You
can fault Enron's senior managers for encouraging their employees to buy
ever more Enron stock—even as they themselves were unloading it. But
those of us who have 401(k) plans have to take personal responsibility for
the portfolio within those plans. Yes, we deserve the help of concerned legislators and regulators—and a basketful of legislative remedies relative to

401(k) and other retirement plans were introduced hastily in the months following Enron's collapse—but we also have to look out for our own interests.
We have to keep the horse *in* the barn rather than reacting after it gets away.

A large percentage of U.S. workers who are shareholders in public corporations are in that relationship through their 401(k) plan. (In other words,
it is still somewhat unusual for people to buy and sell stocks in individual
corporations through brokerage accounts.) The popularity of the 401(k) program surged over the last two decades mainly because corporations were
eager to escape the burden of traditional pension plans.

In fact, the number of companies that offer pensions as the core component of their retirement benefits has been declining precipitously in recent
years. According to the *Wall Street Journal*, in 1980, 64 percent of all retirement savings went into old-style pension plans. In 1999, *85 percent* went
into accounts with employee control.[2] According to a Hewitt Associates survey, in 1999, 67 percent of companies with retirement schemes offered both
401(k) and pensions; this percentage dropped to 54 percent in 2001.[3]

Obscured within these aggregate statistics are some even more alarming
trends. Increasingly, the richer workers are being looked after, whereas the
poorer workers are not. According to the *Wall Street Journal*, "Roughly half
the workers on private payrolls don't have any employer-sponsored retirement
plans at all. About 74 percent of the best-paid fifth of American workers
participate in some form of pension plan on the job, but only 17 percent of
the worst-paid fifth do, according to number-crunching of Labor Department
data by the Economic Policy Institute, a Washington think-tank."[4]

A report sponsored by the same Economic Policy Institute was released
in May 2002. The study, headed by New York University economist Edward
N. Wolff, found that

> Between 1989 and 1998, the share of households whose projected
> retirement income is less than half their preretirement income
> rose from 29.9 to 42.5 percent. Figures were worse for African-
> American and Latino households, which saw an increase to 52.7
> percent.
>
> For households at the median of the nation's economic landscape,
> overall retirement wealth declined by 11 percent from 1983 to
> 1998.
>
> Only the very richest of near-retirees, those with a net worth of $1
> million or more, saw their retirement wealth increase in that
> period. All other groups—even those with net worth between
> $500,000 and $1 million—saw a decline.[5]

The disappearance of the traditional pension plan was somewhat obscured by the extraordinary scope and duration of the bull market that ran from 1982 to 2000. Yes, individuals were financially disadvantaged by the disappearance of the pension plan—but their healthy 401(k) nest eggs obscured that loss. Now, unfortunately, we can see the tradeoffs more clearly.

I am pretty sure that most people whose retirement assets are in 401(k)s know relatively little about how they work. For example, I doubt that many 401(k) investors realize that their savings are guaranteed neither by the company that runs the plan on behalf of its employees nor by the federal government. (To this extent, at least, we should be grateful for the publicity afforded to the woes of the Enron shareholders.) I doubt that many such investors understand that the part of their plans that consists of allocation into stock depends crucially on a healthy stock market.

As of this writing, the market is not healthy. (For this, of course, we have the Enrons and Andersens of the world to thank.) No one knows when the market will again become bullish, but we should keep in mind that there have been entire decades—most recently the 1970s—in which the market remained anemic. The lesson? Your 401(k) should only be one of the components of your larger retirement strategy.

Enron in the Bigger Picture

Enron had three retirement plans: a 401(k), an employee stock ownership plan, and a traditional pension plan. Traditional pensions are characterized as *defined-benefit plans* because they guarantee a predetermined monthly income in retirement. Because the corporation is responsible for funding these programs, responsibility for making the investments that will fund them rests entirely with the employer. The 401(k) program is a *defined-contribution plan,* meaning that (1) employees (and sometimes employers) make predetermined contributions to their plans and (2) employees make all the decisions about the allocation of those funds.

Enron's 401(k) plan had assets of $2.1 billion, of which $1.3 billion, or 63 percent, was in Enron stock. Some 57 percent of Enron's 21,000 employees participated in the company's 401(k) plan. In addition, Enron had 7600 participants in its employee stock ownership plan (ESOP), which at its peak was worth $1.1 billion, nearly all in company stock. Its defined-benefits plan, with nearly 20,000 participants, had assets of $270 million, partially in Enron stock.

Because it was Enron's policy to match employees' 401(k) contributions with company stock, and because employees also could join in the ESOP, the company's downfall caused an overall loss of $1 billion in about 16,000 401(k) employee and 5000 retiree accounts. On December 14, 2001, 12 days after Enron's bankruptcy filing, the company issued a news release entitled, "Enron Explains Basic Facts About Its 401(k) Savings Plan." Enron's spokesman, Mark A. Palmer, explained that the company's policy with 401(k) plans was in no way unusual within the American corporate landscape:

> "Until recently [meaning prior to Enron's Chapter 11 filing], the company provided a 50 percent match on employees' 401(k) contributions of up to 6 percent of their base pay. The match comes from Enron holdings. As is the case with most company matching programs, the match was provided in company stock."

> "As is also the case in many company 401(k) programs, until recently, stock holdings from the company match could not be transferred into other investment options until the employee reached age 50."

Insofar as this statement went, Palmer was absolutely right. (I will return to the subjects he *did not* talk about shortly.) The miseries being endured by Enron's past and present employees were the result of the plunge in the value of Enron's stock to a pathetic 75 cents rather than any eccentricities in Enron's 401(k) plan. And yes, Enron was very much in the mainstream of corporate America when it came to employer contributions. Of the 85 percent of companies that match an employee's contribution one way or another, about a quarter of them do so with employer stock, just as Enron did. According to the Investment Company Institute in Washington, "19 percent of 401(k) assets are now in company stock. At large companies, the share is 25 percent."[6]

Another research group, the Institute of Management and Administration, emphasizes the growing trend for companies to match employee contribution with employer stock. The *Wall Street Journal* quoted the Institute to the effect that, based on a survey of 219 large companies, "In 1995, 33 percent of the value of the total assets in 401(k)s, Employee Stock Ownership Plans (ESOPs), and profit-sharing plans was in employer's stock."[7] This percentage had risen to 44 percent by mid-1999, dropping back to 34 percent with the slump in the stock market. "American workers now put more money into pension and retirement savings plans sponsored by their employers than the companies themselves do. . . . According to the most recent data, companies were still the primary contributors to retirement programs of all types in 1998, accounting for 50 percent of new money flowing into the plans. Nearly a decade earlier, in 1989, companies contributed 70 percent. (Those percentages include contributions in the form of company stock.)."[8] At Procter & Gamble and Abbott Laboratories, more than 90 percent of the assets are in employer stock.

Are these companies being generous? In some cases, certainly. However, in addition, they derive considerable tax and accounting benefits from matching employees' contributions to a 401(k) plan with their own stock. Going one step further, a company can combine the 401(k) with an ESOP, thereby creating a hybrid retirement plan called a *KSOP*. In a KSOP, dividends on the stock are tax-deductible. To take advantage of those dividend deductions, companies often design a special type of preferred share paying higher dividends. Procter & Gamble (P&G), in particular, has taken advantage of such structures: "Procter & Gamble has shares used exclusively for its retirement plan that pay annual dividends of as much as $2.06 a share, compared to a dividend of $1.40 a year on common shares. The plan's $10.8 billion in P&G stock, accounting for 12.6 percent of the company's shares outstanding, would garner $346 million in dividends—or a tax deduction of some $127 million, using the company's tax rate of 36.7 percent."[9]

The numbers involved in these tax-minimization efforts are staggering. As Warren Vieth reported in the *Los Angeles Times*, "The tax deduction granted to employers for their retirement plan contributions reduces federal revenue by about $90 billion a year. It's the government's biggest tax subsidy, more costly than the deductions allowed for mortgage interest or employee health insurance."[10]

It was as a result of its 401(k) plan and its stock-option program that Enron managed to pay taxes in only one year out of the most recent five, paying a paltry $17 million in 1997. In each the other four years, it managed to get substantial rebates: $3 million in 1996, $13 million in 1998, $105 million in 1999, and $278 million in 2000.

Ironically, new legislation pushing harder in the direction of promoting employer stock as the main component of a 401(k) plan was making its headway at the same time that the Enron drama was unfolding. Tellingly, corporate lobbyists had been pushing for that particular change in the law for a number of years. It became part of President Bush's tax-cut bill in 2001.

To the extent that a company can "lock up" its stock in the 401(k) plans of its own employees with restrictions on the sale of that stock, those shares are in "reliable hands." And this, in turn, is a reliable tax-advantaged way to prop up that stock price. "Employers are using their contributions to employees' 401(k)s as a strategy to manipulate the value of their stock," comments Teresa Ghilarducci, a University of Notre Dame economist. "That's become a key tactic in keeping their share prices stable. They're using the nation's pension system for purposes it was never intended."[11]

The Pitfalls of 401(k) Plans

The biggest pitfall of a 401(k) plan has already been introduced: *There are no guarantees*. They are not guaranteed by the employer, the federal government, or anybody. However, there are also other perils and pitfalls that deserve some attention.

Restrictions on Sale and How Executives Bypass Them

One common restriction in 401(k) plans is that employees are not allowed to sell company stock in their 401(k) before they have reached a particular age. At Enron, the restriction on sales got lifted at age 50; in other companies, the age is 55; in still other companies, you have to reach "retirement age," whatever that is defined to be. In any case, these kinds of restrictions on sales of stock apply in 85 percent of the 23 percent of companies that match employee contribution to their 401(k) with their own stock.

In the wake of its Chapter 11 filing, as noted earlier, Enron tried to convey the message that there had not been anything wrong with its 401(k) plan. It was mainly a case of the *number* of accounts hit—21,000—and, of course, the swoon of the stock price. Never quite stated, but certainly implied, was the notion that Enron employees who persisted in complaining about the devastating results were in some way misbehaving.

But Enron's employees—angry, scared, and burdened by staggering losses—would have none of this.[12] And one thing that fueled their anger was the discovery that Enron's executives got preferential treatment when it came to selling company stock in their portfolios. Indeed, executives have access to a financial tool protecting them against the lack of diversification inherent in a personal portfolio that consists mainly of company stock. The tool is variably called *swap funds* or *exchange funds.*

To understand this device, you need to understand the principle of a financial swap. Briefly stated, with a swap, at agreed-on dates, one of the two parties involved receives from the other a cash flow indexed in a particular way, whereas the counterparty receives a cash flow based on a different index. For the trade to be meaningful, at least one of the indices must be floating. The particulars of the deal are determined at initiation so that the current fair values of the future flows in opposite directions are equivalent.

A *swap fund,* by extension, allows an executive to swap company stock revenue for that of a more diversified portfolio of securities. And here's a neat trick: In addition to achieving diversification, through the mechanism of the swap, the company stock is not sold—its ownership remains with the executive, permitting him or her to avoid taxation on any of the proceeds.

In 2001, Representative Richard Neal (Democrat, Massachusetts) introduced a bill limiting the use of swap funds, regarding them as a tax-avoidance scheme. In February 2002, Neal sent an impassioned letter to his House colleagues. "While the employees of Enron looked on helplessly," he wrote in part, "one director was able to use exchange funds to hedge his bets, diversify his portfolio, and postpone taxes."

It is schemes like these that (justifiably) convince the "little person" that the game is rigged against him or her—and ultimately reduce investor confidence and hurt *everybody* with a stake in the larger game.

Lockout Periods

Enron employees knew, too, that during a crucial period when the company was in free fall—between October 29, 2001, and November 12, 2001—they had been prevented from selling their Enron stock. In this same time period, however, executives were free to sell *their* Enron stock. According to company spokesman Mark A. Palmer, there was a purely technical reason for that temporary restriction; there was nothing sinister going on. A change of administrators for Enron's 401(k) had been underway for some time, and the transition occurred, coincidentally, just after the infamous "Non-Recurring Charges of $1.01 Billion After Tax" news release of October 16, 2001. During such a transition period, "a temporary shutdown, typically lasting several weeks, is required to allow employee account information to be accurately and completely transferred to the new administrator."

The situation was not unprecedented. In October 2000, employees at telecommunications company Lucent Technologies went through a nearly identical predicament. They were prevented from selling company stock while the share price was plummeting, losing 32 percent of its value, when (on October 10) the company announced that it would miss quarterly targets. In this case, the justification for the lockout was that the plan administrator needed time to balance assets after Lucent had spun off a major division.

The same applied to 8000 of the 63,000 employees of Qwest Communications International, Inc., a telecommunications company mentioned in previous chapters, during a 1-month period from December 21, 2001, to January 21, 2002. During this period, Qwest was switching administrators while it was merging the company's 401(k) plan with that of US West, a regional "Baby Bell" that the Denver firm had acquired in 1999. About 31 percent of the plan's assets were in company stock. The stock price declined by 7 percent during the lockout period.

Palmer's news release also had this to say on the already-notorious Enron lockout period:

> After selecting a new 401(k) administrator, Enron notified all affected employees in a mailing to their homes on October 4, stating that a transition period would begin on October 29. Between the first notification and the first day of the transition period, the company sent several reminders to employees over the internal e-mail system.

> The transition period during which employees were unable to change investments in their 401(k) accounts lasted a total of just 10 trading days, beginning on October 29 and ending on November 12, 2001. The transition applied to all plan participants, including senior executives.

> From October 29, the first day of the temporary shutdown, through November 13, the first day participants could transfer stock, the Enron share price went from $13.81 to $9.98, a drop of $3.83. On five of those trading days, Enron's share price closed below $9.98.

Unfortunately, those particular days had not been uneventful for the company. On October 29, the Securities and Exchange Commission (SEC) announced that its inquiry into a possible conflict of interest in the running of Enron's partnerships, initiated on October 22, had been upgraded to a formal investigation. On November 8, Enron published its second news release of devastating consequences: "Enron Provides Additional Information about Related Party and Off-Balance-Sheet Transactions; Company to Restate Earnings for 1997–2001." On November 8, Enron announced that Dynegy, Inc., would purchase the company for over $8 billion in stock and cash and that, as part of the agreement, Chevron Texaco would inject $1.5 billion in fresh capital. On November 29, the deal with Dynegy fell through. Four days later, Enron filed for bankruptcy protection.

Other than what follows in subsequent paragraphs, I have no particular insight into the motivations of Enron's executives or the coincidence of timing that led to a lockout—preventing employee sale of Enron stock—at precisely the juncture when a wholesale flight from that stock became an urgent priority. I will observe, however, that the mechanics of 401(k) plans can be extremely cumbersome and that employers—who have a legal obligation as fiduciaries of the 401(k) plans under their wings—are not able to move quickly even if they want to. Changes in administrators, for example, take months (or years) and require a whole forest's worth of paperwork. Thus, even if a corporation were inclined to manipulate this process, such a manipulation would be difficult (and dangerous) to pull off.

The Administration of Retirement Plans

This raises the larger question of plan administration. In hindsight, how convincing is Enron's claim that the administration of its 401(k) plan was beyond reproach?

Section 404a of the Employee Retirement Income Security Act (1974) articulates two basic requirements governing how 401(k) programs should be run:

> Fiduciaries "must administer the plan with skill and prudence, maintain diversified investments and must follow their own guidelines for the plan."
>
> Programs are under an "exclusive benefit rule": Fiduciaries must operate the plan for the sole benefit of the participants and beneficiaries.

Taking the latter provision first, in February 2002, the Department of Labor's Pension and Welfare Benefits Administration told a journalist that it was investigating a claim by an Enron employee that the company used 401(k) plan assets to pay other expenses.[13] If this were true, of course, criminal charges could be brought.

As for the first rule—that fiduciaries "must administer the plan with skill and prudence, maintain diversified investments and must follow their own guidelines for the plan"—there soon emerged a passionate debate. Had the administrators of Enron's 401(k) program displayed appropriate prudence?

At issue, in particular, was the conduct of Cindy Olson, an Enron executive vice-president who served as a 401(k) plan trustee. In February 2002, in front of a Senate panel, Olson revealed that she was one of the people who had been approached in August 2001 by Enron's whistleblower, Vice-President Sherron Watkins, who was at the time looking for advice before sending her anonymous (but soon to be infamous) e-mail to Chief Executive Officer (CEO) Kenneth Lay.

Commenting on Olson's subsequent course of action, Eli Gottesdiener—a Washington lawyer representing Enron workers and retirees suing over their ruined accounts—stated that the proper response of "any prudent, disinterested fiduciary" would have been to convene an emergency meeting of the plan administrative committee, disclose Watkins' allegations, and "immediately suspend any further use of Enron stock as a plan investment . . . pending a committee investigation conducted independent of Enron" and its accountants and lawyers.[14] On February 8, the *Wall Street Journal* reported that "James Prentice, a senior vice president at Enron affiliate EOTT Energy and chairman of Enron's 401(k) administrative committee, testified at a Senate Education and Labor Committee hearing on February 7, 2002, that he 'and other trustees didn't take steps to evaluate whether the company stock was a prudent investment . . . until early November, when they hired outside counsel to look into the issue.'"[15]

This belated action on the part of the trustees was not deemed sufficient by the Department of Labor, which announced on February 10, 2002, that it was "seeking to remove, through court action if necessary, the Enron Corp. officials who oversee the company's retirement plans and replace them with independent experts."[16]

Thus, on the question of Enron's prudence in the administration of its 401(k), the jury is still out. However, the swirl of questions, allegations, and lawsuits certainly suggests that, to the extent possible, investors in 401(k) plans need to be prepared to look out for their own interests.

An Investor's Own 401(k): The Rules of Elementary Prudence

In Chapter 7 I advised you to *ignore strategies that only work in a bull market*. This lesson applies equally to 401(k) plans, at least for the component that is supported by equity. And especially when the market is not bullish, a 401(k) should be one only of the building blocks of a retirement strategy.

Defined-contribution plans such as 401(k)s have not fared particularly well in recent years—even in the later years of the bull market—to such an extent that some states have started amending their laws to protect contributing employees against further deterioration. "The state of Nebraska," the *Wall Street Journal* reported, "alarmed that state workers were floundering, recently passed a law effectively phasing out its employee-controlled retirement plan. A recent study found Nebraska state employees who were managing their own retirement funds averaged a paltry 4.9 percent a year between 1997 and 2001, while the state's pension plan managed returns closer to 8 percent. Starting in January, new employees will be required to join what state officials call a modified pension plan that guarantees an annual return of at least 7 percent."[17]

Thus self-management of the 401(k) is not a sure bet. In fact, George Feiger, a partner at the financial services consulting firm of Capco—quoted in the *Wall Street Journal*—likened the self-management of a 401(k) to a "do-it-yourself appendectomy kit." Colorful—and discouraging! So what are some of the mistakes that are commonly made—and which may be avoided?

A recent study showed that 20 percent of employees who are entitled to a 401(k) plan ignore the opportunity. This is a mistake on several counts. First, the employee loses the opportunity to shelter pretax dollars today and gain use of those dollars in the future, when his or her tax rate almost certainly will be lower. Second, the employee loses the opportunity to build a nest egg outside the capital gains tax system. (Purchases and sales of assets inside a retirement plan are nontaxable events.) And anyone who has had to keep track of gains and losses on taxable stock transactions will understand this advantage. And finally, many companies match (or partially match) the employee's contribution to his or her 401(k). Under the right circumstances, this is an unparalleled opportunity to salt away money for retirement.

However, as we have seen, the circumstances are not always right. If a company matches the employee's contribution with company stock, the investor should be aware of both the upsides and downsides of this benefit.

The upside is that the value of the stock may go up, and the downside is that it may come down. Most of us will not ever experience the exuberance of owning a portfolio loaded up with a runaway stock, like Enron was in its heyday, so this particular piece of wisdom will not help many investors, but *stay level-headed.* Do not succumb to other people's enthusiasm and optimism. Make your own judgments. This applies, of course, to *all* stocks in a 401(k) plan, not only to employer stock.

Similarly, if a company offers its employees an opportunity to purchase stock at a discount through an employer stock purchase plan, such an opportunity should not be ignored, but a diversification approach holds that the stock should not be retained.

If a company matches employees' contributions to a 401(k) plan only with company stock, then employees obviously have no choice but to accept that stock. By the same token, employees are free to limit company stock in their portfolio to that particular level—that is, at the level of the contributions made by the employer. Employees should *not* feel obliged to put their own money into company stock.

In fact, they should think hard before doing so. This is so because you want to achieve some level of diversification in your portfolio—that is, not "put all your eggs in one basket."

The soundness of diversification was shown mathematically by Harry Markowitz in 1952 in his theory of portfolio selection.[18] What is often overlooked in Markowitz' work is that diversification only works as a return optimizer if the stocks chosen are the best available. (In other words, you cannot have any duds among your diverse eggs.) Even knowledgeable authors have sometimes said that a few underperforming stock cannot hurt, since they help at diversification. This is, of course, nonsense. These authors are confusing *volatility*—which gets lowered with each additional stock in the basket—with *performance,* which can be hurt by that additional stock if it underperforms. An underperforming stock in the basket naturally will make the overall performance drop.

Thus optimism and misplaced loyalty are no-nos because they work against diversification. To counter these natural tendencies toward overconcentration in employer stock, lawmakers have been thinking of capping the allowable proportion of employer stock in 401(k)s. However, as we have seen in previous chapters, there are often unexpected negative consequences to such well-meaning countermeasures. As the *Washington Post* reported recently, "A number of Democrats, including Senators Barbara Boxer (California) and Jon S. Corzine (New Jersey) . . . think the government ought to limit employer stock to no more than a fixed percentage of a 401(k) plan's assets. Boxer and Corzine peg that at 20 percent. . . . Boston College professor and former Federal Reserve official Alicia H. Munnell noted that a specific percentage limit would be most likely to have an impact when a stock is rising. If the employer's stock were falling in value, the company and the workers could put more and more in. If it were rising, workers would be forced to sell when they hit the cap—which might occur for no other reason than the stock had soared."[19]

Therefore, although I am leery of a government-imposed cap, I strongly endorse the idea of you imposing your *own* cap on the percentage of employer stock in your own 401(k). And as you diversify, think across economic sectors and look to debt instruments as well as to shares of stock. In stormy weather, there is nothing like a nice high-yield T-bill.

And finally, a well-worn but still valuable piece of advice: As you get older, reduce the level of risk in your 401(k). As a general rule, lower the proportion represented by shares of stock and increase the proportion of debt instruments, such as bonds. So-called life-cycle funds do this automatically; the breakdown of stock, bonds, and cash varies according to the participant's age and current savings.[20]

LESSONS FOR THE INVESTOR

Save for retirement outside your 401(k). Because it depends so much on the stock market being bullish, a 401(k) plan should be only one of the components of a retirement plan.

Seek advice. Do not try running your 401(k) on your own. Ask advice from your company's appointed advisor. Seek a second opinion, too.

Take advantage of your company's 401(k) plan. If your contribution is matched, there is simply no better savings plan. Even if it is not, the company bears the cost of running the plan. Also, roll over your 401(k) if you change jobs.

Once a month, check the stocks in your 401(k). You need to know what is going on. This applies to employer stock as well.

Be hard-nosed about the ESOP. Yes, by all means, buy stock at a discount through your company's ESOP, but plan to sell it as soon as possible.

Limit your loyalty. If your company matches your 401(k) with company stock, do not go overboard: Do not add more!

Diversify. Do not let employer stock exceed 20 percent of your retirement portfolio. I would be more comfortable at 10 percent.

Diversify, but do not diversify for the sake of diversifying. Choose the best. An underperforming stock will hurt your portfolio's performance.

Do not overdiversify. There is a ceiling to useful diversification. By choosing four or five of the possible allocation options in your 401(k), you probably cover the full range of possible investment choices. Adding even more is redundant.

Counterbalance the remainder of your 401(k). If your company is technological, counterbalance with a solid-value fund. If your company is industrial or a utility, diversify with a tech fund.

Sell employer stock as soon as allowed. When you meet the conditions to sell company stock (age of 50 or 55 or retirement), do so. Have a scheduled plan. For instance, sell 25 percent of your stake over four quarters. Move them to an individual retirement account (IRA) or to a taxable account and sell (you will benefit from the long-term capital gains taxation clause).

15

The Last Word

Much of what has been included in previous chapters has focused on what the investor in the post-Enron world should *not* do. In this chapter I will articulate some general principles about what such an investor *should* do, based on the information presented in previous chapters. And toward the end of this chapter I will offer some concluding thoughts about the overriding lessons derived from our recent collective experiences in the realm of personal investment.

The Alternatives to Stock Picking and Mutual Funds

Obviously, there is more to investment than purchasing individual stocks or buying shares in mutual funds. This book is not meant to be an investment guide per se; there are lots of good books out there that already serve this purpose.[1] However, let me present a couple of investment guidelines deriving from the book's main arguments.

The first thing to keep in mind is that there are two general factors that influence the returns of any type of investment: the investment's *size* and the *risk factor*.

Size of Investment

This point is seldom mentioned, but it is nonetheless true. The more money you have got to invest, the better deal you will get out of the financial markets. The reason why this is true should be obvious. If you pay a yearly fee that is proportionate to your investment, the higher the fee, the better service it will command. In particular, you will have access to more expensive research and be invited to use investment methods that are more costly to deploy. There is no mystery here and—unfortunately—no miracle!

Risk Factor

The higher the risk, the higher is the return. This is a sentence that for the purposes of emphasis should read with its terms reversed: *The higher the return, the higher is the risk.* And *high risk* means that the return may not materialize or may even turn into a loss.

Investment theory holds that *the higher yield commanded by shares of stock compared with bonds reflects the higher risk involved.* This risk may not materialize for a number of years; it will still be there nevertheless, lurking ominously in the background. Thus any comparison between stocks and debt instruments should be made with this same investment horizon in mind. For instance, if you intend to keep your stock for 5 years, the investment should be evaluated comparing the yield with the coupon of a 5-year Treasury note.

The notion that higher returns should reflect higher risk makes a lot of sense within financial theory. Markets are presumed to be efficient. If there were an arbitrage opportunity between capital markets—for example, between lending your money to the government or to firms for the short or the long term (bonds) and buying shares of corporations (stocks)—arbitrageurs would spot that opportunity and start working on it. They would create "money machines" that borrowed money (from CDs to 30-year Treasuries) and invest it in stock. The arbitrageurs' activity gradually would eliminate the spread between equities and debt instruments. Eventually, an equilibrium would be reached, and the rate charged for borrowing the capital and the returns from investing in stock would become the same.

If this were true, there would be no difference between investing in equities for so many years or in debt instruments with the same duration. (The *no-arbitrage* or *one-price* principles would imply that it amounts to the same.) In real life, of course, this is *not* true. Stocks (most) entail risks that bonds (most) do not. The point, again, is to make sure that you are comparing risks and returns on an apples-to-apples basis over comparable time periods.

With these general principles in mind, let's look at some specific investments options.

Short Selling

The first thing you can do as an alternative to just picking stocks or buying into mutual funds is *shorting* the market or *short selling*. This is a technique that is becoming increasingly popular among individual investors.

How does it work? When you buy shares in a particular stock, you are either voting for the returns represented by that dividend stream—unlikely, for reasons already discussed—or you are betting that the price of this stock will be going up. If over time you are not satisfied with the way the stock has behaved, there is no alternative open to you but to sell it. Once you own the stock, there is no direct way for you to benefit from a downward move of that stock. (You lose.)

However, there is an indirect way of doing so, whereby you build a synthetic position in the stock and then bet on the stock value going down. This is called *selling short.*

Here's how to become a short-seller: You approach someone who holds shares in the stock, and you arrange to borrow those shares from him or her in exchange for a borrowing fee or premium.[2] As soon as you get hold of those shares, you sell them at the current market price. Then you wait to find out whether your prediction was correct—that the price would get substantially lower. Assuming that it does, you buy back a number of shares equal to those you borrowed and return the borrowed block to your lender.

In the process, of course, you pocket the difference between the price at which you sold the stock at the inception of your selling-short scheme and the much lower current price. Naturally, you would like your profit to at least offset the sum you paid as a premium to borrow the shares in the first place. Moreover, if you are really serious about this, you will want the profit to offset not only that premium but also the interest that would have accrued on the premium at current market rates for a period of a similar duration as that of your selling short.

A money machine? Well, yes, if you guessed right about the direction that your stock was going to go. If the price goes up rather than down, you will have to buy back at a loss the shares you borrowed in order to be able to return them on schedule to their owner.

Thus a short position on the stock market is achieved through buying and selling, just like a traditional long position. The difference is that a short position implies first selling (the shares that were borrowed) and then buying (in order to return the shares that were borrowed to their owner). Some people disapprove of short selling—it is "un-American"—on the grounds that it constitutes "betting against" a stock—or even against the overall market. Indeed, if you sell because you believe that the stock price is going down, by doing so you are swelling the size of the party of sellers. It is true that there is a quasi-moral argument around the issue: Individual investors as a group only win on the rising side of stock prices, and by short selling, you are working against them.

At the same time, as we have seen, you are only effectively pushing the price down by selling if there is at the time a majority doing just the same as you, meaning that in this case you are just simply right about the direction of the market, and you can hardly be blamed for being right! On the contrary, if you are selling when there is a majority buying, the price will go up anyway, and at the end of the day, you will be losing on your short selling. In other words, there is nothing more to short selling than being rewarded for being right and punished for being wrong. This is no different than the lot of the ordinary investor who either owns the stock or simply abstains. The only thing is that with short selling you have added to the range of your strategies one that makes money when the stock price drops.

This is why I leave it to you to buy or not that quasi-moral argument. Smart people are encouraged to make money off the rising stars in the market; why shouldn't they be encouraged to make money off the setting suns as well?

Index Funds

Index funds track stock market indices such as the Dow Jones Industrial Average, the Nasdaq Composite, Standard & Poor's 500 (S&P 500), or the Russell 2000. Fees are very low because there is no research input from fund managers.

Index funds are a great idea when the price of stocks, on average, is going up. Of course, they are a lousy concept in a bearish market. Index funds do not pass the litmus test for elementary sound investment: that the strategy works also in a bear market environment.

Enhanced Index Funds

The *enhancement* in enhanced index funds is in the additional research provided. And as I said, you pay for research, so fees are much greater, running as high as 2 percent of the assets. This is something like 10 times more than with a "plain vanilla" index fund. Do not jump too quickly to buy this extra service, though. A comparative study of such funds in recent years has shown that the enhancement achieved is only minimal. In the dismal 2000–2002 period, for example, enhancement funds (like their less expensive cousins) failed to operate in the black.

In addition, enhanced index funds are ineffective from a tax point of view. They are better used as part of a tax-deferred plan such as a 401(k) or an individual retirement account (IRA). And to engage our final measure, in a bear market, enhanced index funds are hardly better than "plain vanilla" index funds. In other words, they do not pass the test either.

Foreign Stock

In times of domestic troubles, some people are drawn to overseas stocks. However, in the period 2000–2002, foreign stocks have not performed any better than U.S. equities. On the whole, foreign stocks are less dearly priced relative to their earnings than U.S. stocks, but as we have seen, this simple fact is no evidence that they will perform any better. Mainly, it expresses what percentage of their savings local investors have decided to inject in their national stock market. This can be rational or irrational.

In addition, overseas stocks may not allow true diversification of an American-based portfolio. Indeed, as a consequence of globalization of the financial world, foreign national stock markets have been highly correlated with the U.S. stock market. And smaller markets, which have a higher chance of being decorrelated from (that is, not closely linked to) the U.S. market, present an exchange-rate risk—that is, a possible depreciation of the local currency compared with the U.S. dollar, which can hurt investors in significant ways.

Savings Accounts

Not knowing what else to do in 2002, investors have turned to the security of savings accounts. From 2001 to 2002, savings accounts in the United States grew 22 percent in value to $2.5 trillion.

However, as we all know, the return from savings accounts is extremely low, on the order of about 1 percent a year in 2002, which barely keeps pace with the current level of inflation. Keep in mind that at 15 percent—the rate obtained by the "friends of Enron"—an investment doubles in value in 5 years. At 1 percent, it will take *70 years* for your investment to double. So start early—or keep an eye out for a better alternative!

Money Markets

Money markets provide a safe haven in the short term. In the week ending July 17, 2002, when the stock markets were crashing, more than three-quarters of the money that flowed out of stock mutual funds ended up in the money markets.

Returns from the money markets tend to be somewhat better than those from savings accounts, and money-market funds are relatively low-risk investments. Again, think of these as safe havens in stormy weather.

Bonds

With their coupons, bonds tell you in absolutely clear terms what their returns will be. Unlike dividends on shares, which represent (in principle) a share in a corporation's capital growth, the interest rate that applies to a bond over its whole lifetime is known in advance.

In times when capital gains on the stock market are negative, even bonds with low coupon rates look like a good deal. Two perils threaten, however: inflation and rising rates. At maturity, the principal of the loan is returned to the lender. With inflation, the value of that principal effectively depreciates over the years. How much it will be worth then *in real terms*, in constant dollars—meaning once inflation has been taken into account—is anybody's guess.

This problem has been eliminated with Treasury inflation-protected securities (TIPS). The face value of TIPS rises with inflation to remove its effect. Be aware, however, that these inflation adjustments are taxable.

Rising market rates represent a danger if the bondholder does not intend to keep the bond until it matures. The issue here is of reselling the bond on a secondary market. If rates rise, the bond value depreciates.

Why? To use a simple example, say that I possess a 10-year bond with 1 year to go. I paid $10,000 for this bond. The bond's coupon is 4 percent. A 1-year bill currently has a 5 percent rate. For how much can I sell my bond? The computation is straightforward. For me to have a chance of selling my bond, it needs to be competitive with all other debt instruments outstanding for 1 year. In other words, it cannot do worse than the 1-year bill—in other words, it needs to return 5 percent at the end of the year. By definition, however, it will only return 4 percent. What should I do? I should discount the price of the bond so that it effectively returns 5 percent.

This is done more easily than it may look like at first. What do I get at the end of the year? I get $10,000, which is the dollar amount of the principal, and $400 in interest ($10,000 × 0.04 = $400). The total is $10,400. To be competitive on a financial market where 1-year debt yields 5 percent, $10,400 needs to represent the combination of 100 percent principal plus 5 percent interest of a particular sum x. That sum x is found easily: It is 100 percent of an amount of which $10,400 is 105 percent. In other words, $x =$ 100 × $10,400/105 = $9904.76.

In short, there are risks inherent in holding bonds if you intend to resell them before they mature. If interest rates go up, the reselling price goes down.

Mortgage-Backed Securities

Mortgage-backed securities are bonds of a very special kind: The holder of one such bond is entitled to the cash flows attached to a pool of home loans, which is the interest flows and reimbursement of principal that monthly payments break down into.

The traded volume of mortgage-backed securities (MBSs) has grown considerably over the past 15 years. In 2002, they represented 45 percent of all outstanding debt instruments. Their yield is higher than that generated by Treasuries. However, as you would expect, there is a price to pay for that higher yield. There is a lot of uncertainty for the bondholder as to how much of the bond's returns in addition to principal eventually will be delivered and at what speed. This uncertainty results from the fact that homeowners have the right to prepay their mortgages, depriving the investor in an MBS of the interest cash flows that otherwise would be expected on the remaining lifetime of the loan.

If the MBS has a high coupon, this means that homeowners in the pool pay a high rate on their mortgages. This has the implication that if mortgage rates drop, these homeowners will be able to refinance their loan and will prepay the principal. Prepayments of principal will speed up, but future interest cash flows attached to those mortgages will be lost. On the contrary, if the MBS's coupon is low, this means that homeowners have managed to lock their loans at low rates. This reduces the chances that they will ever be tempted to refinance at an even lower rate. The risk for the investor here is not that of prepayment but of *extension*. Interest-rate cash flows attached to the mortgages will be fully paid, but there will be precious few anticipated payments of principal.

This is the situation encountered in 2002. Homeowners are able to obtain historically low mortgage rates, making it highly unlikely that they will refinance any time soon. Any prepayment in those pools will result from the ordinary rotation in housing, due to people moving to a bigger or smaller house or relocating.

Real Estate

Real estate is the great American investment alternative to the stock market. Despite all the recent talk about households' stock portfolios and 401(k)s, these still represent only about 20 percent of household wealth, whereas 60 percent of the average family's wealth is the market value of their home.

The great effectiveness of real estate as an investment has two sources. The first is the *direct* government subsidies in housing, as in Federal Housing Authority/Veterans Administration (FHA/VA) mortgages. The second is the *indirect* subsidies that derive from the fact that the government-sponsored entities Fannie Mae and Freddie Mac—the hybrid organizations that gobble up and securitize the lion's share of all home loans—benefit from the "AAA" credit rating of the American government and are not subject to a variety of taxes.

For the past 27 years, home prices have outpaced inflation by just 1 percentage point per year. However, this is not the whole picture. In 1999, Alan Greenspan reckoned that "over the past five years, the average capital gain on the existing home net of transaction costs was more than $25,000, almost a fifth of the average purchase price."[3]

In many cases, therefore, making extra payments on your mortgage is not a bad strategy: You increase by so much your equity in your house while you decrease the amount on which interest is calculated. Alternatively, if your household budget permits, you may want to refinance your mortgage into a new one with a shorter maturity. Say you refinance a 30-year mortgage into a 15-year one. Your monthly payments will be higher—but not as much higher as you might think—but the time when you have repaid a sizable part of the principal is considerably shortened. In other words, you are building equity in your house at an accelerated pace.

Remember, however, that a house is like anything else: The escalator goes both ways. We have gotten used to the idea that house prices only go up, but there is no God-given law that says that it needs to be thus. Say that you make a down payment of $30,000 on a house worth $200,000. You only need to experience a 15 percent drop in the value of your home for your equity in the house to be wiped out.

Keep in mind that investing in a house with a mortgage is a way of leveraging debt—that is, there is a multiplier in the risk associated with the debt. If there is a foreclosure because of default on monthly payments, for example, you have lost it all.

In some ways, we have been rescued by Enron. More accurately, we have been rescued by the death of Enron, and the mortal wounds to Arthur Andersen, and the punishment of the individuals at those companies—and others—that continues to unfold.

With the corpses of these once-formidable companies lying around on the front pages of our newspapers and all over the evening news, we couldn't *help* but get an anatomy lesson. What we learned was that the system was rigged.

We learned that there was a chasm between what we had been told about how the system worked and how it actually worked. We learned that we had been invited to the banquet—after buying a ticket, of course—but that there was another room, an "inner circle," where the "big people" would get together and play a game that worked to our disadvantage.

We were appalled to learn that at companies like Enron, a two-tiered system was taken for granted; it was a way of life. In the outer circle, employees lost their shirts. In the inner circle, the cronies got paid in multiple ways—big salaries, outlandish stock options, and $50 million bonuses. We learned that there were people and institutions called the "friends of Enron" who were able to command a 15 percent interest rate—multiples of any standard commercial rate—for lending big money to the company in the weeks before the quarterly report. We learned that top executives, although not running a notably successful enterprise, were able to earn a 2500 percent return on investment.[4]

We learned that Enron was running a corrupt school—getting paid to teach other companies to behave like Enron. We learned that there were scores of companies waiting in line to get schooled.

We learned that arrogance, complacency, and self-satisfaction can become the operating principles of a major corporation.

And we learned that when a company like Enron goes under, there are corporate lifeboats—but only for those in the inner circle.

With one exception, I will not attempt to summarize the lessons of this book in this closing chapter. And that exception is: *Encourage companies that pay dividends.*

In August 2002, Federal Reserve Chairman Alan Greenspan sketched out a postmortem on the dot-com craze. For the first time since his earliest days at the Fed, Greenspan's statement fell on skeptical ears. He said that we do not understand how speculative bubbles develop and that we cannot tell for sure when we are seeing one. "Bubbles . . . appear to primarily reflect exuberance on the part of investors in pricing financial assets," he said. "Bubbles appear to emerge when investors either overestimate the sustainable rise in profits or unrealistically lower the rate of discount they apply to expected profits and dividends."[5]

Not true, as I have tried to illustrate in this book. We know where bubbles come from—from the death of dividends. With dividends gone, there is nothing left to anchor a stock's value. Like a hot-air balloon, it rises, at least until the hot air cools off or the balloon bursts.

Dividends determine the value of a stock. They are the most effective way—if not the only one—for us to support the "share" system. You own a share; you deserve better than the elusive promise of capital gains. You deserve a share of the proceeds. This is the basic premise of the game.

Dividends cannot be massaged; they are either being paid or they are not. And in a bear market, making 2 percent in dividends is better than making a negative figure—in single or double digits—on capital gains. Almost by definition, companies that pay dividends are solid, profitable, and committed to their shareholders over the long run. Standard & Poor's noted that in 2001, dividend payers in the S&P 500 fell by 0.1 percent, whereas non-dividend payers saw their stock price drop by 5.4 percent.[6] Which sounds better to you?

A principle central to Confucianism, the ancient Chinese philosophy and way of life, is the "rectification of names." In the West, a name is mainly a label—a convenience. Not so in traditional China, where a word used to refer to something was regarded as an element of the nature of the *thing itself*, just like its color or its taste. A name did not represent a thing but truly *was* the thing in an essential manner. When chastizing his decadent and morally corrupt society, Confucius would say, "Let the father be a father. Let the Prince be a Prince."

When a father will act again like a father and a prince will act again like a prince, we will be back on track. This is the hidden and beneficial power of the rectification of names—getting things back to their true nature. In this spirit, let us resolve to *let a share system be a share system.* Let a share in a corporation's capital growth be a share in capital growth.

And may we all profit as investors in the post-Enron world!

Notes

Chapter 1

1. Steve Liesman, "Investors Cast Aside Enron Concerns to Place Focus on Changing Economy," *Wall Street Journal,* April 1, 2002.
2. E. S. Browning, "Simple and Solid, New Stocks Emerge as Market's Leaders," *Wall Street Journal,* June 17, 2002.
3. Robert Sobel, *Dangerous Dreamers: The Financial Innovators from Charles Merrill to Michael Milken* (New York: Wiley, 1993).
4. Michael Moore, "Bandwidth Trading: The New Commodity Gold Rush," in Peter C. Fusaro and Jeremy Wilcox (eds.), *Energy Derivatives: Trading Emerging Markets* (New York: Energy Publishing Enterprises, 2000), p. 109.
5. Lin S. Frank and Terrence M. Gee, "Bandwidth Trading: Developing a Market," in Peter C. Fusaro and Jeremy Wilcox (eds.), *Energy Derivatives: Trading Emerging Markets* (New York: Energy Publishing Enterprises, 2000), p. 95.
6. *Ibid.,* p. 102.
7. Jonathan D. Day and James C. Wendler, "Best Practice and Beyond: Knowledge Strategies," *The McKinsey Quarterly* 1(1998):19–25.
8. Greg Ip, "The Rise and Fall of Intangible Assets Leads to Shorter Company Life Spans," *Wall Street Journal,* April 4, 2002.
9. Paul Krugman, "Death by Guru," *New York Times,* December 18, 2001.
10. Remarks by Chairman Alan Greenspan, "Corporate Governance," at the Stern School of Business, New York University, New York, March 26, 2002.
11. June Kim, "Will Your 401(k) Go the Way of Enron?" *SmartMoney,* December 4, 2001.

Chapter 2

1. Paul A. Volcker, "A Litmus Test for Accounting Reform," *Wall Street Journal,* May 21, 2002.
2. Ronald Brownstein, "Enron Fallout Proves Personal Loss Can Have Big Political Consequences," *Los Angeles Times,* February 20, 2002.
3. Janet Whitman, "For Competence, Accounting Gets a 'D' in Poll of Businesses, *Wall Street Journal,* April 10, 2002.
4. Floyd Norris, "Leaderless at Arthur Andersen When Direction Is Needed," *New York Times,* March 30, 2002.
5. "Arthur A., Takin' It to the Streets," *http://www.eraider.com,* March 24, 2002.
6. Kurt Eichenwald, "Andersen Misread Depths of the Government's Anger," *New York Times,* March 18, 2002.

7. Arthur A., "Materiality and the Single Accountant," *http://www.eraider.com,* August 31, 2001.
8. Ken Brown, "In Memo Last September, Andersen Urged Firm to Be Especially Careful," *Wall Street Journal,* April 12, 2002.
9. "Report of Investigation by the Special Investigation Committee of the Board of Directors of Enron Corp," William C. Powers, Jr., chair, February 1, 2002, p. 132.
9. Walter Hamilton, "Securities and Exchange Commission Chairman Concedes Missteps in Pursuit of Market Reforms but Presses Ahead," *Los Angeles Times,* March 10, 2002.
10. Jerry Hirsch, "Accountants Can't Keep Up with Financial Complexity," *Los Angeles Times,* February 24, 2002.
11. "Text of Watkins' Testimony at House Hearing on Enron," *New York Times,* February 14, 2002.
12. Dennis K. Berman, "Regulators Are Taking a Look at Andersen's 'Swaps' Method," *Wall Street Journal,* March 19, 2002.
13. Robert Sobel, *Dangerous Dreamers: The Financial Innovators from Charles Merrill to Michael Milken* (New York: Wiley, 1993), p. 183.
14. Greg Ip, "The Rise and Fall of Intangible Assets Leads to Shorter Company Life Spans," *Wall Street Journal,* April 4, 2002.

Chapter 3

1. Dennis K. Berman, "Regulators Are Taking a Look at Andersen's 'Swaps' Method," *Wall Street Journal,* March 19, 2002.
2. James C. van Horne, *Financial Market Rates and Flows,* 4th ed. (Englewood Cliffs, NJ: Prentice-Hall, 1994), p. 5.

Chapter 4

1. Transcript of Senate Commerce Committee Hearing on Enron, February 26, 2002.

Chapter 5

1. Robert S. Shiller, *Irrational Exuberance* (New York: Broadway Books, 2000), p. 15.
2. This is at least the name that Burton G. Malkiel gives it in *A Random Walk Down Wall Street* (New York: Norton, 1999), pp. 31–33.
3. *Ibid.,* Chap. 4.
4. Alfred Rappaport and Michael J. Mauboussin, *Expectations Investing* (Boston, MA: Harvard Business School Press, 2001).
5. Randall Smith and Susan Pulliam, "Two More Wall Street Firms Are Targeted in Trading Probe," *Wall Street Journal,* April 25, 2002.
6. Benjamin Graham, David L. Dodd, and Sidney Cottle, *Security Analysis: Principles and Techniques* (New York: McGraw-Hill, 1962), p. 480.
7. *Ibid.,* p. 742.
8. Burton G. Malkiel, *A Random Walk Down Wall Street* (New York: Norton, 1999), p. 85; Jeremy J. Siegel, *Stocks for the Long Run* (New York: McGraw-Hill, 1998), pp. 102–103.
9. Jeremy J. Siegel, *Stocks For the Long Run* (New York: McGraw-Hill, 1998), p. 78.

10. Richard Foster, "The Welch Legacy: Creative Destruction," *Wall Street Journal,* September 10, 2001.

11. Remarks by Chairman Alan Greenspan, "Corporate Governance," at the Stern School of Business, New York University, New York, March 26, 2002.

12. Alfred Rappaport and Michael J. Mauboussin, *Expectations Investing* (Boston, MA: Harvard Business School Press, 2001).

13. Remarks by Chairman Alan Greenspan, "Corporate Governance," at the Stern School of Business, New York University, New York, March 26, 2002.

14. Jeremy J. Siegel, *Stocks for the Long Run* (New York: McGraw-Hill, 1998), p. 100.

15. James O'Shaugnessy, *What Works on Wall Street* (New York: McGraw-Hill, 1997), pp. 123–132.

16. Peter Eavis, "Trusts Keeping Enron Off Balance," *http://www.TheStreet.com,* November 22, 2001.

17. Gretchen Morgenson, "How 287 Turned into 7: Lessons in Fuzzy Math," *New York Times,* January 20, 2002.

18. Thornton O'Glove (with Robert Sobel), *Quality of Earnings: The Investor's Guide to How Much Money a Company Is Really Making* (New York: Free Press, 1987), p. 160.

19. Robert S. Shiller, *Irrational Exuberance* (New York: Broadway Books, 2000), p. 67.

Chapter 6

1. Robert T. Daigler, *Financial Futures and Options Markets: Concepts and Strategies* (New York: HarperCollins, 1994), p. 142.

2. Michael Brick, "What Was the Heart of Enron Keeps Shrinking," *New York Times,* April 6, 2002.

3. Jack D. Schwager, *The New Market Wizards: Conversations with America's Top Traders* (New York: HarperBusiness, 1992), p. 155.

4. The French mathematician Louis Bachelier was the first to notice this. He wrote in his 1900 Ph.D. thesis that "contradictory opinions concerning [market] changes diverge so much that at the same instant buyers believe in a price increase and sellers believe in a price decrease . . ." [*Theory of Speculation*, quoted in Peter L. Bernstein, *Capital Ideas: The Improbable Origins of Modern Wall Street* (New York: Free Press, 1992), p. 20].

5. Philip L. Carret, *The Art of Speculation* (New York: Wiley, 1997), p. xv.

6. Burton G. Malkiel, *A Random Walk Down Wall Street* (New York: Norton, 1999), p. 146.

Chapter 7

1. Gretchen Morgenson, "How 287 Turned into 7: Lessons in Fuzzy Math," *New York Times,* January 20, 2002.

2. Kurt Eichenwald, "Enron Ex-Chief Is Said to Suspect Fraud in a Unit," *New York Times,* April 24, 2002.

3. David Barboza, "Enron Offered Management Aid to Companies," *New York Times,* April 10, 2002.

4. Kurt Eichenwald and Michael Brick, "Enron Investors Say Lenders Took Part in Fraud Scheme," *New York Times,* April 8, 2002.

5. David Barboza, "Enron Tried to Raise Cash Two Years Ago," *New York Times,* March 9, 2002.

6. *Ibid.*

7. *Ibid.*

8. David Wallace, "One-Stop Energy Shop," *http://www.business2.com/ebusiness/2000/06,* June 2000.

9. Michael Brick, "What Was the Heart of Enron Keeps Shrinking," *New York Times,* April 6, 2002.

10. Rone Tempest and Myron Levin, "Generating Pure Profits with Electricity Trading," *Los Angeles Times,* March 23, 2002.

11. Patricia Hemsworth, "Electricity Trading: Europe and North America," in Peter C. Fusaro and Jeremy Wilcox (eds.), *Energy Derivatives: Trading Emerging Markets* (New York: Energy Publishing Enterprises, 2000), p. 15.

12. Nancy Rivera Brooks, Thomas S. Mulligan, and Tim Reiterman, "Memo Shows Enron Role in Power Crisis," *Los Angeles Times,* May 7, 2002.

13. "Report of Investigation by the Special Investigation Committee of the Board of Directors of Enron Corp," William C. Powers, Jr., chair, February 2, 2002, p. 78.

14. Andy Kessler, "Bernie Bites the Dust," *Wall Street Journal,* May 1, 2002.

15. Jonathan R. Laing, "The Bear That Roared: How Short-Seller Jim Chanos Helped Expose Enron," *Barron's,* January 28, 2002.

16. Suzanne Kapner, "Use of Stock to Finance Deals Haunts Telecom Companies," *New York Times,* March 14, 2002.

Chapter 8

1. "Summary of Statement No. 123, Accounting for Stock-Based Compensation," Financial Accounting Standards Board, October 1995.

2. Steven Pearlstein, "Here's the New Take on Stock Options: They Reward Corporate Leaders for All the Wrong Things," *Washington Post,* March 24, 2002.

3. Alfred Rappaport and Michael J. Mauboussin, *Expectations Investing: Reading Stock Prices for Better Returns* (Boston: Harvard Business School Press, 2001), p. 171.

4. Jeremy J. Siegel, *Stocks for the Long Run* (New York: McGraw-Hill, 1998), p. 77.

5. Robert S. Shiller, *Irrational Exuberance* (New York: Broadway Books, 2000), p. 15.

6. Remarks by Chairman Alan Greenspan, "Corporate Governance," at the Stern School of Business, New York University, New York, March 26, 2002.

7. Bill Gross, "Buffetting Corporate America," *PIMCO—Investment Outlook,* March 2002.

8. Jerry Hirsch, "Accountants Can't Keep Up with Financial Complexity," *Los Angeles Times,* February 4, 2002.

9. J. Nellie Liang and Steven A. Sharpe, "Share Repurchases and Employee Stock Options and Their Implications for S&P 500 Share Retirements and Expected Returns," Federal Reserve Board, November 1999.

10. Joann S. Lublin, "CEO's Pay Last Year Was Lowest Since 1989," *Wall Street Journal,* March 5, 2002.

11. Andrew Tobias, *The Only Investment Guide You'll Ever Need* (San Diego: Harcourt, 2002), p. 126.

12. Burton G. Malkiel, *A Random Walk Down Wall Street* (New York: Norton, 1999), p. 329.

13. Aaron Lucchetti, "Restricting Options: Fund Manager Gets Tough on Issue of Executive Pay," *Wall Street Journal,* April 15, 2002.

14. Jerry Guidera, "Computer Associates' Revenue Is Probed by Federal Officials," *Wall Street Journal,* May 20, 2002.

15. Gretchen Morgenson, "Outrage Is Rising as Options Turn to Dust," *New York Times,* March 31, 2002.

16. Tracy Byrnes, "Stock-Option Accounting Hides in the Shadows of the Financials," *Wall Street Journal Online,* March 21, 2002.

17. Tracy Byrnes, "More on Stock Option Accounting Practices," *Wall Street Journal Online,* March 28, 2002.

18. Alfred Rappaport and Michael J. Mauboussin, *Expectations Investing: Reading Stock Prices for Better Returns* (Boston: Harvard Business School Press, 2001), pp. 179–180.

19. *Ibid.,* pp. 173–174.

20. *Ibid.,* p. 181.

21. Remarks by Chairman Alan Greenspan, "Corporate Governance," at the Stern School of Business, New York University, New York, March 26, 2002.

22. Greg Hitt and Jacob M. Schlesinger, "Stock Options Come under Fire in the Wake of Enron's Collapse," *Wall Street Journal,* March 26, 2002.

23. Tracy Byrnes, "Stock-Option Accounting Hides in the Shadows of the Financials, *Wall Street Journal Online,* March 21, 2002.

24. Summary of Statement No. 123, *Accounting for Stock-Based Compensation* (New York: Financial Accounting Standards Board, 1995).

25. Remarks by Chairman Alan Greenspan, "Corporate Governance," at the Stern School of Business, New York University, New York, March 26, 2002.

26. Greg Hitt and Jacob M. Schlesinger, "Stock Options Come under Fire in the Wake of Enron's Collapse, *Wall Street Journal,* March 26, 2002.

27. David M. Blitzer, Robert E. Friedman, and Howard J. Silverblatt, *Measures of Corporate Earnings* (New York: Standard & Poor's, originally released November 7, 2001, revised May 14, 2002), p. 5.

28. Jeffrey L. Seglin, "Do Stock Options Buy Silence?" *New York Times,* February 17, 2002.

29. Greg Hitt and Jacob M. Schlesinger, "Stock Options Come under Fire in the Wake of Enron's Collapse," *Wall Street Journal,* March 26, 2002.

30. Rob Wells, "Major Fight Looms over Options Accounting," *Los Angeles Times,* February 18, 2002.

31. Remarks by Chairman Alan Greenspan, "Stock Options and Related Matters," at the 2002 Financial Markets Conference of the Federal Reserve Bank of Atlanta, Sea Island, Georgia, May 3, 2002.

32. This could be done very easily through taking an index for the sector as a *trend* and *detrend* or through "standardizing" the company's own stock by dividing its price by the contemporaneous value of the index.

33. Alfred Rappaport, "To Avoid a Tumble, Look for These Red Flags," *Wall Street Journal,* February 25, 2002.

Chapter 9

1. Carol Hymowitz, "Does Rank Have Too Much Privilege?" *Wall Street Journal,* February 26, 2002.
2. Transcript of Senate Commerce Committee Hearing on Enron, February 26, 2002.
3. Gretchen Morgenson, "Pushing the Pay Envelope Too Far," *New York Times,* April 14, 2002.
4. Jake Tepper, "Enron's Last-Minute Bonus Orgy," *Salon.com,* February 8, 2002.
5. Paul Beckett, "American Express CEO's 2001 Pay Leapt," *Wall Street Journal,* March 11, 2002.
6. Kathy M. Kristof, "CEOs Paid 70% More at Firms under Scrutiny," *Los Angeles Times,* August 26, 2002.
7. Carol Hymowitz, "Does Rank Have Too Much Privilege?" *Wall Street Journal,* February 26, 2002.
8. Neal Gabler, "Desperately Seeking Celebrity," *Los Angeles Times,* August 11, 2002.
9. David Barboza, "Some Houstonians Whom Enron Called Friends," *New York Times,* March 21, 2002.
10. Michael G. Goldstein, Michael A. Swirnoff, and William A. Drennan, *Taxation and Funding of Nonqualified Deferred Compensation: A Complete Guide to Design and Implementation* (Chicago: American Bar Association, 1998), p. 234.
11. *Ibid.,* p. 235.
12. Jason Leopold and Jessica Berthold, "Enron's Filings Show Lavish Compensation Was Awarded to Many Senior Executives," *Wall Street Journal,* March 18, 2002.
13. John D. McKinnon, "Treasury Moves to Close Tax Loophole Used to Lift Executives' Compensation," *Wall Street Journal,* March 18, 2002.
14. Jerry Knight, "Tracking the Trouble Caused by WorldCom's Bernie Ebbers," *Washington Post,* March 18, 2002.
15. Floyd Norris, "Company Loans Linked to Stock," *New York Times,* March 28, 2002.
16. Jason Leopold and Jessica Berthold, "Enron Unit Chiefs' Compensation Raises Fresh Questions," *Wall Street Journal,* March 15, 2002.

Chapter 10

1. "Fact Sheet FAQs: Measures of Corporate Earnings for Equity Analysis," Standard & Poor's, May 14, 2002.
2. Henny Sender, "Accounting Standards Board Learns Hindsight Is 20/20 in Telecom Swaps," *Wall Street Journal,* March 26, 2002.
3. David M. Blitzer, Robert E. Friedman, and Howard J. Silverblatt, *Measures of Corporate Earnings* (New York: Standard & Poor's, originally released November 7, 2001, revised May 14, 2002).
4. "Pro Forma Financial Information: Tips for Investors," Securities and Exchange Commission (SEC), Washington, December 4, 2001.
5. Bill Gross, "Buffetting Corporate America," *PIMCO—Investment Outlook,* March 2002.
6. Andrew Tobias, *The Only Investment Guide You'll Ever Need* (San Diego: Harcourt, 2002), p. 169.
7. Mark Maremont and William M. Bulkeley, "IBM Is Resolute on Accounting Cited by SEC," *Wall Street Journal,* February 28, 2002.

8. Peter Behr, "Broadband Strategy Got Enron in Trouble," *Washington Post,* January 2, 2002.
9. Dan Feldstein, "What Was Bottom Line at Enron? Disturbing Signs Not Easy to Spot in Annual Report," *Houston Chronicle,* March 17, 2002.
10. Ellen Nakashima and Peter Behr, "Army Secretary's Enron Role Probed," *Washington Post,* February 18, 2002.
11. Jonathan R. Laing, "The Bear That Roared: How Short-Seller Jim Chanos Helped Expose Enron," *Barron's,* January 28, 2002.
12. "Cautionary Advice Regarding the Use of 'Pro Forma' Financial Information in Earnings Releases," SEC, December 4, 2001.
13. Seth Schiesel and Simon Romero, "WorldCom: Out of Obscurity to Under Inquiry," *New York Times,* March 13, 2002.
14. Floyd Norris, "Company Loans Linked to Stock," *New York Times,* March 28, 2002.
15. Roger H. Hermanson and James Don Edwards, *Financial Accounting: A Business Perspective,* 6th ed. (Chicago: Irwin, 1995), p. 150.
16. *Ibid.,* p. 412.
17. David M. Blitzer, Robert E. Friedman, and Howard J. Silverblatt, *Measures of Corporate Earnings* (New York: Standard & Poor's, originally released November 7, 2001, revised May 14, 2002).
18. Andy Kessler, "Winnick's Voyage to the Bottom of the Sea," *Wall Street Journal,* March 21, 2002.
19. Shawn Young, "Qwest Predicts Charge on Its Assets in 2002 of $20 Billion to $30 Billion," *Wall Street Journal,* April 2, 2002.
20. Anonymous, "What the SEC Examines During Financial Reviews," *Los Angeles Times,* April 4, 2002.

Chapter 11

1. Dennis K. Berman, "Regulators Are Taking a Look at Andersen's 'Swaps' Method," *Wall Street Journal,* March 19, 2002.
2. Dan Feldstein, "What Was Bottom Line at Enron? Disturbing Signs Not Easy to Spot in Annual Report," *Houston Chronicle,* March 17, 2002.
3. Peter Eavis, "Why Enron's Writedown Unnerves Some Investors," *TheStreet.com,* October 22, 2001.
4. Dan Feldstein, "What Was Bottom Line at Enron? Disturbing Signs Not Easy to Spot in Annual Report," *Houston Chronicle,* March 17, 2002.
5. Jonathan R. Laing, "The Bear That Roared. How Short-Seller Jim Chanos Helped Expose Enron," *Barron's,* January 28, 2002.
6. Arthur A., "The End of Enron (and Maybe Andersen)," *http://www.eraider.com,* November 13, 2001.
7. Mark Maremont, "Firm Acquired by Tyco Sped Payments to Bolster Cash Flow, E-Mail Indicates," *Wall Street Journal,* March 19, 2002.
8. David Barboza, "Enron Offered Management Aid to Companies," *New York Times,* April 10, 2002.
9. Floyd Norris, "Can Investors Believe Cash Flow Numbers?" *New York Times,* February 19, 2002.

10. Seth Schiesel and Simon Romero, "WorldCom: Out of Obscurity to Under Inquiry," *New York Times,* March 13, 2002.

11. Marcelo Prince and Mylene Mangalindan, "Siebel Revenue from Swap Deals Increased Dramatically in 2001," *Wall Street Journal,* April 4, 2002.

12. Michael Brick, "What Was the Heart of Enron Keeps Shrinking," *New York Times,* April 6, 2002.

13. Gregory Zuckerman and Rachel Emma Silverman, "Why Bond Guru Gross Decided to Attack GE's Finance Practices," *Wall Street Journal,* March 22, 2002.

14. David Barboza, "Some Houstonians Whom Enron Called Friends," *New York Times,* March 21, 2002.

15. Rebecca Smith, "Lay Sold Shares Back to Company Even as Price Fell," *Wall Street Journal,* February 19, 2002.

16. Allan Sloan, "One Enron Lesson: Some Insider Trading Falls Outside the Timely-Reporting Rule," *Washington Post,* March 5, 2002.

17. David Ivanovich, "S&P, Moody's Blast Enron Firm's New President Accused of Deception," *Houston Chronicle,* March 21, 2002.

18. Daniel Altman, "The Taming of the Finance Officers," *New York Times,* April 14, 2002.

Chapter 12

1. Remarks by Chairman Alan Greenspan, "Corporate Governance," at the Stern School of Business, New York University, New York, March 26, 2002.

2. "Study Sheds Light on Value of Analysts' Stock Recommendations, Finds That 2000 Was Disaster," Berkeley, June 14, 2001.

3. Supreme Court of the State of New York, County of New York, in the Matter of an Inquiry by Eliot Spitzer, Attorney General of the State of New York, Petitioner, Affidavit in Support of Pursuant to Article 23-A of the General Business Application for an Order Law of the State of New York with regard to the Pursuant to General Acts and Practices of Business Law Section 354, Merrill Lynch & Co., Inc., pp. 35–36.

4. Charles Gasparino, "New York Attorney General Turns Up Heat on Wall Street," *Wall Street Journal,* April 10, 2002.

5. Ben White, "Tired of Stock Answers? Independent Research Firms Are Drawing Investors as Analysts' Troubles Mount," *Washington Post,* April 14, 2002.

6. Charles Gasparino, "Exiting Merrill Analyst Blodget Faces New York Investigation," *Wall Street Journal,* December 10, 2001.

7. Supreme Court of the State of New York . . . , pp. 31–32.

8. Robert O'Harrow, Jr., and Caroline E. Mayer, "N.Y. Investigation of Analysts Broadens," *Washington Post,* April 11, 2002.

9. Richard A. Oppel Jr., "The Man Who Paid the Price for Sizing Up Enron," *New York Times,* March 27, 2002.

10. Patrick McGeehan, "Public Anger on Wall Street Research Reaches Political Arena," *New York Times,* April 12, 2002.

11. James K. Glassman, "Faulty Analysis," *Wall Street Journal,* April 12, 2002.

12. Ben White, "Tired of Stock Answers? Independent Research Firms Are Drawing Investors as Analysts' Troubles Mount," *Washington Post,* April 14, 2002.

Chapter 13

1. Gregory Zuckermen, "Enron Quietly Ran Risky Hedge Fund That Turned Over Millions in Trades," *Wall Street Journal,* April 11, 2002.
2. Kurt Eichenwald with Diana B. Henriques, "Web of Details In as Warnings Went Unheeded," *New York Times,* February 10, 2002.
3. Liz Pulliam Weston, "Get Loan Rate Based on Your Credit Score," *Los Angeles Times,* March 1, 2002.
4. Tanya Azarchs, "Enron Credit Exposure Widely Dispersed Through Global Financial System," Standard & Poor's *RatingsDirect,* December 6, 2001.
5. Richard A. Oppel, Jr., "Credit Agencies Say Enron Dishonesty Misled Them," *New York Times,* March 21, 2002.
6. Laura Goldberg and Michael Davis, "What Went Wrong with Enron?" *Houston Chronicle,* November 8, 2001.
7. Testimony of Chairman Alan Greenspan, Federal Reserve Board's Semiannual Monetary Policy Report to the Congress, Committee on Financial Services, U.S. House of Representatives, February 27, 2002.
8. Peter Eavis, "Trusts Keeping Enron Off Balance," *http://TheStreet.com,* October 22, 2001.
9. Gregory Zuckerman, "Sinking Commercial Paper Market Broadens Effects of Enron Troubles," *Wall Street Journal,* March 28, 2002.
10. Unsigned editorial, "Fannie's Progress," *Wall Street Journal,* April 2, 2002.
11. James V. Grimaldi, "Enron Pipeline Leaves Scar on South America. Lobbying, U.S. Loans Put Project on Damaging Path," *Washington Post,* May 6, 2002.
12. James V. Grimaldi, "Enron's Overseas Boondoggle," *Washington Post,* February 18, 2002.

Chapter 14

1. Liz Pulliam Weston, "Pensions Are Losing Popularity," *Los Angeles Times,* March 18, 2002,.
2. David Wessel, "Enron and a Bigger Ill: Americans Don't Save," *Wall Street Journal,* March 7, 2002.
3. Liz Pulliam Weston, "Retire: Lessons from Enron," *Los Angeles Times,* January 28, 2002.
4. David Wessel, "Enron and a Bigger Ill: Americans Don't Save," *Wall Street Journal,* March 7, 2002.
5. Peter G. Gosselin, "Near-Retirees Don't Have Enough Saved. Pensions: Study's Surprising Conclusion Is That Most Older Workers Lost Ground During the 1990s Economic Boom," *Los Angeles Times,* May 3, 2002.
6. David Leonhardt, "Sweetening Pensions at a Cost to Workers," *New York Times,* February 17, 2002.
7. Ellen E. Schultz and Theo Francis, "Companies' Hot Tax Break: 401(k)s," *Wall Street Journal,* January 31, 2002.
8. Edward Wyatt, "Pension Change Puts the Burden on the Worker," *New York Times,* April 5, 2002.

9. Ellen E. Schultz and Theo Francis, "Companies' Hot Tax Break: 401(k)s," *Wall Street Journal,* January 31, 2002.
10. Warren Vieth, "Sponsors Fight 401(k) Plan Limits," *Los Angeles Times,* February 18, 2002.
11. *Ibid.*
12. "Staggering losses" is the phrase used in a lawsuit filed by more than 400 Enron employees on Monday, January 28, 2002 (Nancy Rivera Brooks, "Enron Workers File Suit Over 'Staggering Losses,'" *Los Angeles Times,* January 29, 2002).
13. Martine Costello, "Did Enron Cross the Line?" *CNNMoney,* February 5, 2002.
14. Albert B. Crenshaw, "U.S. to Seek Retirement Plan Control at Enron," *Washington Post,* February 11, 2002.
15. Kathy Chen, "Enron 401(k) Chief Defends Handling of Plan, Discloses He Sold Stock in June," *Wall Street Journal,* February 8, 2002.
16. Albert B. Crenshaw, "U.S. to Seek Retirement Plan Control at Enron," *Washington Post,* February 11, 2002.
17. Jeff D. Opdyke, "More Firms Turn to Money Managers as Do-It-Yourself Retirement Falters," *Wall Street Journal,* April 30, 2002.
18. Harry M. Markowitz, "Portfolio Selection," *Journal of Finance* 7(1):77–91, 1952.
19. Albert B. Crenshaw, "Fear, Greed: The Players in Pension Debate," *Washington Post,* February 8, 2002.
20. Kathy M. Kristof, "Proposals for 401(k) Reform Fall Short," *Los Angeles Times,* February 17, 2002.

Chapter 15

1. A very good investment guide in my mind—and very funny too—is Andrew Tobias' *The Only Investment Guide You'll Ever Need* (San Diego: Harcourt, 2002).
2. It might happen that a company has reached such dire straits that there are no shares left on the market to be borrowed for the purpose of short selling (see, for some examples, Dave Kansas, "Squeeze May Soon Turn Short Sellers' Jubilation into Gloom," *Wall Street Journal,* August 22, 1994).
3. Remarks by Chairman Alan Greenspan, "Mortgage Markets and Economic Activity," before a Conference on Mortgage Markets and Economic Activity sponsored by America's Community Bankers, Washington, November 2, 1999.
4. Kathryn Kranhold, Rick Wartzman, and John R. Wilke, "As the Enron Inquiry Intensifies, Midlevel Players Face Spotlight," *Wall Street Journal,* April 30, 2002.
5. Remarks by Chairman Alan Greenspan, "Economic Volatility," at a symposium sponsored by the Federal Reserve Bank of Kansas City, Jackson Hole, WY, August 30, 2002.
6. Erin Schulte, "Long in the Shadows, Dividends Take Stage," *Wall Street Journal Online,* April 20, 2002.

Index

A

AAA grade, 185, 186
Abbott Laboratories, 201
Acceleration of payments, 157
Accomplices, 21
Accounting for Stock Issued to Employees
  (Accounting Principles Board), 115
Accounting Principles Board (APB),
  115-116
Accounting/accountants, 13-27
  aggressive, 137
  low standards for, 19-20
  and overpriced stocks, 23-24
  regulatory environment for, 20-21
Acquisitions, 101, 150, 157
Adelphia, 3, 100, 133, 148
Advances, 31
Adventurousness, 10
African-American households, 198
Aftermarket, 50, 51
Agency costs, 103
Aggressive accounting, 137
AIG, Inc., 195
Allen, Senator, 154
Alpha Equity Research, Inc., 177
Alternative minimum tax (AMT), 110
Amazon.com, 25
American Electronics Association, 114
American Express, 127
AmeriCredit, 163
Amin Badr el-Din, 85
AMT (alternative minimum tax), 110
Analysts, 165-179
  and conflicts of interest, 167-170
  and enhanced index funds, 214-215
  examples of, 172-174
  finding good, 176-177
  and negotiating stock ratings, 171-172
  and problems with ratings, 171
  role of, 166-167

truthfulness of, 177-178
  value of, 175-176
Annual reports, 152
  accountant's role in, 14
  organization of, 139
Anticorrelated products, 131
AOL Time Warner, 149
APB (see Accounting Principles Board)
Appreciation, 31
Arbitrage, 60-61, 212
The Art of Speculation (Philip L. Carret),
  77
Arthur A. (Web gadfly), 16-17, 154-155,
  156
Arthur Andersen, 10-12, 13-20
  and Enron's culture, 21-22
  patterns of abuse at, 15-18
  Jeffrey Skilling on, 18-19
Ask price, 66, 69, 70, 71-74
As-reported earnings, 100, 138
Asset-light companies, 8-10
At the money, 107
AT&T, 140, 157
Avici, 92
Azarchs, Tanya, 186
Azurix, 154

B

Bandwidth, 6
Bandwidth market, 86-87
Bankruptcy:
  of Enron, 2, 3, 11, 183
  of Global Crossing, 149
  and retention bonuses, 126
  and shareholders, 45-46
Baptist Foundation, 16
Barber, Brad, 175-176
Barboza, David, 84-85, 130, 157-158
Barter-based economies, 29-30, 159
Bass, Carl, 21

Baxter, John Clifford, 81
Bear Stearns & Co., 119, 169
Berce, Daniel E., 163
Berman, Dennis K., 151
Bid price, 66, 69, 70, 71-74
Bills, 38
Black-Scholes valuation method, 67, 116
Blackstone Group, 70
Blodget, Henry, 166, 170, 172-173, 178
Bloomberg, 70
Boeing Co., 115
Bond ratings, 185
Bonds, 38, 44-45, 216-217
Boneparth, Peter A., 125-126
Bonuses, 104-105, 126-127
Book value, 143
Borrowing fee, 213
Boundary phenomenon, 66, 72, 73
Boxer, Barbara, 18-19, 90, 91, 208-209
Brick, Michael, 88
Bridge-Telerate, 70
Broadband, 6, 85-88
Broadband/bandwidth industry, 6, 7, 144
Brown, Thomas, 169
Bubble game, 1, 25
Buffet, Warren, 25
Bull market, 93-94
Bunning, Jim, 187
Bush, George W., 21, 201
Business model, Enron's, 1-12
    Arthur Andersen's role in, 10-12
    asset-light, 8-10
    bandwidth and stock prices in, 6-8
    collapse of, 2-4
    innovative, 4-5
Buy and hold strategy, 77
Buyers, 51
Byrnes, Tracy, 110-111, 115

C
California energy crisis, 88, 89-91, 192
California Independent System Operator
    (Cal-ISO), 89-91
Call options, 41, 108
Callard Asset Management, 177
Capacity swaps, 29-30
Capital, 30
Capital gains, 25, 58-59, 112
Capital growth, 37-47
    and bonds, 44-45
    and gain/loss, 40-41

and lenders/borrowers, 43-44
and rent, 38-39, 41-42
and shares, 38-40, 42-43, 45-46
Capitalism, 29-36
    and buying/selling/leasing, 29-30
    and growth through diversification, 32-34
    and loans, 30, 34-35
    and profit/loss, 31-32
Capitalized reputation, 190
Caps, 209
Carmichael, Douglas R., 144-145
Carnahan, Jean, 85
Carret, Philip L., 77
Cash swaps, 158, 159
Castle-in-the air theory, 50, 53, 62
Catastrophe Bonds credit cliff, 195
La cavalerie, 61
Celebritization of wealth, 128
"Certain transactions," 148
CFSB (Crédit Suisse First Boston), 169
Chanos, Jim, 93, 147, 156
"Charges," 147
Checkbox style of accounting, 20
Chenault, Kenneth, 127
Chevron Texaco, 205
Chewco, 22, 83, 85
Chinese walls, 169, 170, 175
Chung Wu, 174
Cisco Systems, Inc., 111, 118
Citigroup, 119
Clapman, Peter, 134
Clark/Bardes Consulting, 105
Clearinghouses, 68, 69
Clinton administration, 114
Coca-Cola, 118
COLI (company-owned life insurance), 131
Collusion, 22
Colonial Realty, 16
Columbus analogy, 40
Commercial paper, 104
Commission rebates, 69
Commissions, 4, 77, 125-126
Commitments and contingencies, 155
Commodities, 30
Common market price, 143
Common shareholders, 46
Company stock:
    and employees as shareholders, 199,
        200-201, 204, 207-208
    and 401(k) plans, 204
    trading in, 7

Company-owned life insurance (COLI), 131
Compensation, other, 148
Computer Associates, 107
Computrade Systems, Inc., 177
Concurrent transactions, 159
Confidence factor, 181
Confidence-sensitive entities, 189-190
Conflicts of interest, 156, 167-170
Confucius, 221
Consumable (term), 86-87
Contingent stock obligations, 155-156
Contrarian strategy, 93
Core earnings, 117-118, 195
Corporate back scratching, 149
Corporate jets, 133
Correlated products, 131
Corzine, Jon S., 209
Council of Institutional Investors, 117
Credit cliffs, 182, 183, 187-188, 188-191
    confidence-sensitive entity, 189-190
    event-specific dependent, 189
    rating trigger situation, 190-191
    and ratings decline spiral, 191-192
Credit line, 133
Credit ratings, corporate, 185-187
Crédit Suisse First Boston (CFSB), 169
Credit swaps, 68, 87
Cuiabá pipeline, 194

D
D grade, 185
Dabhol project, 125
Dangerous Dreamers (Robert Sobel), 5
Davis, Gray, 89
"Death by Guru" (Paul Krugman), 9
Debt:
    reporting (omissions) of, 155
    retirement of, 102
Decision making, financial reports as basis for, 24
Decks, 69
Deep-discount brokerages, 78
Deferred compensation, 129
Defined-benefit plans, 199
Defined-contribution plans, 199, 207
Dell Computer, 112
Demme, Karen, 118
Depreciation, 31
Deregulation, energy, 90
Derivatives, 5, 10, 86, 91-93, 92

Deutsche Telekom, 93
Dietert, Jeff, 188
Direct government subsidies in housing, 218
Direct public offering, 51
Discounting, 45
Diversification, 10, 32-34, 203, 208, 215
Dividends, 25, 39, 46, 53, 58-60, 220
Dividend-stream theory, 49-50, 52-54, 57
Dodson, William D., 125
Dollar cost average, 77
Donaldson, Lufkin & Jenrette, 169
Dorgan, Byron, 37, 123-124, 126
Dorton, Patrick, 21
Dot-com bubble, 4, 25, 128
Dow Jones Industrial Average, 56, 214
Dow-Jones, 24
Drucker, Peter F., 134
Duncan, David, 17, 169
Dunn, Joe, 90
Dyke, James, 182
Dynegy, Inc., 182-183, 186, 189, 191, 205

E
Earnings, 99-104
    and debt retirement, 102
    quality of, 149
    and reinvestment, 101
    reporting of, 152-153
    and share buybacks, 102-104
Earnings before bad stuff (EBBS), 138
Earnings before interest and taxes (EBIT), 100
Earnings per share (EPS), 112-113
Earnings-focused, 25
Earnings-obsession, 25, 81-95
    broadband model risk as factor in, 85-88
    bull market as factor in, 93-94
    California energy crisis as factor in, 89-91
    derivatives as factor in, 91-93
    and Enron culture, 82-84
    entrepreneurial culture as factor in, 83-84
    Project Summer as factor in, 84-85
    and reporting, 153
Eavis, Peter, 61, 155-156, 191
EBay.com, 25
Ebbers, Bernard, 92-93, 133, 158-159
EBBS (earnings before bad stuff), 138

EBIT (earnings before interest and taxes), 100

EBS (Enron Broadband Services), 6

Economic Policy Institute, 198

The Economist, 139

ECT Investments, 181

E.D.S (Electronic Data Systems), 158

Eichenwald, Kurt, 16

Electricity, 6, 86

Electronic Data Systems (E.D.S.), 158

Eli Lilly and Co., 146, 157

Elias, Amy Jean, 173

EMC Corp, 134

Emissions swaps, 88

Employee Retirement Income Security Act, 205

Employee stock ownership plans (ESOPs), 24, 26, 54, 199-201

Employees as shareholders, 197-210

   and administration of retirement plans, 205-206

   and company stock, 199, 200-201, 204, 207-208

   dual standards for, 198

   at Enron, 199-200

   with 401(k) plans, 202-205

   knowledge of 401(k) plans by, 199

   and self-management of plan, 207-209

   and tax minimization efforts, 201

Employer stock purchase plans, 208

Energy derivatives, 86

Energy forwards, 88

Energy trading, 1, 4, 6

Enhanced index funds, 214-215

Enrico, Roger A., 123, 127

Enron, 174, 177, 186, 189

   business model of, 1-12

   culture of, 21, 82-84

   deferred compensation at, 130

   401(k) administration changes at, 203-205

   401(k) plan trustees, 206

   as Government-Support Dependency, 193-194

   marking to market approach of, 144-146

   and ratings agencies, 182-184

   stock options at, 118-119

   tax-minimization efforts of, 201

Enron Broadband Services (EBS), 6

Enron Capital and Trade Resources, 8, 84

Enron Communications, Inc., 6

Enron press releases:

   "additional information about related party and off-balance-sheet transactions" (November 8, 2001), 205

   "explaining basic facts about its 401(k) plan" (December 14, 2001), 200

   "non-recurring charges of $1.01 billion after tax" (October 16, 2001), 203

   "non-recurring charges totaling $1.01 billion after-tax" (October 15, 2001), 11

   restatement of reported income (November 8, 2001), 11

"Enronitis," 59

Entrepreneurs, 31

EPS (see Earnings per share)

Equilibrium theory, 74

Equity, building, 219

Equity method, 142, 154-155

Equity variation, 130

ESOPs (see Employee stock ownership plans)

European structure (of accounting), 20

Evans, Donald L., 182

Event-specific dependent credit cliffs, 189

Excessive compensation, 123-135

   burden of, 126

   and celebritization of wealth, 128-129

   commission fees as, 125-126

   and executive freedom, 125-126

   and perks, 132-133

   reporting of, 127

   retention bonuses as, 126-127

   for retired executives, 129-132

   shareholder actions on, 133-134

Exchange funds, 203

Exchange-rate risk, 215

Exchanges, 30

Exclusive benefit rule, 205

Executive compensation, 101, 103

Exercise price, 108

Expectations Investing (Alfred Rappaport and Michael Mauboussin), 57, 112-113

Expectations theory, 50

Expensing (of options), 117-118

Export-Import Bank, 194

Extensions, 218

Extrinsic evidence, 74

F

Face value (of loan), 30, 33

Fads, 9
Fair, Isaac & Company (FICO), 184
Fair value, 115, 116, 143-144
Fairness, 134
Fannie Mae, 160, 193
FASB (see Financial Accounting Standards Board)
Fastow, Andrew S., 83-85, 125, 156
Federal Energy Regulatory Commission (FERC), 90
Federal Home Loan Mortgage Corporation (FHLMC), 193
Federal Housing Authority (FHA), 218
Federal National Mortgage Association (FNMA), 193
Federal Reserve, 105, 189, 190
Feedback loops, 72
Feeding (company), 56
Feiger, George, 207
Feldstein, Dan, 154
FERC (Federal Energy Regulatory Commission), 90
FHA (Federal Housing Authority), 218
FHLMC (Federal Home Loan Mortgage Corporation), 193
Fiberoptic cable, 6
FICO (Fair, Isaac & Company), 184
Filter strategy, 65, 75-78
Financial Accounting Standards Board (FASB), 98, 114-115, 143, 149
Financial Institutions Reform Recovery and Enforcement Act, 23
Financial reports, decision making based on, 24
Financial statements, stock options in, 114-116
Financial swaps, 203
Firm-foundation assessment of price, 50
First Call/Thomson Financial, 170
Fitch Ratings, 185
Fitzgerald, Peter, 19, 111
Fixed-income investments, 38-39
FleetBoston, 129
FNMA (Federal National Mortgage Association), 193
Food and Drug Administration, 71
Footnotes (in annual reports), 127, 139, 147-148
Foreign stocks, 215
Form 4 (SEC), 161, 162
Form 5 (SEC), 161, 162

Forward purchases, 30
Forwards, energy, 88
401(k) plans:
  administration changes in, 203-205
  benefits of, 207
  as defined-contribution plans, 199
  at Enron, 199-200
  Enron's, 197
  lockout periods with, 203-204
  restrictions on sale of, 202-203
  stock manipulation with, 202
  support for regulation of, 14
  trustees for, 206
France Télécom, 93
Fraud, 16, 178
Freddie Mac, 160, 193
Freedom (of executives), 125-126
Frequency (of trading), 144
Frevert, Mark A., 159
Friedman, Karen, 197
Full disclosure, 162-163
Fundamentals (explanation of stock price), 49-50
Fungible (term), 87

G
GAAP (see Generally Accepted Accounting Principles)
Gabler, Neal, 128
Gain-on-sale accounting, 147
Gas banks, 84
GATX Corp., 192
General Electric, 104, 118, 160
General expenses, 140
Generally Accepted Accounting Principles (GAAP), 92, 138, 139, 141
Ghilarducci, Teresa, 202
Glassman, James K., 175
Global Crossing, 3, 23, 30, 149, 151, 158
Global Network, 140
Globalization, 215
Gold standard, 67
Goldman Sachs Group, 169, 170, 177
Goods, 30
Goodwill, 148-149
Gottesdiener, Eli, 206
Government-Sponsored Entities (GSEs), 192-193
Government-Support Dependencies (GSDs), 192-194
Grading system, credit, 185

Graham, Benjamin, 53
Gramm, Wendy L., 86
Greenspan, Alan, 99
  on confidence sensitivity, 190
  on death of recession, 81
  on diminishing role of shareholders, 103
  on dot-com post-mortem, 220
  on evolution of dividends and earnings,
    58-59
  on expensing stock options, 116-117
  on growth and uncertainty, 10
  on home transactions, 218
  on management and stock options, 119-
    120
  on research analysts, 165
  on share repurchase plans, 113-114
  on share valuation, 57
Griep, Clifford M., 183
Grimaldi, James V., 194
Gross, Bill, 104, 139, 147, 160
Growth, 10
Grubman, Jack B., 166, 173-174
GSDs (see Government-Support
  Dependencies)
GSEs (see Government-Sponsored
  Entities)

H
Haas School of Business, 176
Hedge funds, 181
Hedges, 131-132
Hershey Foods Corp., 160
Hewitt Associates, 198
High-tech sector, 114
Hitt, Greg, 114
Home Depot, 148
Houston Chronicle, 145
Hymowitz, Carol, 128

I
Iacocca, Lee, 128
IBM, 140-141
"The IBM footnote," 140
ILIT (irrevocable life insurance trust), 130
Illegal trading, 161
ImClone, 71
"In the money," 41, 108
Income, 31
Inconvenience, 34
Independence (of auditors), 21
Independent equity research, 177

Index funds, 214
Indexed option programs, 120
Individual retirement accounts (IRAs), 215
Inflation, 216
InfoSpace, 171-173
Initial public offerings (IPOs), 50
Innovation, 9
Insider trading, 160-162
Institute of Management and Administra-
  tion, 200
Institutional investors, 52, 69, 75, 104, 117
Insurance, 88
Insured Ratings credit cliff, 194-195
Intel, 118
Interest cash flows, 34
Interest (on loan), 33
Interest rate, 33
Internal Revenue Service (IRS), 110
Internet, 6
Intrinsic evidence, 74
Intrinsic value based method of accounting,
  115-116
Intrinsic value of a call option, 107-108,
  110
Investment Company Institute, 200
Investor confidence, 11, 24
Investor-owned utilities (IOUs), 89, 90
Investors:
  and accountants, 14
  responsibility of, 24-26
IOUs (see Investor-owned utilities)
IPOs (initial public offerings), 50
IRAs (individual retirement accounts), 215
Irrevocable life insurance trust (ILIT), 130
IRS (Internal Revenue Service), 110

J
Janitor life insurance, 131
JEDI, 22
Jensen, Michael, 98
Jets, corporate, 133
Joint ventures and affiliates, 142
Jones Apparel Company, 125-126
Jumping-off points, 187
Junk bonds, 23, 38, 185, 186
Junk-bond status, 11, 183

K
Kapner, Suzanne, 94
Kessler, Andy, 92-93
Keynes, John Maynard, 50

Knowledge, 8
Kopper, Michael J., 125
Krugman, Paul, 9
KSOP, 201

L
Laddering, 52
Laing, Jonathan R., 93
Larsen, Lars, 157
Latino households, 198
Law of one price, 61
Lay, Kenneth, 87, 125, 131, 133, 161, 162, 182, 194, 206
Lazard Freres, 169
Lease agreements, 142
Leases, 30
Lehavy, Reuven, 175
Lehman Brothers Holdings, 169
Letter-of-the-law mentality, 20
Leverage, 154, 182
Levin, Carl, 111, 119
Levitt, Arthur, Jr., 21
Lieberman, Joseph I., 187
Liesman, Steve, 1
Life insurance, 130, 131
Life the Movie (Neal Gabler), 128
Life-cycle funds, 209
Line of credit, 133
Liquidation value, 143
LJM1, 125, 156
LJM2, 83, 125, 155
LJM Cayman, 83
Loans, 29, 30
    reporting of, 148
    to Jeffrey Skilling, 133
Lockheed Martin, 157
Lockout periods, 203-204
Long selling, 76
Long-term Treasury bonds, 44-45
Loophole-Sensitive Entities credit cliff, 195
Los Angeles Times, 14, 184
Loss, 31-32
Lucent Technologies, 111, 204

M
Malkiel, Burton, 50, 77, 78, 107
Manipulating reports, 151-164
Margin accounts, 109
Margin calls, 109
Mark, Rebecca, 125

Market makers, 69, 87
Markets, 30
Marking to market, 22-23, 61-62, 143-146
Markowitz, Harry, 208
Martin Act (New York), 168
Materiality standard, 16-17
Maturity:
    bond, 216
    loan, 30
Mauboussin, Michael, 57, 112-113
MBS (see Mortgage-backed securities)
McCain, John, 111
McConnell, Pat, 118
McCullough, Robert F., 61-62, 83, 88
McGeehan, Patrick, 175
McKinsey & Company, 8
The McKinsey Quarterly, 8
McMahon, Jeffrey, 162-163
McNichols, Maureen, 175, 176
Mean reversion, 74
Medium-term Treasury notes, 45
Megagrants, 105
Melnick, Andy, 170
Mentor Graphics Corp., 134
Merrill Lynch, 167, 168, 170, 171-172, 172-173, 178
Microsoft, 55, 111, 112
Milken, Michael, 5
Miller, William, 107
Model risk, 87, 88
Money markets, 216
Moody's Investors Service, 11, 182, 185, 193
Morgan, J. P., 63, 134
Morgan Stanley, 169
Morgenson, Gretchen, 61-62, 126
Mortgage industry, 193
Mortgage-backed securities (MBS), 217-218
"Mother of All Corporations," 2
Mulford, Charles, 141
Munnell, Alicia H., 209

N
Nacchio, Joseph P., 133
NASD (see National Association of Securities Dealers)
Nasdaq Composite, 214
Nasdaq Index, 7, 92
National Association of Securities Dealers (NASD), 52, 167, 168

"Naturally Occurring Ponzi Process," 62
Neal, Richard, 203
Nebraska, 207
Negative-feedback loops, 192
Negotiation:
    of credit ratings, 186
    of stock ratings, 171-172
Net earnings, 46
Netting, 150
The New Market Wizards (Jack D. Schwager), 73
New Power Company, 92
New York State, 167, 178
New York Stock Exchange (NYSE), 167, 172
New York Times, 84, 148, 159, 163, 174, 175
News agencies, 70
Noise, 67
Nominal amount (of loan), 33
Non-core businesses, 7-8
Non-dividend paying companies, 54-56
Nonlinearity, 68, 187-188
Nonqualified plans, 130
Normal, 141
Northwest Natural Gas Co., 189
Notes, 38
NYSE (New York Stock Exchange), 167, 172

O
Off-balance-sheet reporting, 142
Olson, Cindy, 206
Olson, John, 154
The Only Investment Guide You'll Ever Need (Andrew Tobias), 106
Open outcry, 66
Operating earnings, 117, 138
OPIC (see Overseas Private Investment Corporation)
Optical-fiber business, 86
Oracle, 119
Organized markets, 68, 87
O'Shaughnessy, James, 59
OTC markets (see Over-the-counter markets)
"Other compensation," 148
"Other revenues," 147
"Out of the money," 41
Overcapitalized, 33
Overseas Private Investment Corporation (OPIC), 193-194
Over-the-counter (OTC) markets, 68, 87

Owens-Illinois, 157
Ownership, transfer of, 29

P
Pacific Gas & Electric, 183, 192
Package buying/selling, 69
PaineWebber, 174
Palmer, Mark A., 200, 203
Partnerships, Enron, 11
Pearlstein, Steven, 98
Pension and Welfare Benefits Administration, 205-206
Pension plans, 198
Pensions assets and liabilities, 142
Performance, 208
Perks, 132-133
Perry, Michael, 101, 106, 113
Peterson, Lowell, 127
Pfizer, Inc., 160
P&G (see Procter and Gamble)
Physiocrats, 31
PIMCO, 104
Pit, 68
Pit recorders, 70
Pitt, Harvey L., 19, 21, 168
Ponzi, Charles ("Carlo"), 60-62
Ponzi schemes, 60-62
Portfolio selection theory, 208
Portland General Electric Co., 189
Positive-feedback loops, 192
Pottruck, David, 175
Powers Report:
    on capitalizing on own stock, 92
    on Chewco and JEDI, 22
    on Andrew Fastow, 83
Preferred shareholders, 46
Preferred shares, 201
Preferred stock, 46
Prentice, James, 206
Present value, 30
Pretax earnings, 100
Price, 30, 46
Price caps, 90
Price gouging, 90
Price-discovery process, 35
Pricing shares, 65-79
    and filter strategy, 75-78
    and market types, 68
    and traders, 68-70
    traders' responses to, 71
    and transactions, 70

and tug-of-war analogy, 66
and uncertainty, 74-75
variation in, 66-68
and volume, 71-74
Primary buyers, 51
Primary markets, 50-51
Principal (of loan), 33
Private placement, 51
Pro forma reporting, 138-139
Procter and Gamble (P&G), 118, 201
Producers, 51
Profit, 31-32, 34
Profit rate, 32, 33
Profit-sharing plans, 200
Project Summer, 84-85, 194
Proprietary trading, 69, 70
Pyramid schemes, 61, 62

Q
Quality of earnings, 149
Quarterly reports (10-Q filings), 152, 160
Quesnay, François, 31
Quote screens, 70, 72
Qwest, 3, 23, 30, 133, 149, 157, 204

R
"Rally in the Valley," 114
A Random Walk Down Wall Street (Burton
  Malkiel), 77, 107
Random-walk view of price formation, 67
Rappaport, Alfred, 50, 57, 112, 120
Raptors partnership, 83, 85
Rate of return, 32
Rating agencies, 11, 68, 181-196
  and corporate credit ratings, 185-187
  and debt, 102
  and Enron, 182-184
  and Enron as GSD, 193-194
  and Enron as insured ratings credit cliff,
    194-195
  Enron as loophole-sensitive credit cliff,
    195
  and nonlinear ratings, 187-188
  and spiral of downgrading corporation,
    191-192
  and triggers by other agencies, 192
  value of, 184-185
Rating cliff, 183
Rating trigger situations, 190-191
Ratings, analysts' stock, 171-172
Raychem Corp., 157

Real estate, 218-219
Rectification of names, 221
Regulatory environment, 20-21
Reinsurance, 88
Reinvestment, 101
Reliability, 137, 152
Reliant Resources, Inc., 191
Rent(s), 34, 39, 53
  profit/risk with, 41-42
  share vs., 43-44
Reported net income, 100
Reporting, 137-150
  cash flow maneuvering in, 158-159
  of certain transactions, 148
  charges, 147
  and earnings management, 157
  Enron's financial, 153-156
  Enron's "full disclosure," 162-163
  Enron's marking to market approach to,
    144-146
  of excessive compensation, 127
  and fair value, 143-144
  footnotes in, 147-148
  gain-on-sale, 147
  of goodwill, 148-149
  impenetrability of Enron's, 156
  on insider trading, 160-162
  maneuvering for quarterly, 160
  manipulation of, 25, 151-164
  off-balance-sheet, 142
  of other compensation, 148
  other revenues, 147
  and pro-forma arguments, 140-142
  SEC targeting of, 149-150
  of stock options, 114-116
  styles of, 138-139
Reputation, 189-190
Reregulation, energy, 89
Research analysts (see Analysts)
Research firms, 75
Responsibility:
  Arthur Andersen's lack of shared, 17-18
  Jeffrey Skilling's lack of, 19
Retention bonuses, 4, 126-127
Retirement:
  administration of plans for, 205-206
  of debt, 102
  executive compensation in, 129-132
Retirement plans:
  at Enron, 198
  executive, 4

Return on investment (ROI), 101
Returns, 31
Revenue recognition, 149
Revenues, other, 147
Rigas family, 133, 148
Risk:
    factor of, 212
    level of, 209
Risk logic, 185
Risk management, 5, 8
    and fixed-income investments, 38
    instruments for, 87-88
    and loans, 31
    and over-the-counter markets, 68
    and rent vs. share, 40-41
ROI (return on investment), 101
Round-tripping, 149, 158
Rule of no arbitrage, 61
Run on the bank, 189-190
Russell 2000, 214

S
Sale of assets, 140
Sales, 29
Salomon Smith Barney, 109, 169, 170,
    173-174
Samson, Solomon B., 182, 183, 188-191
Savings accounts, 215-216
Schlesinger, Jacob M., 114
SEC (see Securities and Exchange
    Commission)
Secondary buyers, 51
Secondary markets, 30, 51, 56-57, 216
Securities and Exchange Commission (SEC):
    Adelphia's filing with, 148
    American Express Co.'s filing with, 127
    and Arthur Andersen, 16, 17
    on charges, 147
    Enron conflict of interest investigation
        by, 204-205
    Enron's 3rd quarter 2001 filing with, 7-8
    excessive compensation investigations
        by, 127
    Global Crossing and Qwest investigated
        by, 30
    insider trading information filing with,
        161-162
    IPO investigations by, 52
    lax regulatory environment at, 20-21
    and nationally recognized ratings organ-
        izations, 185
    on pro forma, 139

reporting targeted by, 149-150, 152
research analysts investigated by, 168
on sale of assets, 140
and share repurchases, 113-114
on Trump Hotels, 141
Self-policing, 152
Sender, Henry, 137-138
Settle price, 66, 70, 71-74
Share, rent vs., 43-44
Share buybacks, 102-104, 111-114
Share price and value, 49-64
    and capital gains, 58-59
    and dividends, 59-60
    dividend-stream theory of, 52-54
    and IPOs, 52
    and non-dividend paying companies,
        54-56
    and Ponzi schemes, 60-62
    primary and secondary markets for, 50-51
    in secondary market, 56-57
    self-limiting nature of, 62-63
Sharecropping, 40
Shareholders, 40, 133-134
Shares, 38, 39
    and bankruptcy, 45-46
    compensation on basis of, 39-40
    price of, 46
    profit/risk with, 42-43
Shiller, Robert J., 49, 62, 103
Short selling, 76, 94, 213-214
Short-term Treasury bills, 45
Shredding of documents, 17
Siebel, Tom, 159
Siebel Systems, Inc., 159
Siegel, Jeremy, 55, 56, 59, 103
Silicon Valley, 114
Size of investment, 211-212
Skilling, Jeffrey K., 5, 6, 8-9, 11, 18-19,
    20, 84, 86, 89, 90, 93, 119, 131, 133,
    145, 153-154, 181, 190, 194
Slippage, 69, 75, 144
Sloan, Allan, 162
Sobel, Robert, 5
Southern California Edison, 183, 192
S&P (see Standard & Poor's 500)
Spartis, Philip L., 173
Special orders, 71
Specialists, 68
Special-purpose entities (SPEs), 93, 142,
    154-155
Speculative bubbles, 2, 220
SPEs (see Special-purpose entities)

Spitzer, Eliot, 167-169, 172, 174, 175, 177
Split-dollar deferred death-benefits plan, 130
Split-dollar life insurance policy, 131
Spread, 72
Staff Accounting Bulletin 101 (SEC), 140
Standard & Poor's, 11, 24, 97, 99, 117, 185, 186
  on credit cliffs, 182
  on dividends, 220
  on goodwill, 148
  on measures of corporate earnings, 117
  on real estate operations, 195
  on reliability of earnings reports, 137
  on reporting styles, 138
Standard & Poor's (S&P) 500, 56, 105, 214
Standardized bandwidth product, 86-87
Standing orders, 75
Starbucks Corp., 160
Statement 123 (FASB), 98, 107, 115, 116
Statement 133 (FASB), 143
Statement 142 (FASB), 149
Stern, Thomas D., 126
Stewart, Martha, 71
Stock:
  issuing new, 112
  repurchase of, 112-113
Stock options, 97-122
  as compensation, 104-105
  cost of, 99
  and earnings, 99-104
  at Enron, 118-119
  in financial statements, 114-116
  Alan Greenspan on, 116-117
  indexed, 119-120
  losing money with, 108-110
  repricing of, 105-107
  and share buybacks, 102-104, 111-114
  Standard and Poor's on, 117-118
  tax treatment of, 110-111
  value of, 107-108
Stock ratings, 171-172
Stock-based employee compensation plans, 98
Stock-price fever, 7
Stock-price pumps, 2
Stocks For the Long Run (Jeremy Siegel), 55, 56
StockScouter, 177
Stop-loss, 76
Strike price, 108

Structured finance, 158
Studebaker, 56
Subscriptions, research, 75
Sunbeam Corporation, 16
Supply-and-demand model, 73
Sutton, Joe, 125
Swap funds, 203
Swing trading, 65, 75-78
Synthetic leases, 82, 195

T
Tappin, Todd, 170
Tax accounting, 20
Tax-deductibility (of KSOP dividends), 201
Tax-deferred plans, 215
Taxes:
  and debt, 102
  and share buyback, 113
Technical analysts, 74
Technology stocks, 7
Telecom Italia, 93
10-K filings (see Annual reports)
10-Q filings (quarterly reports), 152
Tepper, Jake, 126-127
Teslik, Sarah, 104, 117
Thresholds, 187
TIAA-CREF, 134
Time periods:
  and dividend stream, 53
  of loans, 31-32
TIPS (Treasury inflation-protected securities), 216
Tobias, Andrew, 106, 139
Traders, 68-70, 71
Trading books, 69, 70
Trading-floor setting, 66
Trailing sell orders, 76
Transactions, 70, 72, 148
Treasury bills, 209
Treasury bonds, 38, 44-45
Treasury inflation-protected securities (TIPS), 216
Triple A (AAA) grade, 185, 186
Trout, Monroe, 73
Trueman, Brett, 175
Trump, Donald, 128
Trump Hotels & Casino Resorts, 141
Trust, 37, 190
Truthfulness, 177-178
Tug-of-war analogy, 66
Tyco International, 3, 101, 157

U

UBS PaineWebber, 169
UBS Warburg, 70
Uncertainty, 74-75
Undercapitalized, 32
Underwriters, 51
Upward-trend buys, 76
U.S. Department of Justice, 14, 15
U.S. Department of Labor, 205, 206
US West, 133, 149, 204

V

Valuation:
    of asset-light companies, 9-10
    fair, 143-144
    and marking to market, 22-23
    in secondary markets, 56-57
    stock, 58-59
Veterans Administration (VA), 218
Victor Talking Machine, 56
Vieth, Warren, 201
Vivendi Universal, 93, 191
Volatility, 208
Volcker, Paul A., 13, 15
Volume, 75

W

Wall Street Journal, 5, 14, 118, 119, 126,
    131, 133, 140, 141, 145, 159, 162, 175,
    177, 178, 181, 191, 193, 198, 200, 206,
    207

Wal-Mart Stores, Inc., 160
Warren, Elizabeth, 134
Washington Post, 133, 144, 175, 177, 208
Waste Management, Inc. (WMI), 16-17
Watkins, Sherron, 20, 92, 127, 206
Weather swaps, 88
Weil, Roman, 20
Weinberger, Mark, 132
West, Ed, 146
Whalley, Greg, 159
Whitewing, 154, 191
William M. Mercer, Inc., 105, 129
Williams Companies, Inc., 191
Winn-Dixie Stores, Inc., 115
WMI (see Waste Management, Inc.)
Wolff, Edward N., 198
Wood, Patrick, III, 90
WorldCom, 3, 23, 92, 101, 109, 133, 147,
    149, 158-159, 173-174
Write-downs of assets, 22-23
Writer, 108

Y

Young, Shawn, 149

Z

Zamansky, Jacob, 174
Zayed bin Sultan al-Nahayan, 85
Zero-coupon yield curve, 87
Zero-sum game, 34